Microservices and Containers

Microservices and Containers

Parminder Singh Kocher

✦ Addison-Wesley

Boston • Columbus • Indianapolis • New York • San Francisco • Amsterdam • Cape Town
Dubai • London • Madrid • Milan • Munich • Paris • Montreal • Toronto • Delhi • Mexico City
São Paulo • Sydney • Hong Kong • Seoul • Singapore • Taipei • Tokyo

Library of Congress Control Number: 2017963682

ISBN-13: 978-0-13-459838-3
ISBN-10: 0-13-459838-5

This book is dedicated to my mom and dad. Without their love and countless blessings, it just wouldn't have been possible.

Contents

Preface xiii

Acknowledgments xv

About the Author xvii

Part I: Microservices **1**

Chapter 1: An Introduction to Microservices **3**

    What Are Microservices? 3

    Modular Architecture 8

    Other Advantages of Microservices 9

    Disadvantages of Microservices 11

Chapter 2: Switching to Microservices **13**

    Fatigues and Attributes 14

    Learning Curve for the Organization 15

    Business Case for Microservices 17

    Cost Components 18

Chapter 3: Interprocess Communication **23**

    Types of Interactions 23

    Preparing to Write Web Services 24

    Microservice Maintenance 25

    Discovery Service 26

        API Gateway 27

        Service Registry 27

    Putting It All Together 28

Chapter 4: Migrating and Implementing Microservices **33**

    The Need for Transition 33

    Creating a New Application with Microservices 35

        Organization Readiness 36

        Services-Based Approach 36

Interprocess (Service-to-Service) Communication 37

Technology Selection 37

Implementation 38

Deployment 39

Operations 40

Migrating a Monolithic Application to Microservices 40

Microservices Criteria 42

Rearchitecting the Services 44

A Hybrid Approach 45

Part II: Containers **47**

Chapter 5: Docker Containers **49**

Virtual Machines 50

Containers 52

Docker Architecture and Components 54

The Power of Docker: A Simple Example 57

Chapter 6: Docker Installation **61**

Installing Docker on Mac OS X 61

Installing Docker on Windows 66

Installing Docker on Ubuntu Linux 68

Chapter 7: Docker Interface **73**

Key Docker Commands 73

Docker Search 73

Docker Pull 75

Docker Images 76

Docker RMI 77

Docker Run 77

Docker ps 79

Docker Logs 80

Docker Restart 85

Docker Attach 85

Docker Remove 86

Docker Inspect 87

Docker Exec 89

Docker Rename 90

Docker Copy 91

Docker Pause/Unpause 92
Docker Create 94
Docker Commit 94
Docker Diff 95
Dockerfile 95
MySQL Dockerfile 96
Docker Compose 100

Chapter 8: Containers Networking **105**
Key Linux Concepts 105
Linking 106
Default Options 110
None 110
Host 111
Bridge 113
Custom Networks 116
Custom Bridge Network Driver 117
Overlay Network Driver 119
Underlay Network Driver or Macvlan 121

Chapter 9: Container Orchestration **123**
Kubernetes 123
Kubectl 124
Master Node 124
Worker Nodes 127
Example: Kubernetes Cluster 128
Apache Mesos and Marathon 129
Mesos Master 130
Agents 130
Frameworks 131
Example: Marathon Framework 131
Docker Swarm 132
Nodes 132
Services 133
Task 133
Example: Swarm Cluster 133
Service Discovery 136
Service Registry 139

Chapter 10: Containers Management 143

Monitoring 143

Logging 144

Metrics Collection 147

docker stats 148

APIs 149

cAdvisor 149

Cluster-wide Monitoring Tools 150

Heapster 150

Prometheus 151

Step 1: Running Prometheus 152

Step 2: Adding Node Exporter and cAdvisor 155

Step 3: Adding Targets 156

Step 4: Bringing Up the User Interface: Grafana 157

Step 5: Viewing the Stats 160

Step 6: Integrating the Alertmanager 165

Part III: Hands-On Project—Putting Learning
into Practice 169

Chapter 11: Case Study: Monolithic Helpdesk Application 171

Helpdesk Application Overview 171

Application Architecture 172

Authentication, Interceptor, and Authorization 173

Account Management 175

Ticketing 178

Product Catalog 181

Appointments 184

Message Board 186

Search 189

Building the Application 190

Setting Up Eclipse 190

Building the Application 193

Deploying and Configuring 198

New Requirements and Bug Fixes 200

Chapter 12: Case Study: Migration to Microservices 203

Planning for Migration 203

Applying Microservices Criteria 205

Conversion Summary 206

Impact on Architecture 207

Converting to Microservices 207

Product Catalog 208

Ticketing 211

Search 211

Application Build and Deployment 212

Code Setup 213

Building the Microservices 213

Deploying and Configuring 213

New Requirements and Bug Fixes 217

Chapter 13: Case Study: Containerizing a Helpdesk Application **221**

Containerizing Microservices 221

Listing Dependencies 222

Build Binaries and WAR files 222

Creating a Docker Image 222

Building the Docker Image 226

DC/OS Cluster Setup on AWS 227

Deploying the Catalog Microservice 235

Submitting a Task to Marathon 236

Inspecting and Scaling the Service 239

Accessing the Service 245

Updating the Monolithic Application 246

Conclusion **247**

What Is DevOps? 247

Only the Beginning 250

Appendix A: Helpdesk Application Flow **251**

Administrator Flows 252

Login 252

Administration and Supported Products 253

Customer Flows 255

My Products 255

Create an Incident 256

View Incident 256

Message Board 257

Make Appointment 258

Search 259

My Profile 259

Support Desk Engineer Flows 260

View All Tickets 260

View Tickets 261

Appendix B: Installing the Solr Search Engine **263**

Prerequisites 263

Installation Steps 263

Configuring Solr for Simple Data Import 265

Index **267**

Preface

As always, the technology sector is in the midst of momentous transitions—the Internet of things, software-enabled networking, and software as a service (SaaS), to name but a few. Because of these innovations, there is a large demand for platforms and architectures that can improve the process of application development and deployment. Companies of many sizes now require frameworks and architectures that can simplify their applications' update processes, allowing their latest versions to go to market more frequently without adding undue overhead to the development and deployment teams.

This transition, like many of its cousins, is still young, yet many technologies and frameworks in the space have already come and gone. The winners remain standing, however, continuing to improve the world's software by allowing its developers—us—to create new applications and update existing ones with more agility than ever before. Two such winners? Microservices and containers, red-hot topics that, in my opinion, also possess staying power. Compared to the monolithic approach, the most common way of developing and deploying applications, microservices simplify those processes, especially with large projects that require multiple teams and increasingly long code. In such cases, even a small change in the code can cause serious delays. Microservices can handle today's large codes by incorporating agility and scalability into application development and deployment, all within a proven paradigm.

That's where this book comes in. When I first started learning about microservices, there were several valuable online resources (in particular, I recommend the websites microservices.io, by Chris Richardson, and martinfowler.com, by James Lewis and Martin Fowler), but I could not find many books that systematically built a case for why a CTO or director of an engineering team should (or should not) make the transition to microservices. There was a clear gap in the market; the more I mastered the subject matter, the more I thought, "Why can't I be the one to fill that gap?" Soon I was brainstorming ideas for a book of my own.

Is This Book for You?

I wrote this book with two audiences in mind. The first group includes students, designers, and architects with experience in software and systems engineering. Although you might be familiar with microservices and/or containers, this is probably your first book dedicated entirely to them. It should provide you not only with a comprehensive overview on the subjects but also with enough information and analysis to help you decide when—and when not—to utilize these technologies. Those of you who already have hands-on experience with microservices and/or containers may want to skim through Parts I and II and dive straight into Part III, which presents a full-fledged service desk example, written by following the standard service-oriented architectures (SOA) methodologies. This case study discusses how one such application's architecture can be converted to a microservices-based architecture as well as how Docker containers fit into the picture. I think this deep dive under the hood will be a real treat and ultimately pique your interest enough to delve into the world of microservices and containers yourself.

My other target readers are non-programmers coming at the topic from a business perspective—executives or project managers interested in learning the basics. Perhaps you read an intriguing blog post about microservices. Could that be the solution your team has been searching for but you couldn't seem to find a good follow-up book? Maybe you've overheard the engineers discussing Docker containers and want to learn enough to fit in and talk the talk. Whatever your reasons, this book—essentially a primer chock full of easy-to-understand examples and minimal jargon—should be ideal for any manager considering new ways to update or develop new applications more effectively.

This book is for anyone trying to accomplish any or all of the following:

- Make his or her organization more effective in building industrial-strength software.

- Transition into microservices and Docker containers while understanding how they differ from SOA.

- Learn microservices and Docker as part of his or her school curriculum to gain new, highly marketable skills.

In short, this book is for anyone who wants to learn more about microservices and Docker containers. I hope you are one of them! Let's get started.

Register your copy of *Microservices and Containers* on the InformIT site for convenient access to updates and/or corrections as they become available. To start the registration process, go to informit.com/register and log in or create an account. Enter the product ISBN (9780134598383) and click Submit. Look on the Registered Products tab for an Access Bonus Content link next to this product, and follow that link to access any available bonus materials. If you would like to be notified of exclusive offers on new editions and updates, please check the box to receive email from us.

Acknowledgments

As someone who has spent his entire career in tech, I never thought I would write a book. I was an engineer, not an author. And so, before embarking on this challenge, I had little idea what went into authoring a book—and how tough it would be. Let's just say, I knew it would be a lot of work, but not *this* much work. Writing this book would have been difficult enough if I had been able to devote my working days to it. Writing it while continuing to work full time seemed downright impossible at times! And it would have been, too, were it not for the many talented and generous people who guided and supported me every step of the way.

First, to the entire team at Pearson, thank you for accepting my proposal and guiding me through the entire editorial process. In particular, I want to thank my main contact there, Christopher Guzikowski for his guidance at every step, for his trust that I could do this, and for his patience while I worked on this book. Also big thanks to Michael Thurston for his indispensable editing and quick turn-around time.

This book would not have been possible without similar aid and support from many friends, starting with Lenin Lakshminarayanan and Anuj Singh, who spent countless evenings and weekends with me helping with all the code-related aspects of the case study, a critical section of this book. Many thanks to Gerald Cantor, who read multiple drafts and provided honest, invaluable feedback; Ravi Papisetti, Nawaz Akther, Sameer Nair, and Gurvinder Singh for providing useful insights and suggestions; and Michael Wolman for reviewing every word of this book.

This book also would have been impossible without the motivation and guidance I received. Whenever I had doubts, I would seek guidance from my mentors, who played a huge role in getting me to this point in my career. In particular, I would like to thank Greg Carter, my mentor for the past 12 years, for his unconditional support and guidance; Sunil Kripalani, for always trusting me and pushing me to be innovative and strive to make an impact; and Antonio Nucci, a true visionary—just talking with him motivates me to accomplish more.

Last but certainly not least, I want to thank my family for putting up with me during this rewarding but frequently stressful experience! To my children, Prabhleen,

Jashminder, and Jasleen, for spending countless weekends without me and understanding that Papa was working on his passion. And finally, especially, to my beautiful wife, Raman, for her inspiration, encouragement, and trust in me. If not for her support, this book would have remained merely a dream, not a reality.

Thank you all so much!

About the Author

Parminder Singh Kocher was born and raised in India and is a lifelong technology learner with two decades of hands-on experience in building enterprise-grade software systems. He has been with Cisco Systems since 2005 and managed the Cisco's Managed Services (CMS) platform, and has since worked as an innovation evangelist leading multiple software groups. Currently, he is engineering director for Cisco Networking Academy platform, where he leads the engineering teams responsible for developing the Academy's next-gen platform accesses in 180 countries. In addition to bachelor's and master's degrees in computer science, Kocher has an executive MBA from Baylor's Hankamer School of Business and an executive certificate in strategy and innovation from MIT's Sloan School of Management. He lives in Austin, Texas, with his wife and three children.

PART I

Microservices

Chapter 1

An Introduction to Microservices

Technology has changed, and continues to change, how the world behaves. In turn, these altered behaviors are putting new, challenging demands on the technology that supports it all. We have progressed from an era of 56k dialup modems to 100Gbps Ethernet in less than two decades. As the speed increased, it placed greater demand on corporations to develop faster software for which advanced and high-level software languages were developed to suit application needs. Similarly, on the systems side, we have evolved from mainframes to high-speed servers to making servers a commodity to virtualization and cloud. Now "containerize" is a verb, as containers are being utilized to use resources more efficiently.

Along the way, new paradigms such as model–view–controller (MVC), enterprise integration patterns (EIPs), and service-oriented architectures (SOAs) were released. Microservices-based architecture is now the talk of the tech world. Let's find out why.

What Are Microservices?

A microservice is an independent, standalone capability designed as an executable or a process that communicates with other microservices through standard but lightweight interprocess communication such as Hypertext Transfer Protocol (HTTP), RESTful web services (built on the Representational State Transfer [REST] architecture), message queues, and the like. What makes microservices unique from a standard application is that each microservice is developed, tested, deployed, and scaled on demand and independent of other microservices.

The microservice concept inherits all the best principles of software development, including being loosely coupled, scalable on demand, and services oriented, to name a few.

What does standalone capability mean? It means that each microservice performs precisely one function, which behaves the same for all consumers. Take, for instance, an order management service that only processes orders and does nothing else; it does not even send notifications. It may call another microservice responsible for sending notifications on processing. This separation of functions provides enormous flexibility, as each microservice can be managed, maintained, scaled, extended, reused, and replaced independently of other microservices.

Given this definition, a microservices-based application is simply a group of several independent, standalone microservices, each offering specific, well-defined functionality, communicating through well-defined protocols to provide overall application functionality. You can describe such a paradigm as a microservice-based architecture in which each microservice runs as a separate process.

You may be wondering how this is different from SOA-based monolithic applications. The difference is that in a monolithic application, all the capabilities are packed into one big executable, or a WAR file, also known as a *monolithic implementation*.

Let's explore this with a simple example: a calculator application you may access from the web. In a monolithic application, all calculator operations—addition, subtraction, and so on—may be written as separate program functions, and one function may call another function directly to complete its action. There is one process running, and the communication is through standard program function calls. The design might look something like Figure 1.1.

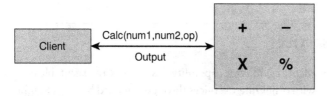

Figure 1.1 *Monolithic architecture for a simple calculator application*

This is a very simple example for which microservices would be overkill, but just for the sake of understanding, let's assume a developer following the microservices paradigm builds the calculator application by constructing each operation offered by the calculator as a separate standalone service, as shown in Figure 1.2. In this case, a microservice calls another microservice through interprocess calls over HTTP or another protocol. In the previous case, if a nasty bug is encountered in any of the functions (say, out of range), it could take the whole application down. With microservices, however, only the impacted service would go down; the rest would still be available for users.

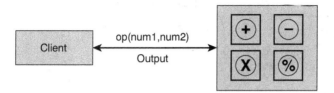

Figure 1.2 *Microservices-based architecture for a simple calculator application*

The purpose of this simple example is to underscore the biggest advantage of following the microservices paradigm: that it can simplify the implementation of a complex application by allowing you to divide the application into manageable, standalone components. This simplicity can help in various ways, such as by enabling you to add many capabilities as required without impacting other services.

Furthermore, each microservice can be independently updated or scaled on demand. For example, suppose we need to create a new operation that uses an existing, available functionality: say, finding the square of a given number. This operation is straightforward and involves minimal to no touching of the existing code. We create a new microservice that calls the standard published API for the "multiply" microservice (see Figure 1.3). Consequently, we have only one microservice to write, compile, and deploy, compared to a monolithic application's need for recompilation, redeployment, and so on, with possible downtime as a result.

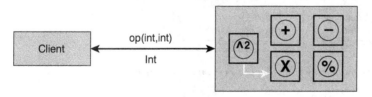

Figure 1.3 *"Square the number" function easily added with new microservice*

We can also have microservices that are called only by other microservices, not directly by the client application, as shown in Figure 1.4. For example, in the figure, a client may be able to call only three microservices under Layer 1, whereas the first microservice under Layer 1 may call the two microservices behind it under Layers 2 and 3, as shown by the arrows. These two microservices are called *helper microservices*.

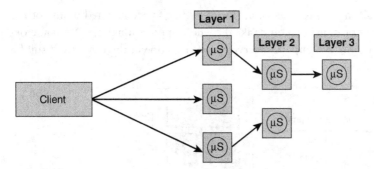

Figure 1.4 *A microservice calling other microservices*

The concept of microservices is not new, but it has been gaining popularity recently because of the challenges posed by monolithic applications.

Let's look at another example to discuss these challenges. Think about an e-commerce system and the components it would involve at a high level, as shown in Figure 1.5.

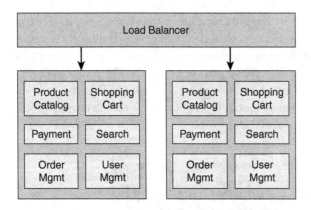

Figure 1.5 *Basic components of a monolithic e-commerce system*

For a small- to medium-size company, this system may work well initially. One package is built and deployed to production by the operations team, and it is easy to provide horizontal scalability by deploying multiple copies of the application and putting a load balancer in front of them. As the business grows, so do the required capabilities, which further extends the code along with the team size and, in turn, complexity to deploy, release, and support the application. Over time, the application will become more complex, making it harder to define the clear ownership of code and functionality to application developers. At that point, things tend to fall apart and organizations begin to face the following challenges:

- Performance issues
- Scalability
- Longer cycles for regression testing
- Longer cycles to upgrade and redeployment, leading to an inability to deploy small fixes and enhancements
- Unscheduled downtime
- Potential downtime during upgrades
- Stuck with the existing technology and programming language
- No way to scale just the required components or functionality

Of the many impacts resulting from these challenges, one that typically goes unseen is the frustration experienced by engineering teams and the increased rate of attrition that follows.

In these situations, the microservices paradigm can be very useful. This paradigm is only useful for large monolithic applications, as it comes with some costs that may not be worthwhile if the application is small or is supporting small businesses. It may take lot of investment to decompose the monolithic application at this point of maturity; organizations usually start developing new capabilities as microservices and then, based on return on investment, may slowly start to decompose the old application.

Imagine if we have to update the shopping cart component in the previous example. Depending on the architecture and legacy of the software, it may require not only adding or updating the code but also doing the regression testing on all the code or functions that touch the shopping cart component. It will also require recompilation, testing, and deployment of the entire application, which may result in downtime or may slow the application. In addition, say a developer feels that it would have been easy and efficient if that particular functionality were coded in some new language such as Scala. That desire will likely remain unfulfilled unless investment is available to recode the complete application in that new language. Basically, the application developer is stuck with the choice his predecessors made, which may have been right at that time but is no longer optimal.

Let's see how microservices can help here. As we discussed, we will break all the major monolithic components into standalone microservices, as shown in Figure 1.6.

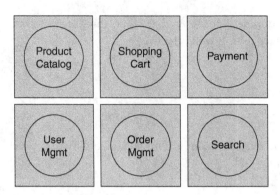

Figure 1.6 *E-commerce system components broken down into standalone microservices*

These microservices are deployed separately, and each performs a single function. If we want to modify the shopping cart microservice, we have less code to work with—that is, just this particular microservice—and it will be much easier to test and deploy. Microservices not only address the challenges posed by monolithic services but also offer several advantages that drive organizations toward continuous delivery.

Modular Architecture

If we look at the history of software projects in the entire industry, only 29 percent of large projects were successful within specified cost, time, and quality, as per chaos manifesto (The Standish Group, "CHAOS Report 2016," 2016). That means 71 percent of projects in 2015 failed or were challenged. Failure may have been due to quality issues, lack of completion, budget overages, and so on. Consequently, a lot of new practices and software management standards were put in place that were meant to be followed by software organizations (e.g., IEEE Software Engineering Standards, Software Testing Standards). The main purpose behind these standards was to control the complexity by using best practices. This helped in two ways: first, by improving the chances of project completion; second, by increasing the shelf life or age of the application.

Software applications or platforms have an average age of four to six years, after which they fall into obsolescence due to various reasons. The reasons may include changing requirements over time, inability to scale due to legacy architecture, outdated technologies given the pace of change in the technology world, and so on. The industry tends to get on the Next Gen bandwagon, which means rewriting the software or platform using the latest technologies, new architecture, and best practices. But at some point, the question must be asked: Does it really require changing every component—that is, the complete package? Not necessarily. Some components or parts may do much better given the new technologies, but that usually is not an option, as the architecture did not provide the modularity, enabling us to replace individual software components or parts with rewritten code.

We have been developing monolithic applications—hence the need to follow the standards to deal with complexity. If we break down this complexity by using a microservices paradigm, we will end up with a modular architecture that significantly increases the shelf life. In addition, we can immediately reduce our dependence on multiple standards and bulky software development processes to save time, thus fast-tracking the overall software development lifecycle.

Apart from the process efficiencies, a modular architecture will also create a lot of savings down the road when we want to upgrade the platform. Instead of starting from scratch, we can surgically remove the outdated microservices and replace them with new ones implemented using the right technology and design. This is one of the key long-term benefits of using the microservices paradigm and one of the distinct advantages that sets it apart from others. However, in most cases, gains from the increased modularity alone make a microservices-based approach worth the investment.

Other Advantages of Microservices

In addition to what we discussed so far, microservices may offer the following benefits to an organization and its engineers:

- **Simplicity.** Each microservice performs only one distinct and well-defined function, so there is less code to take care of, less cohesion and dependency within the code, and a lower probability of bugs.

- **Scalability.** To scale a monolithic application, we need to deploy resource-heavy applications on multiple servers behind a load balancer. It is not possible to scale just a portion of an application; it is all or nothing. With microservices, we can scale out only the components that are expected to be highly loaded, as shown in Figure 1.7. Providing differentiated levels of scalability is very easy and a salient feature of microservices.

- **Continuous delivery.** Because of fewer interdependencies within the code bases and faster development cycles, the microservices paradigm enables and actually lends itself to a culture of continuous delivery and DevOps.

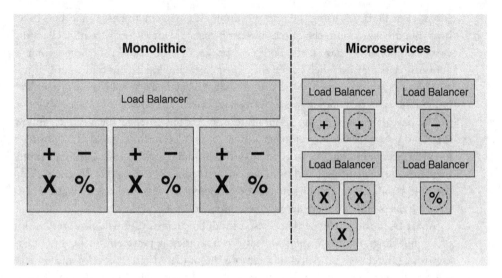

Figure 1.7 *Scalability comparison*

- **More freedom and fewer dependencies.** Microservices are meant to be stan-dalone and independent. A development team can focus on its microservice and freely enhance functionality without worrying about breaking another microservice as long as they keep the interface contract intact or implement a new contract that is backward compatible.

- **Fault isolation.** Fault isolation is a phenomenon in which a fault in one part of a system does not bring down the entire system. That is, the fault is isolated from the entire system. In a monolithic application, a fault in any part of the system will bring down the entire system, as the system is a single executable/process. With microservices, a fault in one microservice may bring down the impacted microservice, but it will not necessarily bring down the entire application because the affected microservice is running in its own process space. For exam-ple, in an e-commerce system based on microservices architecture, if the product review microservice crashes, users will still be able to see inventory, select items, view cart, and place an order. However, they will not be able to see reviews until the reviews microservice issue is resolved. If the same application were mono-lithic, the review service issue would possibly shut down the entire application.

- **Data segregation and decentralization.** Unlike monolithic applications, where all the data typically is stored and shared in a central database, microservices provide us an opportunity to segregate this data. Each microservice usually owns its data and does not share its data directly with other microservices.

- **Choices.** Unlike a monolithic application, where all application components have to use a single database, platform, and programming language, microservices-based applications offer the opportunity to use the best tool for each specific job. One microservice might use Oracle with Linux OS, and another might use a NoSQL database on a Microsoft platform. Long-term commitment to technology stacks is no longer necessary.

Disadvantages of Microservices

Nothing comes for free; there has to be some cost in achieving all the benefits offered by microservices. If we move toward microservices, we need to be aware of the challenges posed by such an architecture. Not to worry, though. In the next part of this book, we learn about how to use certain systems and applications to overcome these challenges. For now, let's list some of the challenges posed by microservices:

- **Troubleshooting complexity.** Microservices provide the overall capabilities through inter-microservices communication, which increases potential points of failure. This makes answering questions such as the following more challenging:

  - Is my system healthy at any given instance?

  - If an end user reports a problem such as slow performance or timeouts, where do I start my troubleshooting?

  In a monolithic application, it is easier to trace a request end to end. However, in a microservices-based application, each end user request might be broken down into multiple requests and might be hitting multiple microservices to get a response. Troubleshooting can become a little tricky.

- **Increased latency.** Intraprocess communication (like the kind used in monolithic applications) is much faster than the interprocess communication used by microservices.

- **Operational complexity.** With several hundreds to thousands of microservices in a real-world application, operations teams have to deal with complex infrastructure, deployment, monitoring, availability, backups, and management. In a way, we are moving the complexities of a monolithic architecture to the systems side of microservices. Still, this complexity can be addressed by a high level of automation.

- **Version control.** Because a microservices-based application may have thousands of microservices, the versioning and management becomes little complex. It requires better version control and management systems.

Chapter 2

Switching to Microservices

Chapter 1, "An Introduction to Microservices," compared and contrasted microservices with monolithic architectures. Now that you understand the distinction between the two, you are probably trying to answer the question, are microservices right for my team? If you are already dealing with the growing pains of monolithic architecture or are planning to build a monolithic system, then it is worthwhile to look at microservices. Otherwise, there is no reason to switch to this architecture, as it is not suitable for small-to-medium service architectures given the work involved. Each microservice comes with a burden of extra work at a scale that is unnecessary with monolithic architectures: API sets, process monitoring, load balancing for performance/high availability, and so on, are required for each microservice rather than just at the application level. You are actually trading monolithic code complexity for the operational complexity of microservices, and if that complexity does not exist in your system, you will unnecessarily add it. For those reasons, you have to be very careful when it comes to moving forward with this paradigm, or it can backfire.

This chapter lays out the criteria that qualify (and disqualify) various applications for a microservices-based architecture. Usually, executives and managers look for potential business cases or return on investment. We discuss these considerations briefly by doing some simple cost–benefit modeling and organization investments.

Fatigues and Attributes

A switch to microservices may best be suited for existing monolithic applications architectures that show some of the following fatigues:

- Difficult and time-consuming deployment process
- Large and complex code base that overloads developer IDEs
- Non-uniform scaling requirements (i.e., some capabilities require more scaling than others)
- High costs of development, testing, and deployments
- Degraded code quality over time because of too many interdependencies
- Application failure due to single component failure

Perform thorough due diligence to understand these fatigues and document them clearly. Then, try to determine whether some of the following characteristics would add value to your current application:

- Services organized around business capabilities
- Standalone and/or partial deployment of services
- Asynchronous communication
- Replacing different platform components, programming languages, and/or databases for different parts of the application services for enhanced performance
- Continuous deployment and continuous integration
- Each engineering team owning and understanding specific business areas such as order management or a shopping cart

Thinking in these terms will give you a pretty good idea of where you stand and whether it makes sense to transition to a microservices paradigm. Once considerable effort has been put into adopting the microservices-based paradigm, there is no turning back. So before you decide, you must also be aware of the unique needs that are put on the organization due to this shift:

- **Culture change.** The organization mindset must embrace a shift in the roles of engineering teams—from functional roles to business-centric roles with shared goals and responsibilities. This means creating joint teams of product managers, developers, testers, and operations to lead collectively and take ownership of the microservices. It also requires investments in fresh talent and in training existing staff, as well as in new systems, tools, and software. In addition, a great deal of automation throughout the software lifecycle is required to ensure success.

- **Operational processes.** With a microservices paradigm, an organization's operational processes and structure need to be changed. The paradigm demands a more cross-functional structure that takes charge of deployment, support, upgrade, and operation of microservices. The existing operational processes of testing and deploying the monolithic application have to be broken down into multiple and extensive processes supporting hundreds or thousands of self-sufficient microservices and supporting communication between them.

Learning Curve for the Organization

There is a whole new learning curve for existing engineering and operational teams who have been working with and supporting the various aspects of monolithic architecture–based applications. This learning curve can be defined by the following new practices required to make the shift toward microservices-based applications:

- **Standalone microservices.** Monolithic applications exist as one large unit deployed on multiple boxes for scalability. With microservices, there are hundreds to thousands of self-contained services, all requiring equal attention.

- **Microservices discovery.** The higher the number of microservices, the more complexity we encounter. For example, we need to think about how the microservices will be discovered—that is, how and where do we create the inventory of microservices? Other challenges include on-demand scalability and version control, including retiring services that are no longer needed. The good news is that various applications, such as Consul, Apache ZooKeeper, and other third-party products, can be used to solve these challenges. These challenges create a need to hire new staff or retrain existing employees, which may take a good part of the investment.

- **Communication between microservices.** Determining how communication will occur between all the services and the outside world includes considering client expectations around response time, latency, number of retries, and so on, as well as what happens when these service level agreements (SLAs) or expectations are not met. It is possible that a standard interface for communication needs to be established.

- **Microservices testing.** Testing practices and principles of monolithic applications are not applicable to microservices-based applications. While testing each self-sufficient microservice is easy, the challenge comes with testing the complete application that is composed of hundreds or thousands of microservices. This requires dealing with lots of moving parts, and integration testing becomes the most important aspect of the overall testing. Some of the testing complexities can be addressed by establishing best practices and automating the test cases.

- **Scaling of microservices.** With microservices, scaling becomes easier and efficient. You can scale up or down the services you need on demand. But it does come at some cost. First, the microservices must be designed to keep scaling needs in mind—that is, know the usage demand for each microservice. Second, scaling must be automated, which requires some investment and learning curve with frameworks such as Mesos and Marathon. We discuss these frameworks in detail in the later chapters.

- **Microservices upgrading.** On the surface, it may sound simple to upgrade every microservice, since each is self-sufficient and consequently should not cause any disruption. It may actually be simple if the new version incorporates simple changes that do not impact the outside world. But when changes impact other dependent services, upgrading may not be that straightforward. It must be ensured that other services are up to speed to consume new functionality or that the new service is backward compatible.

- **Microservices security.** Security has always been important, and given today's cybersecurity threats, it has become especially crucial to acknowledge security during design time. A few aspects that need to be dealt with include microservice-to-microservice security, client-to-microservice security, data-in-motion, and data-at-rest security. Several standards, such as OAuth and OpenID, are available to address some aspects of security, but others must be thought through to balance the security needs with ease of consumption.

- **Microservices management.** No matter which software architecture or paradigm is in place, application management is a key requirement for overall operational and support success. Managing microservices is more complex than managing a monolithic application. The existing monitoring and managing tools or practices may not be that helpful. Instead of a handful of servers and applications, we have to deal with more complex new systems and technologies such as containers. Therefore, a single pane of glass (i.e., a single interface) to configure, monitor, and diagnose may be very helpful.

- **Monitoring in microservices.** With hundreds to thousands of microservices spread out over distributed systems, there are going to be lot of moving parts. Proper checks and balances must be put in place, both in the infrastructure (CPU, memory, I/O performance) and granularly at the application level (application log files, API call performance). The data extracted from this level of monitoring should be easily and readily available for operations and engineering teams to act with and improve the services.

- **Configuring microservices.** For any service, there are various configuration options provided by developers that provide flexibility in production and make it easy to adjust the services depending on the conditions. Such configuration includes settings such as caching, scaling parameters, thread counts, application feature–specific flags, database connections, and so on. Managing these aspects for thousands of services may well be a cumbersome task. A lot of tools exist to address some of these concerns, so a right combination of tool sets must be selected to create a common interface for simplicity.

- **Failure handling in microservices.** When a microservice fails, the check and balances discussed in the previous bullets may help, but the system needs to be designed keeping in mind that failure is inevitable. Each microservice should be built in such a way that a failure in a dependent service should not cause any issues with the performance of its own service, let alone bring the entire system down. The overall intention should be to build toward self-healing systems.

In light of all this information, the organization must be fully prepared for this change and able to allocate the proper resources to make the transition successful. A decision should be made only after all of these concerns are weighed. It is recommended to create a gap list to easily convey and understand the level of investment required to move to a microservices paradigm.

Business Case for Microservices

Given all the issues we have discussed so far, it may be difficult to understand and build the business case for microservices. You may be thinking, if it is more complex to build and maintain microservices-based applications, why should you invest in doing so? It is certainly going to be more complex, and the initial effort may be very high to train existing staff and change the organization culture, yet the long-term benefits would not only outweigh initial investment but also create savings and other advantages in the long run. What you need is a very basic analysis to help you understand or build the business case for the organization.

The average life of a software platform built on monolithic architecture is typically 4 to 5 years and is based on the following factors:

- Changing needs and customer demands driving existing functionality out of date
- New business needs
- Lack of flexibility to adjust or change existing architecture
- Lack of scale
- Outdated technologies
- Slowness caused by outdated systems and increased traffic over time

When faced with these factors, organizations start looking at new technologies and generally decide to invest in a new or next-generation platform. This is called the *platform refresh cycle*. From a business perspective, all the changes required are fair because customer expectations and delivery models change over time. What organizations worry about is the high investment in each cycle in terms of both dollars and time. The worry is fair, as it impacts the bottom-line profits of any organization. That's where microservices can help. Let's do a high-level analysis to prove this point.

Cost Components

Let's use a hypothetical example to look into the cost components of a monolithic platform's lifecycle:

- **Cost to build.** Cost to build a software platform from scratch that includes all the phases of the software development lifecycle, such as analysis, design, development, testing, and release. This is going to be the biggest investment of the cycle. Let's call this cost M_{CTB}.
- **Cost to maintain.** Normal care and feeding of the software platform, such as applying OS-level patches and maintaining infrastructure. Let's call this cost M_{CTM}.
- **Cost to change/update.** Cost of adding new features, bug fixing, retesting, regression testing, and releasing over the lifecycle of the project. Let's call this cost M_{CTU}.

- **Cost to scale.** Cost to appropriately scale the platform to maintain system response time and performance over time as the user base increases. Let's call this cost M_{CTS}.

- **Time to market.** Time taken to build the software platform or a given update. Time between analysis and release on the platform or an update. Let's call this cost M_{TTM}.

For comparison purposes, let's assume the following costs for the same software built using microservices architecture since these costs will be different:

- **Cost to build:** S_{CTB}
- **Cost to maintain:** S_{CTM}
- **Cost to change/update:** S_{CTU}
- **Cost to scale:** S_{CTS}
- **Time to market:** S_{TTM}

So, which platform architecture is more cost effective? Let's compare monolithic and microservices based on each of the preceding variables.

- **Cost to build: $M_{CTB} < S_{CTB}$.** If you already have an application in place, you have to account for all the new investment that may be required, such as training the staff, changing the culture, hiring new talent, and updating tools and systems. Given these considerations, the cost to build a microservices-based application may be very high compared to building a monolithic one. By contrast, if you are starting a brand-new software project, then the costs may not differ much depending on current organizational capabilities. Given system and tool needs, the cost of building a monolithic application may still be lower but not by a lot.

- **Cost to maintain: $M_{CTM} > S_{CTM}$.** Maintaining hardware and applying patches may cost downtime in certain conditions. There are lots of open source technologies that enable all kinds of automations from deployment to fault isolation. We cover many of these tools later in the book. For example, containerizing microservices and moving toward DevOps would enable spinning up new service containers on demand, which can save a lot of IT time and create efficient resource utilization, hence bringing down the overall cost of maintenance while reducing the possibility of downtime.

- **Cost to change/update: $M_{CTU} > S_{CTU}$.** One of the key advantages of using the microservices paradigm is that updating an existing functionality (microservice) or adding a new one is quite simple compared to dealing with complexity of a monolithic project where you might need to rebuild the entire application. The key differentiation is the time and effort it takes to update, build, test, and deploy microservice that performs just one function versus a complete monolithic application, which may take hours just to build and is very prone to human errors. Also, when you compare the testing and deployment efforts, microservices would be shorter and quicker, as discussed earlier, than monolithic applications, which in some cases may require downtime.

- **Cost to scale: $M_{CTS} > S_{CTS}$.** Scaling on demand and only where needed is a key value provided by microservices as compared to a monolithic application that requires spinning up another instance of the whole application. Unlike with a monolithic application, you could scale up only the components (microservices) that show signs of stress by spinning up service containers automatically and similarly destroy these containers when service demand goes down. This approach saves not only effort but also hardware/software resources, as shown in Figure 2.1.

- **Time to market: $M_{TTM} > S_{TTM}$.** There are two ways to look at time to market. First, adding a new service and going live in production is, in most cases, much faster than updating a monolithic application. Second, given the modular architecture of the microservices paradigm, it, along with containers, enables another software delivery method that organizations have been struggling with called DevOps. In fact, microservices and containers are key for the success of DevOps. DevOps provides the four key ingredients required to run a successful software platform:

  - Speed

  - Stability

  - Performance

  - Collaboration

DevOps enables agility and hence time to market. Organizations strive to take their offering quickly to market to maintain a competitive edge. Quick time to market itself may be the highest payback for transitioning to a microservices paradigm.

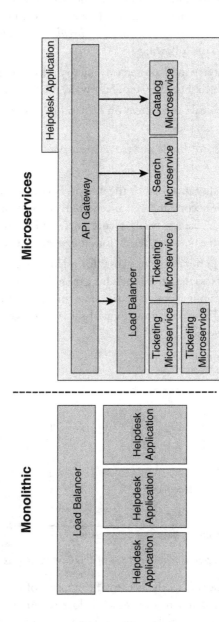

Figure 2.1 *Scaling comparison*

- **Future refresh cycles.** As discussed, a monolithic architecture–based software application has a finite average lifetime. Once that lifetime ends, the organization usually begins a new cycle, which ends up costing it an initial M_{CTB} again, and so on. *But microservices actually break this whole concept of cycles* because they can do the following:

  - Provide flexibility to add or remove microservices according to business requirements, which should be straightforward given the modular architecture.

  - Upscale or downscale the system on demand by adding and removing services under load balancer.

  - Replace outdated technologies per microservice as required, which minimizes the cost.

  Given all the flexibility provided by the microservices paradigm, new business requirements can be accommodated as required, and systems can be kept up to speed with changing business needs. Hence, there will be no need to replace the entire platform with a new generation for quite a few years, if not ever.

Keeping all the costs in mind, the net costs for microservices-based architecture will surely come to much less than total costs for a monolithic architecture. Spending over time may look something like that shown in Figure 2.2, with the net cost much lower for microservices. The intersection point of the two costs really depends on the project type, scope, and size.

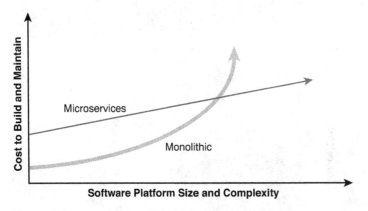

Figure 2.2 *A simplified graphical representation of this cost comparison*

To conclude the business case, the net benefit in terms of cost savings will come with microservices, but it happens over time. It does require the initial investment and organizational buy in. As noted earlier, the mere gain in time to market may outweigh all other benefits for most organizations.

An organization must consider the advantages, the learning curve involved, and the cost–benefit analysis when deciding whether to invest in a microservices-based architecture.

Chapter 3

Interprocess Communication

In monolithic architectures, the communication within the components happens via function, method, or module calls and is very straightforward in most cases. When building microservices architecture, designing and implementing interprocess communication is more complex. Although there are proven techniques for managing interprocess communication in a microservices architecture, and it is not a key subject of this book, in this chapter we review some of the best practices.

Types of Interactions

Microservices typically expose their functionalities through APIs or web services. To consume the web services over the network, there are fundamentally two types of communication/interaction patterns.

- **Synchronous communication.** An interaction in which the client expects immediate response while blocking everything else (e.g., HTTP request/response).

- **Asynchronous communication.** An interaction in which the service response is not expected immediately. The client makes the service call and continues with its work. Examples include publish/subscribe and HTTP request/asynchronous response.

As we discussed in Chapter 1, "An Introduction to Microservices," asynchronous communication is the preferred method of interaction between microservices. Think what would happen if we were to use synchronous communication between microservices. The client would be blocked until it received a response by another service before continuing its work. What would happen if the service were down or has error? This approach would not scale very well, and we would lose most of the advantages of microservices. Therefore, asynchronous communication is the better alternative.

With asynchronous communication, the client makes the request to another microservice and continues with other work while listening for incoming responses through the listener thread. The listener thread processes the responses as and when they come in. Problems within the called microservice would have no impact on the client. The result is improved scalability with loosely coupled services.

Another approach is to use publish/subscribe, where the publisher publishes the messages on, say, a message bus such as Kafka. Subscribers register for messages that are of interest on the message bus and pick those up for processing while ignoring the rest. Once processed, they may publish the results, which may be picked up by the original publisher, depending on the message exchange patterns in use.

Preparing to Write Web Services

Overall, developers have to decide three things when preparing to write web services:

1. **Protocol.** When it comes to web services protocols, we all know that HTTP is the gold standard. It is the same protocol used by web browsers, so it has withstood the test of time. The biggest advantage is that it is very light and based on a simple request/response model in which the client forms and sends an HTTP request and the server executes the actions required and forms and sends back an HTTP response.

2. **Web service standard.** There are three primary choices:

   - *RESTful* is widely accepted and recommended.

   - *SOAP* is bulky enough that it requires client- and server-side implementation.

   - *Data* is an open protocol used for building and consuming RESTful APIs.

   RESTful is based on HTTP request and response. It is much lighter than SOAP, and that's where it wins. Also, RESTful services are stateless and cacheable, which makes them faster—crucial in supporting mobile requests.

3. **Message format.** There are plenty of commonly used and entirely acceptable message formats to choose from, including XML, RSS, and JSON. A favorite of many developers, however, is JSON, primarily because it is text based and human readable, and there are a variety of libraries that can easily convert JSON to objects and back to the textual representation. Because JSON does not suffer the overburden of syntax, JSON data is smaller than XML data. This means faster processing, since it takes less bandwidth to send and receive messages. JSON works especially well for handheld and mobile devices such as cell phones and tablets, which have limited storage, light computing, and low bandwidth requirements to transmit the messages over the web.

Different people have different needs and preferences, so what we present in this chapter are just recommendations. Make your own choices according to your needs, performance requirements, and comfort level.

Microservice Maintenance

Once you build the communications between microservices, you need to keep them up to date and maintain them. The broadly applied adage, "change is constant," is applicable to your software also. Requests to adjust existing functionality will always accompany new requirements that pour in, in some cases necessitating changes to these web services. That is one complexity of microservices, as we have already discussed. Here are some things that will need to be taken care of to address the changing needs:

- **Supporting existing client implementations.** There may be times when you have to update the interfaces as you modify the core functionality of your microservice. You must take care of backward compatibility of your microservice because chances are that one or more other microservices (consumers) are making use of this published interface for communication. So you have to make sure you still support the old version until the consumer microservices team changes its implementation to consume your new interface.

- **Failsafe design.** If a called web service is down, you can address it in few ways, but the simplest is to add timeout in your client code. On the provider side, cover the error cases by returning proper error codes or, in some cases, default values. This practice also improves troubleshooting efforts.

- **Monitoring.** Proactively monitor microservices by calling each at regular intervals or through other methods. Take appropriate action if any of the microservices is down. You may have to create a fine balance, as monitoring calls cause extra traffic. You can use frameworks such as Marathon to achieve availability, orchestration, and the like. If, for instance, you want two microservices instances to be running and one goes down, Marathon has the heartbeat mechanism to detect it and will spin up another web server instance.

- **Queue.** Use the publish/subscribe method when building asynchronous web services. The advantage is that even when the service goes down, it will pick up the request from the bus when it comes back up.

When we convert a monolithic application to a microservices architecture, it results in several hundreds of microservices and thousands of web services or messaging services for communication between these microservices, so following the best practices in these areas are paramount.

Discovery Service

What happens when you have hundreds or thousands of microservices? In addition, perhaps you may have to provide multiple web services per microservice even for same function—for example, a different client-based web service. This is not a big issue in a monolithic architecture, since the client will make one call and the rest will be taken care of by the application. But in microservices-based architectures, two big issues arise:

- Clients have to call multiple services at same time to achieve the same functionality that they previously got with just one call in a monolithic application.
- Clients will have to know the location of the services.

Let's illustrate with an example. Say a user is accessing a library management application and wants to review his account page. The account page shows the book checkout history, recommendations, current cart, payments, account settings, and so on. If the application is based on a monolithic architecture, when the user clicks *My Account*, the service call shows him the My Account page while, in the backend, the application does the magic by calling various functions and looking up the database. For handheld and mobile devices, a different set or subset of calls may be required given the real estate and processing power, which adds to the complexity.

With a microservices-based architecture, a client would be responsible for calling all the required microservices, such as the checkout cart, payment information, and account settings. This approach would be very inefficient and would result in a rigid, or "hardcoded," way of doing things. We would lose the flexibility to make changes such as further dividing a microservice into multiple microservices when required, or vice versa.

In addition, the client would have to know the location of all the microservices that need to be called for the My Account page. We therefore need a system that would act as the overall entry point for the clients and the external calls and another system that stores the up-to-date locations of the microservices.

API Gateway

An API gateway addresses the first problem and will act as an entry point for all the calls. It is responsible for receiving the client requests, calling all the required microservices and sending back the aggregated results from microservices to complete the client request. With an API gateway, the client makes only a single call to invoke the service. This model offers various advantages:

- Internal complexity of the application is hidden from the client, thus simplifying the client code.

- It provides more flexibility for changing, combining, dividing, adding, or removing microservices as required.

- It reduces the round trips between client and application, hence increasing efficiency.

The API gateway can also serve as a point for load balancing, authentication, monitoring, and management. It may provide different APIs for different clients, such as web and mobile, and may prioritize the requests.

The biggest drawback of this model is that API gateway can become a single point of failure and a bottleneck from both a performance and a development perspective. Understand that this API gateway has to be customized, configured and maintained by multiple teams, so the process must be efficient and lightweight. For example, it must be kept up to date as we modify, add, or delete the microservices. From an operational performance perspective, an elastic load balancer would make sure performance and availability metrics are met.

Service Registry

With thousands of microservices in place, our API gateway also needs to know locations such as the IP addresses of all the services so that it can do its job. The idea behind service registry is that it provides a database of all the microservices and their locations, and the database can be queried when required. The microservice developer needs to take care of creating and maintaining a service registry.

The logic should be such that when a microservice comes up, it registers itself with this service registry. When a client makes a call, the API gateway looks up the location of the required microservices, makes those calls, and aggregates the results to complete the client request. At a high level, this is what is required, but as we know, things are not that simple.

What if we lose the registry data? To solve this problem, we have several open source tools, such as Consul and SkyDNS, that actually discover the microservices and make sure they are up and running. For example, Consul is a matured discovery tool that can use custom DNS names to access the microservices and store this information in the registry. It can also perform constant health checks and keep the clusters healthy.

Putting It All Together

Let's look at a simple system and then extend it on the basis of what we have learned. Figure 3.1 shows a simple microservices-based model. At this point, the client is responsible for calling all the microservices to complete the user request.

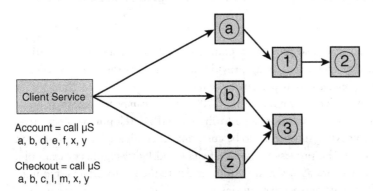

Figure 3.1 *Simple model in which client is responsible for calling each microservice*

Let's add an API gateway to encapsulate all the business logic of the application and hide the complexity from the client service. This makes the client much simpler by enabling a single call to get the job done, as seen in Figure 3.2.

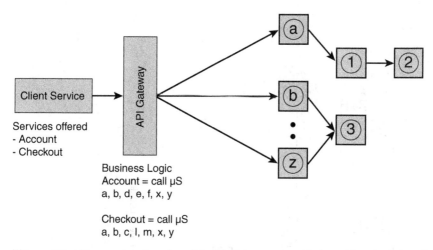

Figure 3.2 *Microservices-based model with API gateway added, enabling a single call to get the job done*

Now let's add a service registry so that the API gateway can query it to know the location of each microservice, as required. As we discussed, all the microservices (a to z and 1 through 3 in the figures) register with a registry service and API gateway. When a new request comes in, the API gateway figures out what microservices need to be called. It then queries for their location from the registry service and makes the calls. Furthermore, it aggregates the results and sends the HTTP response back to the client. See Figure 3.3.

This looks a little complex but is really straightforward. Let's take it a step further and try to scale our individual services, as one of the key advantages of microservices is the ability to scale to accommodate the usage. All that is needed is an additional load balancer where required. Load balancing should be done at the microservices level, which is critical for scalability, and also at the API gateway and service registry levels, as they can become bottlenecks. A model like the one depicted in Figure 3.4 would make sense.

We learn more about scaling microservices-based applications in Part III, "Hands-On Project—Putting Learning into Practice," where you will see a hands-on example with Docker.

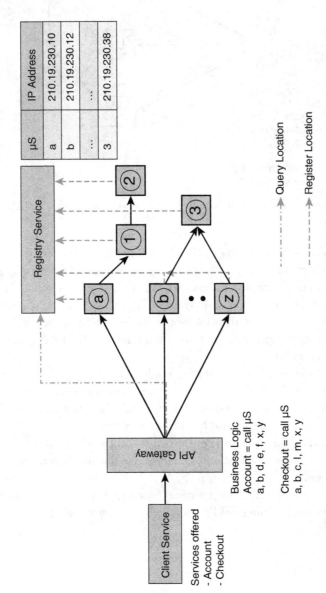

Figure 3.3 *Microservices-based model with registry service incorporated*

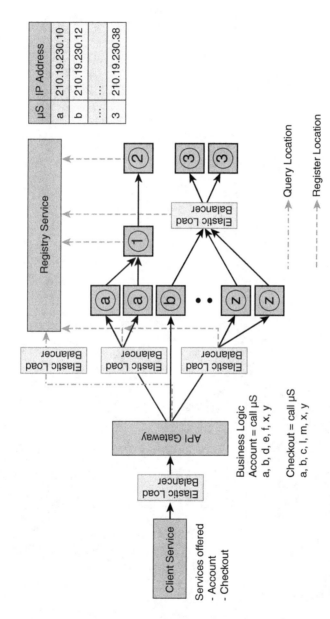

Figure 3.4 *Microservices-based model with additional load balancer*

Chapter 4

Migrating and Implementing Microservices

By this point you know what microservices are and how they work. If you're still reading, I have accomplished my first goal: piquing your interest enough that you are considering implementing microservices yourself! Now it's time to get down to brass tacks: namely, the very critical topic of how to approach the transition to microservices.

The Need for Transition

You'll recall that a monolithic application is very large (in terms of lines of code [LoC]) and complex (in terms of functions interdependencies, data, etc.), serving hundreds of thousands of users across geographical regions and requiring several developers and IT engineers. A monolithic app may look something like Figure 4.1.

Sometimes, even with all these characteristics, the application might run fine at first. You may not encounter challenges in terms of application scalability or performance. But with time and usage, issues will arise, and they may be different for different applications. For example, for a cloud or web application, you may hit scalability issues due to more users consuming your services, or it may become costly and hard to release regular new updates due to longer build times and regression testing. As shown in Figure 4.2, monolithic application users or the developers may experience one or more issues listed on the right.

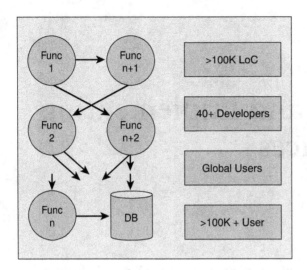

Figure 4.1 *Basic structure of a monolithic app*

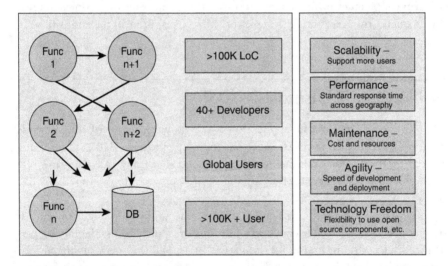

Figure 4.2 *Potential issues with a monolithic app*

That's when a migration to microservices may start sounding like more than a trendy idea; it will sound like a lifesaver. We already learned a bit about microservices in previous chapters, so we know our transition will look something like the application shown in Figure 4.3.

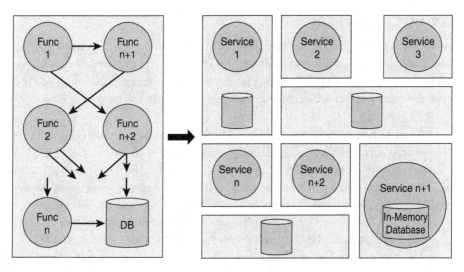

Figure 4.3 *Transition from monolithic to microservices*

So, how do we go about making such a change? There are two possible scenarios: creating a brand-new application or converting or migrating a monolithic application that already exists. The latter scenario is far more likely, but it is worth knowing the ins and outs of both scenarios regardless of the current situation.

Creating a New Application with Microservices

Before we begin, let me say that I have not seen many real-world scenarios of building a microservices-based application from scratch. Typically, an application is already in place, and most applications I have worked on are more of a transition to a microservices architecture from a monolithic architecture. In these cases, the intention of architects and developers has always been to reuse some of the existing implementation. As skills become readily available in the market and some successful implementations are published, we will see more examples of building microservices-based applications from scratch, so it is certainly worthwhile to discuss this scenario.

Let's say you have all the requirements figured out and ready to go into the architecture design of the application you are going to build. There are many common best practices you need to think about as you get started, which are covered in the following sections.

Organization Readiness

As we discussed in Chapter 2, "Switching to Microservices," the first question you have to ask yourself is whether your organization is ready to transition to microservices. That means the various departments of your organization now need to think differently about building and releasing software in the following ways:

- **Team structure.** The monolithic application team (if one exists) needs to be broken down into several small high-performance teams aware of or trained in microservices best practices. As you saw in Figure 4.3, the new system will consist of a set of independent services, each responsible for offering a specific service. This is one key advantage of the microservices paradigm—it reduces the communication overheads, including those multiple nonstop meetings. Teams should be organized by business problems or areas they are trying to address. The communication then becomes about the timing and set of standards/ protocols to follow so that these microservices can work with each other as one platform.

- **Agility.** Each team must be prepared to function independently of others. They should be the size of a standard scrum team; otherwise, communication will become an issue again. Execution is the key, and each team should be able to address the changing business needs.

- **Tools and training.** One of the key needs is the organization's readiness to invest in new tools and people training. The existing tools and processes, in most cases, would need to be retired and new ones picked up. This will require a large capital investment as well as investment in hiring people with new skills and retraining existing staff members. In the long term, if the decision is right to get on microservices, organizations will see savings and recoup the investment.

Services-Based Approach

Unlike with monolithic applications, with microservices you need to take a self-sustained services-based approach. Think of your application as a bunch of loosely coupled services that communicate with each other to provide complete application functionality. Each service must be thought of as an independent, self-contained service with its own lifecycle that can be developed and maintained by independent teams. These teams may select from a variety of technologies, including languages or databases that best suit their services' needs. For example, for an e-commerce site, the team would write a completely independent service, such as a shopping cart microservice, with an in-memory database, and another one, such as an ordering microservice, with a relational database. A real-world application may employ microservices for basic functions such as authentication, account, user registration, and notification with the business logic encapsulated in an API gateway that calls these microservices based on the client and external requests.

Just a reminder: a microservice may be a small service implemented by a single developer or a complex service requiring a few developers. With microservices, the size does not matter; it all depends on one function that a service has to provide.

Other aspects that must be considered at this point are scaling, performance, and security. Scaling needs can be different and provided on an as-needed basis at each microservice level. Security should be thought of at all levels, including data at rest, interprocess communication, data at motion, and so on.

Interprocess (Service-to-Service) Communication

We discussed the topic of interprocess communication in depth in Chapter 3, "Interprocess Communication." Key aspects that must be thought of are security and communication protocol. Asynchronous communication is the way to go, as it keeps all requests on track and does not hold resources for extended periods of time.

Using a message bus such as RabbitMQ may prove to be beneficial for this kind of communication. It is simple and can scale to hundreds of thousands of messages per second. To prevent the messaging system from becoming a single point of failure if it goes down, the messaging bus must be properly designed for high availability. Other options include ActiveMQ, which is another lightweight messaging platform.

Security is key at this stage. In addition to selecting the right communication protocol, industry standard tools such as AppDynamics may be used to monitor and benchmark the interprocess communication. Any anomalies must be reported automatically to the security team.

When there are thousands of microservices, it does become complex to handle everything. We already discussed how to address such issues through discovery services and API gateways in Chapter 3.

Technology Selection

The biggest advantage of transitioning to microservices is that it enables choices. Each team can independently select the language, technology, database, and so on, that is the best fit for the given microservice. Usually in a monolithic approach, the team does not have this flexibility, so make sure you do not overlook and miss the opportunity.

Even if a team is handling multiple microservices, each microservice must be looked at as a self-contained service, and it needs be analyzed. Scalability, deployment, build time, integrations and plugins operability, and so on, must be kept in mind when choosing the technology for each microservice. For microservices with lighter data but faster access, an in-memory database may be most suitable, whereas others may share the same relational or NoSQL databases.

Implementation

Implementation is the critical phase; this is where all the training and best practices knowledge comes in handy. Some of the critical aspects to keep in mind include the following:

- **Independency.** Each microservice should be highly autonomous with its own lifecycle and treated as such. It needs to be developed and maintained without any dependencies on other microservices.

- **Source control.** A proper version control system must be put at place, and each microservice must follow the standards. Standardizing on a repository is also helpful, as it ensures all the teams use the same source control. It helps in various aspects, such as code review, providing easy access to all the code in one place. In the long term, it makes sense to have all the services on the same source control.

- **Environments.** All different environments, such as dev, test, stage, and production, must be properly secured and automated. The automation here includes the build process—that way the code can be integrated as required, mostly on a daily basis. There are several tools available, and Jenkins is widely used. Jenkins is an open source tool that helps automate the software build and release process including continuous integration and continuous delivery.

- **Failsafe.** Things can go wrong, and software failure is inevitable. Handling failures of downstream services must be addressed within the microservice development. Failure of other services must be graceful to the extent that the failure should be invisible to the end user. This includes managing service response times (timeouts), handling API changes for downstream services, and limiting the number of auto-retry.

- **Reuse.** With microservices, don't be shy about reusing the code by using copy and paste, but do it within limits. This may cause some code duplication, but it's better than using shared code that may end up coupling services. In microservices, we want decoupling, not tight coupling. For example, you will write code to consume the output response from a service. You can copy this code every time you call the same service from any client. Another way to reuse code is by creating common libraries. Multiple clients can use the same library, but then each client should be responsible for maintaining its libraries. It can sometimes become challenging when you create too many libraries and each client is maintaining a different version. In that case, you may have to include multiple versions of same library, and the build process may become difficult due to backward compatibility and similar concerns. Depending on your needs, you can go either way as long as you can control the number of libraries and versions by clients and put a tight process around them. This will certainly save you from lot of code duplication.

- **Tagging.** Given the sheer number of microservices, debugging a problem may become difficult, so you need to do some kind of instrumentation at this stage. One of the best practices is to tag each request with a unique request ID and log each one of them. This unique ID will identify the originating request and should be passed by each service to any downstream requests. When you see issues, you can clearly track back through logs and identify the problematic service. This solution will be most effective if you establish a centralized logging system. All the services should log in all the messages to this shared system in a standardized format so that teams can replay the events as required all from one place, from infrastructure to application. A shared library for centralized logging is worth looking into, as we previously discussed. There are several log management and aggregation tools out there in the market, such as ELK (Elasticsearch, Logstash, Kibana) and Splunk, that are ideal.

Deployment

Automation is the key during deployment. Without it, success with a microservices paradigm would be almost impossible. As we discussed, there may be hundreds to thousands of microservices, and for the agile delivery, automation is a *must*.

Think of deploying thousands of microservices and maintaining them. What happens when one of the microservices goes down? How do you know which machine has enough resources to run your microservices? It becomes very complicated to manage this without automation in place. Various tools, such as Kubernetes and Docker Swarm, can be used to automate the deployment process. Given the importance of this topic, a whole chapter, Chapter 9, "Container Orchestration," is dedicated to deployment.

Operations

The operations part of the process needs to be automated as well. Again, we are talking about hundreds to thousands of microservices—organizational capabilities need to mature enough to handle this level of complexity. You'll need a support system, including the following:

- **Monitoring.** From infrastructure to application APIs to last-mile performance, everything should be monitored, and automatic alerts with proper thresholds should be put in place. Consider building live dashboards with data and alerts that pop up during issues.

- **On-demand scalability.** With microservices, scalability is the simplest task. Provision another instance of your microservice you want to scale and just put it behind the existing load balancer and you are all set. But in a scaled environment, this also needs to be automated. As we will discuss later, it is a matter of setting up an integer value to tell the number of instances you want to run for a particular microservice.

- **API exposure.** In most cases, you will want to expose the APIs externally for external users to consume. This is best done by using an edge server, which can handle all the external requests. It can utilize the API gateway and discovery service to do its job, and you can use one edge server per device type (e.g., mobile, browser) or use case. An open source application created by Netflix, called Zuul, can be utilized for this function and beyond.

- **Circuit breaker.** Sending a request to a failed service is pointless. Hence, a circuit breaker can be built that tracks the success and failure of every request made to every service. In the case of multiple failures, all the requests to that particular service should be blocked (break the circuit) for a set time. After the set time expires, another attempt should be made, and so on. Once the response is successful, reconnect the circuit. This should be done at the service instance level. Netflix's Hystrix provides an open source circuit-breaker implementation.

Migrating a Monolithic Application to Microservices

While most of the best practices for building a new microservices-based application apply to migrating from an existing monolithic application as well, there are some additional guidelines that, if followed, will make the migration simpler and more efficient.

Although it may sound correct to convert the whole monolithic application to a completely microservices-based application, it may not be efficient or may be very costly in some cases to convert every function or capability into microservices. You might end up writing the application from scratch, after all. The right way to migrate may require a stepwise approach, as shown in Figure 4.4.

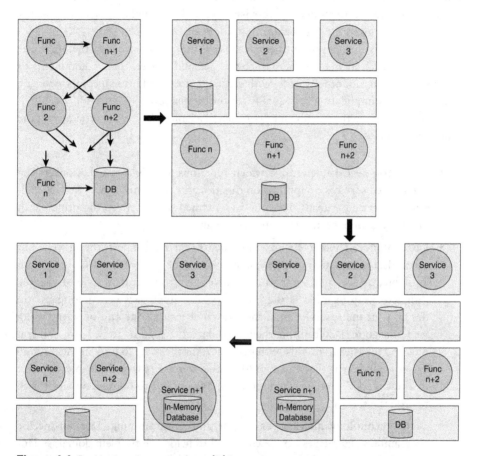

Figure 4.4 *Basic migration steps, monolithic to microservices*

The next question is, Where do we start with the current monolithic application? If the application is really old and it would be time consuming and difficult to take pieces out (i.e., if there is very high level of cohesiveness), then it is probably better to start from scratch. In other cases where parts of the code can be disabled quickly and the technology architecture is not completely outdated, it is better to start with rebuilding the components as microservices and replace the old code.

Microservices Criteria

The question then becomes what components should be migrated first or even migrated at all. That brings us to what I call the "microservices criteria," which outline one of the possible ways to select and prioritize the functions that should be migrated to microservices. They are a set of rules you establish that either qualifies or disqualifies the conversion of your existing monolithic application's components to microservices given the organization's needs at that time.

That "time" is very important here because with time the needs of the organization may change, and you may have to come back and convert more components to microservices later. In other words, with changing needs, additional components of your monolithic application may qualify for the conversion.

Here are best practices that can be considered as microservices criteria during the conversion process:

- **Scale.** You need to determine which functions are highly used. Convert the highly used services or application functionality as microservices first. Recall, a microservice performs only one well-defined service. Keep the principle in mind and divide the application accordingly.

- **Performance.** There likely are components that are not performing well, and other alternatives are readily available. It may be there is open source plugin available, or you may want to build a service from scratch. One of the key things to keep in mind is the boundary of a microservice. As long as you design your microservice in such a way that it does one and only one thing well, it is good. Determining the boundary is often going to be hard, and you will find it easier to do this with practice. Another way to look at the microservice boundary is that you should be able to rewrite the whole microservice in a few weeks' time (if/when required) as opposed to taking few months to rewrite the service.

- **Better technology alternatives or polyglot programming.** Domain-specific programming languages can be employed to help with problem domains. This is particularly applicable to components for which you received many enhancement requests in the past and you expect that to continue. If you think not only that such a component's implementation can be simplified using a new language or capability in the market but also that future maintenance and updates would become easier, then now is the right time to address such changes. In other cases, you may find another language provides easier abstractions for concurrency than the current one used. You can leverage the new language for a given microservice while the rest of the application can still be using a different language. Likewise, you may want some microservices to be extremely fast and may decide to write them in C to get the maximum gains rather than writing in another high-level language. The bottom line is to take advantage of this flexibility.

- **Storage alternatives or polyglot persistence.** With the rise of big data, some components of the application may provide value by using NoSQL databases rather than relational databases. If any such component in the application may benefit from this alternative, then it may be right time to make the switch to NoSQL.

These are the key aspects you should consider for each service or feature within your monolithic application, and you need to prioritize the conversion of such items first. Once you have derived the value from high-priority items, you can then apply other rules.

- **Modification requests.** One important thing to track in any software lifecycle is the new enhancements requests or changes. Features that have a higher number of change requests may be suitable for microservices because of the build and deployment time. Separating such services reduces the build and deployment time, as you will not have to build the entire application, just the changed microservice, which may also increase availability time for the rest of the application.

- **Deployment.** There are always some parts of the application that add deployment complexity. In a monolithic application, even if a particular feature is untouched, you still must go through the complete build and deployment process. If such cases exist, it is beneficial to cut out such pieces and replace them with microservices so your overall deployment time is reduced for the rest of the monolithic application. We talk more about this after we learn about containers.

- **Helper services.** In most applications, the core or main service depends on some of the helper services. The unavailability of such helper functions may impact the availability of the core service. For example, in our helpdesk application, discussed in Chapter 11, ticketing depends on the product catalog service. If the product catalog service is not available, the user will be unable to submit a ticket. If such cases exist, helper services should be converted to microservices and appropriately made highly available so they can better serve core services. These are also called *circuit-breaker services*.

Depending on the application, this criteria may require most of the services to be converted to microservices, and that is okay. The intention here is to simplify the conversion process so that you can prioritize and define the roadmap for your migration to a microservices-based architecture.

Rearchitecting the Services

Once you have identified the functions to be migrated as microservices, it's time to start rearchitecting the selected services following the best practices from the earlier scenario. Here are the aspects to keep in mind:

- **Microservices definition.** For each function, define the appropriate microservices, which should include communication mechanism (API), technology definition, and so on. Consider the data your existing function uses, or create and plan accordingly the data strategy for microservices. If the function was on heavy databases such as Oracle, would it make sense to move to MySQL? Determine how you are going to manage the data relationship. Finally, run each microservices as a separate application.

- **Refactor code.** You may reuse some of the code if you are not changing the programming language. Think about the storage/database layer—shared vs. dedicated, in-memory vs. external. The goal here is not to add new functionality unless required but to repackage the existing code and expose the required APIs.

- **Versioning.** Before you begin coding, decide on the source control and versioning mechanism, and make sure these standards are followed. Each microservice is to be a separate project and deployed as a separate application.

- **Data migration.** If you decide to create a new database, you will have to migrate the legacy data also. This is usually handled by writing simple SQL scripts depending on your source and destination.

- **Monolithic code.** Initially, leave the existing code in place in the monolithic application in case you have to roll back. You can either update the rest of the code to use the new microservices or, better, split your application traffic, if possible, to utilize both the monolithic and microservices version. This provides you the opportunity to test and keep an eye on performance. Once confident, you can move all the traffic to microservices and disable/get rid of old code.

- **Independent build, deploy, and manage.** Build and deploy each microservice independently. As you roll out new versions of microservices, you can again split the traffic between the old and the new version for some time. This means that you may have two or more versions of the same microservice running in the production environment. Some of the user traffic can be routed to the new microservice version to make sure the service works and performs right. If the new version is not performing optimally or as expected, it would be easy to roll back all the traffic to the previous version and send the new version back to development. The key here is to set up the repeatable automated deployment process and move toward continuous delivery.

- **Old code removal.** You can remove your temporary code and delete the data from the old storage location only after you have verified that everything is migrated correctly and operating as expected. Be sure to make backups along the way.

A Hybrid Approach

When writing a brand-new application, developers can directly follow the microservices architecture principles and blueprint to build the software application, as we have discussed. Developers sometimes follow a kind of hybrid approach of microservices and monolithic. In this case, they can develop part of their application as microservices and the rest following standard SOA/MVC practices based on certain criteria. The idea is that not all the components of the application may qualify as microservices.

As we discussed in Chapter 3, microservices offer lot of flexibility, but this flexibility comes at some cost. The hybrid approach is to balance the flexibility and cost aspects with the understanding that, over time, components can be pulled out of the monolithic part and converted to microservices on an as-needed basis. The key is to keep both approaches in mind, along with microservices criteria, during this transition.

PART II

Containers

Chapter 5

Docker Containers

This chapter covers another trending topic, Docker containers. As companies expand, they experience growing pains due to software deployment and scalability. Over time, with more users and features, the software tends to get complex, and then the real software deployment and scalability nightmares begin. We discussed in Chapter 1, "An Introduction to Microservices," that microservices can address the development challenge by simplifying the architecture, but we also discussed that it pushes down the complexity of operations, which includes deployment and scalability. Further complicating the challenge is that, with microservices-based architecture, you are probably going to have thousands of services to host, deploy, and manage. That's where containers come in to address most of our issues.

Docker is an open source technology initiative that addresses the deployment and scalability problems by separating applications from the infrastructure dependencies. It addresses these problems with containers, which allow us to package the application with all its dependencies, including the directory structure, metadata, processes space, sets of ports, and so on. We can run the packaged application the same way, always, across all machines and environments. That's what makes Docker interesting and is the single biggest factor in its meteoric rise. You might be thinking, that's what virtual machines (VM) do. To understand the difference, let's see how these technologies are different.

Virtual Machines

In its simplest form, a virtual machine is a self-contained system that includes everything from its own operating system (called guest OS) to an application environment and the application itself. Multiple virtual machines per host or physical machine can be installed using a layer called a *hypervisor* on top of the host machine OS. This hypervisor, also called type 2 hypervisor, acts as a proxy for hardware, giving the impression to guest OSs that they are running on their dedicated hardware. See Figure 5.1. The type 1 hypervisor directly runs on top of the hardware without a host OS in place and is considered a bare-metal hypervisor.

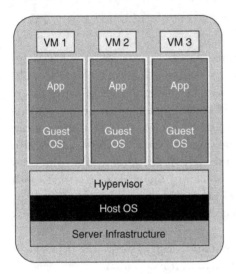

Figure 5.1 *Basic virtual machine architecture with hypervisor atop the host operating system (type 2 hypervisor)*

The VM concept gained lot of traction and created a multibillion-dollar industry because it allowed organizations to utilize the available hardware resources to the best extent possible. Before virtualization, companies used to run dedicated servers for an application. Sharing this infrastructure was okay in a development environment, but in production, all of the server resources were dedicated to one application as a best practice. This resulted in a wastage of resources when the application couldn't use all the resources at all times. We all know how powerful these servers and machines have become over time. Hence virtualization provided this huge opportunity to utilize the server resources more efficiently, at the same time providing the application segregation such that each application can run on its own OS as a separate virtual machine. This model has been widely successful, and it's actually how cloud originated—the rest is history. Virtual machines offered many advantages:

- **Efficiency.** A virtual machine feels and works like a separate machine. The key advantage is efficient resource usage and isolation from a security standpoint.

- **Flexibility.** Resources can be allocated as needed. CPUs, memory, and the like can all be distributed on an initial requirements basis and when needed. Further, resource allocation can auto-adjust to some higher rate. This concept is also known as *elasticity*.

- **Backup and recovery.** Virtual machines can be stored as a single file that can be easily backed up on another source. If and when required, it can be copied back.

- **OS freedom.** Different guest OSs can exist on the same hypervisor. Therefore, you can support multiple applications catering to their specific OS needs.

- **Performance and moving.** It is very easy to move a virtual machine from one host to another in case of performance degradation on the host machine. Most hypervisors support this feature automatically. VMware, a very successful virtualization software, provides this capability with a feature called VMotion, which enables the live migration of a running virtual machine from one host to another.

There are many other advantages, such as cost saving, but this discussion covers the key ones.

Why use containers? To answer that question, we need to also understand some of the issues with virtual machines. If you look again at Figure 5.1, you can likely point out the issues. We have a machine with a host OS. Then we have a hypervisor and an extra OS per virtual machine. We all know an OS is bulky in terms of resource consumption and size. First, it consumes a good chunk of storage and requires a lot of processing power. Second, when we take a backup of a virtual machine, even though it is mostly a single file, it is very big because it contains an OS (Window, Linux, etc.), the installed application with the dependencies, and its local data. Some VM backups may run more than 20GB. This results in a few challenges:

- **Sharing virtual machines.** Moving and sharing virtual machines across a WAN takes lot of time due to sheer size.

- **Portability.** When a coder ships a virtual machine to a fellow coder, over time changes will likely be made to the application, databases, environment, and so on.

The coder will have to ship the whole VM file again, and there is no way for him to do a diff between two VM files. Similar issues occur when we go from development to test to production environments. Either the code needs to be recompiled on every virtual machine, or we need to transfer the complete environment.

- **Performance overhead.** The whole concept of an application talking to its guest OS, which in turns talks to a hypervisor, which then talks to the host OS that controls hardware to get the request fulfilled, is inefficient in the case of a type 2 hypervisor. You can sense some performance issues here due to extra layers. In the case of type 1 hypervisors, the hypervisors are directly installed on the hardware, so the extra overhead of the hypervisor interacting with the host OS goes away. However, the rest of the overheads previously listed still exist.

- **Efficient resource utilization.** Resource usage on a virtual machine is certainly better than running applications on physical machines with a single OS, which leaves the resources idle when an application is lightly used. At same time, virtualization isn't perfect, either, because of the replicating of multiple OSs with a hypervisor.

These are the challenges with virtualization, and the good news is that containers address all of these issues and more. Let's get right into containers.

Containers

Containers also provide a virtual environment that packages the application processes, metadata, and file system—everything that is required by an application to run. But unlike virtual machines, containers do not require their own OSs. Instead, they are just wrappers around a UNIX process that directly talks to the kernel to request and use the resources. Check out Figure 5.2.

As you can see, containers clearly provide the application and process isolation where one application is completely unaware of the existence of another application. But all the processes run on and share the same kernel used by OS. How does this happen? Containers use resource isolation features of the Linux kernel, such as control groups and namespaces, to allow independent processes to run within a single Linux instance. This goes back to why each application does not have its own OS, as VMs do. This also means that virtual machines provide better isolation than containers provide. However, that's what makes containers very lightweight, making them easy to ship and move around. Because of this lightweight nature of containers, you can run more containers on a given hardware combination than if you were to run VMs. With containers, you use your hardware resources much more efficiently.

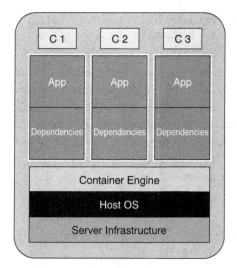

Figure 5.2 *Basic container architecture. Dependencies: directory structure, libraries, process space, and so on*

These containers are also known as *Linux containers* or *LXCs*. The containers concept has been around forever but has only recently gained significant popularity due to Docker. As we discussed, Docker is an open source initiative that introduced several changes to Linux-based containers to make them more portable, easy to use, and flexible. It did that by implementing set of utilities that enable the containers portability and flexibility. These utilities allow you to easily create, ship, copy, and run containers. Using Docker containers, you can overcome most of the disadvantages of using VMs.

There are some subtle differences between Linux and Docker containers:

- **Processes.** Within LXC, you can run multiple processes, whereas Docker containers are restricted to run as a single process. If your application consists of multiple processes, then you must run an equal number of Docker containers. Although it creates a containers management problem, it provides immense flexibility to the application system. Since there is one container per process, you can manage and change behavior at a granular/process level. This is a key advantage and represents the solution that was most needed for microservices: a self-contained service with one process.

- **Persistent storage.** Docker containers are stateless, as they do not support persistence storage. You must attach an external storage by mounting the storage as a Docker volume.

- **Portability.** Docker provides more portability than does LXC, which is the reason Docker become very popular. With LXC, the portability is not guaranteed; that is, when you move an LXC container from one host to another, it may not run smoothly due to different server configuration. Docker, by contrast, guarantees that portability will not be an issue because it abstracts the OS, networking, and storage details from the application better than LXC does. So, when a developer is done with development and testing, he or she can create an image, which can be downloaded on production and is guaranteed to work on the production. This is a key complexity that Docker containers address, making engineers' lives a little easier.

Docker Architecture and Components

Docker uses a client–server architecture whereby the client talks to the Docker daemon, which mainly provides all the services. Let's review the components that provide the workflow and toolsets to manage and deploy the containers, completing the Docker ecosystem:

- **Docker server or daemon.** This resides on the host system and manages all the containers running on the host machine.
- **Docker container.** This is a standalone virtual system that contains the running process, all the files, dependencies, process space, and ports that are required to run the application. Since every container has all the ports available, we do the mapping at the Docker level. We talk more about this later.
- **Docker client.** A user interface or a command-line interface is used to communicate with the Docker daemon.
- **Docker images.** These are read-only template files of a Docker container that you can move around and distribute. Unlike with virtual machines, these files can be version controlled. Not only that, you can run `docker diff` to see changes between two images. Each image consists of multiple layers that may be shared across images. Suppose you have to upgrade the existing application. The update will create a new layer on top of the existing image. This means you can ship and deploy just the new layer, making the overall process lighter and faster, and that's what makes containers lightweight.

- **Docker registry.** This is a repository for sharing and storing Docker container images. A well-known registry is Docker Hub (just like GitHub) that allows you to pull or push the container images with public or private access. You can have your own private registry within your organization.

- **Dockerfile.** This is a very simple text file where you can specify the commands to build Docker images. It allows you to set up instructions to install software; set up environment variables, working directories, and ENTRYPOINT; and add new code using Docker commands. This result in a customized software. We review Docker commands in Chapter 7, "Docker Interface."

- **Docker Machine.** Docker Machine allows you spin up Docker hosts on your local machine or within your public or private cloud, including on various service providers such as Amazon and Microsoft Azure. It also provides a way to manage the hosts through Docker Machine commands—start, stop, inspect, and more. For the latest information, refer to Docker online documentation.

- **Docker Swarm.** Swarm provides out-of-the-box clustering capability wherein a pool of Docker nodes act as one large Docker host. It is a separate tool, which you can install using Docker Machine or, manually, by pulling the Swarm image. At the time of writing, it is being integrated into the Docker Engine. The setup process is pretty straightforward: configure the Swarm manager on all the nodes, and you have it. The beauty is that we can just tell Swarm to start our containers, and it will decide which node to start them on, thus hiding all the complexity. In order to dynamically configure and manage the services in the container, you use a discovery service. The integrated option is called *Swarm mode*, and it works same as the Swarm tool. It also supports load balancing and service discovery and hence acts as a full-fledged orchestration engine. To enable Swarm mode, you use the simple init command and add workers using the join command. We learn more about Docker Swarm later in the book.

- **Docker Compose.** An application will have multiple components and consequently will be running multiple containers. Docker provides the Compose tool, which allows you to define and run multiple container applications. You can define the application environment in a single Dockerfile and the services in the docker-compose.yml file, which will automatically spin up the required containers per the instructions in these files. Like Docker Machine, Compose provides commands for managing the application services with a single command.

Figure 5.3 shows how everything fits together from a logical architecture perspective.

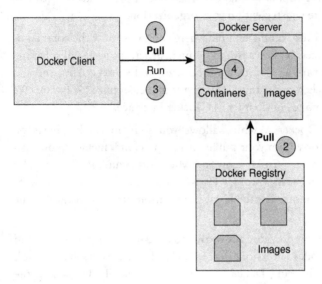

Figure 5.3 *Docker architecture: how it all fits together*

In upcoming chapters, we present a detailed example of pulling and standing up a Docker container. But first we go through the Docker installation (Chapter 6) and commands (Chapter 7). The key point for now is that Docker containers provide a virtual environment, and the rest of the components are the toolsets to manage and operationalize these containers.

So what are the advantages of using Docker technology? It not only addresses many of the issues encountered with virtual machines but also provides VM benefits and other advantages that make it a perfect fit for DevOps:

- **Lightweight.** Docker containers do not have their own OS, so their size is reduced. Also, containers can be stored as images, which are simple files that can be version controlled and distributed easily.

- **Portable.** A Docker container is the sum of an application and all its dependencies bundled together independently of the deployment model, OS version, and so on. This container can be easily transferred to another host machine in the form of an image and run without any issues. You can build it once and run it everywhere.

- **Reuse.** Docker images are simply a set of layers, and successive commands create new layers of images to create a final image. Once an image is built, Docker reuses it for new builds, which makes the builds faster and images smaller, since it reuses or shares these images. For example, we may have an image with, say, file 1 on top of an Apache web server running on Ubuntu. Suppose we need another image with file 2 on top of Apache web server running on Ubuntu. Since we already have the first image, Docker will reuse all the layers of first image except the file 1 layer to create a second image. That means both final images will share the Ubuntu and Apache layers, and each image will have a file layer of its own, which will be the only difference between these two images.

- **Fast deployment.** Docker containers are fully self-sufficient, lightweight packages that are easy to distribute and are completely tested during the testing cycle. The same container can be deployed in production with no or very minimal changes, hence expediting the deployment and reducing the rollbacks due to environment dependencies. This feature is also key for continuous development.

- **Efficient use of resources.** Like virtual machines, Docker uses the resources efficiently, perhaps better than virtual machines do, because of the Docker containers' lighter weight. At the same time, it provides acceptable isolation. Because of their size, a higher number of containers can be installed on a host machine compared to the number of virtual machines installed on the same host.

In many cases, Docker containers are preferable to virtual machines, but let's be very clear: Docker is not going to replace virtual machines. In fact, typical deployments have been taking advantage of the power of both technologies by running Docker inside virtual machines, making the use of resources very efficient.

The Power of Docker: A Simple Example

By now, you probably understand the power of Docker at a theoretical level. You will learn a lot more in upcoming chapters, but let's discuss a small Docker-based deployment and the value it offers.

Assume you have to set up a basic WordPress site that has three parts: a web server with all your WordPress applications, a relational database such as MySQL, and storage to store this data. In a VM world, you can have all these parts on one or more virtual machines. You need to create a VM using your VM manager and then install the OS-specific software (MySQL, WordPress) on each virtual machine. A typical deployment may look like Figure 5.4.

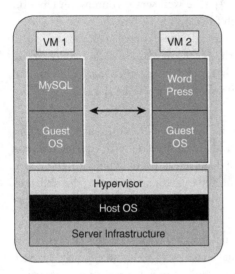

Figure 5.4 *Typical virtual machine deployment*

Let's deploy the same configuration using Docker, keeping microservices in mind. Remember what we discussed earlier: this will provide us independent and standalone capability as an executable/process that communicates with other services or programs through standard interprocess communication.

Similarly, we discussed that each Docker container runs just one process. You make the containers work together by using link options—that's what brings them together. In this example, we need to create three containers:

Step 1: Data container. You can easily pull an existing basic Linux image such as Ubuntu from the Docker Hub and run it. This way, you can create the local storage, which is equivalent to creating a directory structure where you want to store the data. You also have ability to allocate memory, storage, and CPU. Following is the command:

```
docker create --name mysql_data_container -v /var/lib/mysql
ubuntu
```

Step 2: MySQL container. Similarly, you can pull the latest MySQL version image from the Docker Hub and run it on your local host. In the same run command, you can map the volume created in the previous step. In less than 2 minutes, your database is up and running. Following is the command:

```
docker run --volumes-from mysql_data_container -v /var/
lib/mysql:/var/lib/mysql -e MYSQL_USER=mysql -e
MYSQL_PASSWORD=mysql -e MYSQL_DATABASE=test -e
MYSQL_ROOT_PASSWORD=test -it -p 3306:3306 -d mysql
```

Step 3: WordPress container. Just as we did in the previous step, we can pull and run the latest image of WordPress. In the same run command, we can link the MySQL database we created in the previous step:

```
docker run -d --name wordpress --link mysql:mysql wordpress
```

You are all set up with a personal WordPress site in less than 10 minutes. See Figure 5.5.

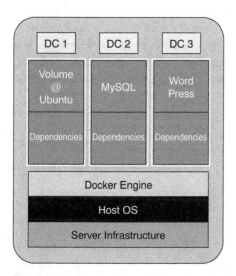

Figure 5.5 *How just three containers can help create a WordPress site*

You can see from Figures 5.4 and 5.5 how lightweight containers are—they don't need their own OSs. Not only that, their lightweight simplifies maintenance and scaling aspects:

- **Very simple upgrade process.** Say you want to upgrade the image of MySQL. All you need is to stop the MySQL container you started in step 2. Pull the latest version of MySQL image and run it along with the mapping to the same volume.

- **Reuse.** Say you want to customize a version of WordPress for your special team. You can pull another WordPress image and run another Docker container and link to the same database.

- **Simple, straightforward clustering.** Docker provides native clustering called Swarm mode. Using just a few commands, you can create a cluster, load balance, and discover your services. We learn more about this in upcoming chapters.

Welcome to the world of containers. A lot is happening is this field, and the Docker community is moving very fast on a daily basis to introduce new capabilities. Also, lots of startup companies are trying to address some challenges and add more automations. While we cover a lot more on Docker containers in upcoming chapters, you should bookmark Docker's community page, https://www.docker.com/docker-community, to stay up to date.

Chapter 6

Docker Installation

Until a year or so, it was a pain to install Docker, but now it's a piece of cake. Docker is based on Linux technology, which is good news, as most of the Linux major distributions such as Centos, Ubuntu, and Amazon Linux support Docker.

In this chapter, we cover installation on Mac OS X, Windows, and Ubuntu Linux.

Installing Docker on Mac OS X

These installation instructions assume your Mac is from 2010 or later, with OS X 10.11 or later. To verify, click the Apple icon and select **About This Mac**. We will download and work with Docker release 17.03.0:. This is the latest release at the time of writing this book.

1. Enter the following URL in your browser: https://docs.Docker.com/Docker-for-mac/install/#download-Docker-for-mac. Click **Get Docker for Mac (Stable)** to start downloading the Docker toolbox in your Downloads folder.

2. Double-click the package to open it. You should see the pop-up shown in Figure 6.1.

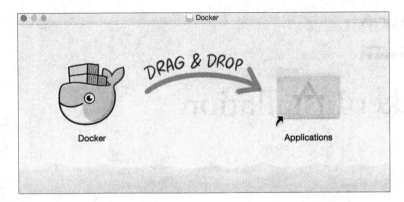

Figure 6.1 *Drag and drop*

3. Drag the Docker whale icon into your Applications folder to download the Docker application to your machine, as shown in Figure 6.2.

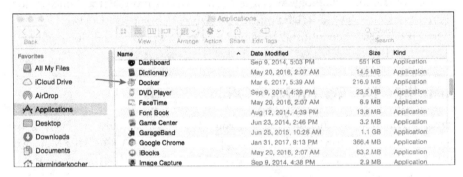

Figure 6.2 *Applications folder with Docker added*

4. Double-click the Docker application and click **Open**. It will give you the screen shown in Figure 6.3; click **OK**.

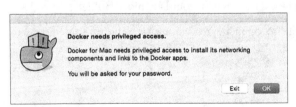

Figure 6.3 *Allow access*

5. You will see another pop-up asking for your Mac OX password. Enter your password.

6. If you have installed Docker toolbox in the past, you will see the pop-up shown in Figure 6.4 giving you the option to copy your existing Docker images and containers. Select **Copy** if you want to copy over existing images; otherwise, select **No.** If it is a fresh install, you will not see this screen.

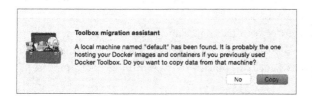

Toolbox migration assistant

A local machine named "default" has been found. It is probably the one hosting your Docker images and containers if you previously used Docker Toolbox. Do you want to copy data from that machine?

No   Copy

Figure 6.4 *Pop-up shown if you have installed Docker toolbox in the past*

7. This will start the installation process; when complete, your Docker engine will start, as shown in Figure 6.5.

Figure 6.5 *Result when installation is complete*

That's it—your installation of the Docker is complete.

Once the environment is up, it gives you an opportunity to register on Docker Hub. Recall that Docker Hub is the cloud-based registry service for storing and distributing Docker images. It has public space where you can share your Docker images, and they will be available for anyone to access. You can also purchase a private option to limit access to only your team.

If you are already registered, enter your username and password (or you can skip it for now). Upon signing in, you are taken to the Docker Hub where you can explore all the publicly available Docker images or you can start creating Docker images, as shown in Figure 6.6.

Figure 6.6 *Docker Hub homepage*

We learn all about Docker commands in the next chapter, but let's try some basic ones now. First, let's verify the Docker version we installed and play with Docker Terminal.

Open a terminal window on your Mac. Execute `docker --version` to confirm the version of Docker installed on your machine, as shown in Figure 6.7.

```
PKOCHER-M-343X:~ parminderkocher$ docker --version
Docker version 17.03.0-ce, build 60ccb22
PKOCHER-M-343X:~ parminderkocher$ ▮
```

Figure 6.7 *Docker version confirmation*

You are all set with Docker version 17.03.0. To list the commands, execute docker --help. You should see all the commands available to you, as shown in Figure 6.8.

```
PKOCHER-M-343X:~ parminderkochers docker --help

Usage:        docker COMMAND

A self-sufficient runtime for containers

Options:
      --config string          Location of client config files [default "/Users/par
                               minderkocher/.docker"]
  -D, --debug                  Enable debug mode
      --help                   Print usage
  -H, --host list              Daemon socket(s) to connect to [default []]
  -l, --log-level string       Set the logging level ["debug", "info", "warn", "error",
                               "fatal"] [default "info"]
      --tls                    Use TLS; implied by --tlsverify
      --tlscacert string       Trust certs signed only by this CA [default "/Users/
                               parminderkocher/.docker/ca.pem"]
      --tlscert string         Path to TLS certificate file [default "/Users/parmin
                               derkocher/.docker/cert.pem"]
      --tlskey string          Path to TLS key file [default "/Users/parminderkocher
                               /.docker/key.pem"]
      --tlsverify              Use TLS and verify the remote
  -v, --version                Print version information and quit

Management Commands:
  checkpoint    Manage checkpoints
  container     Manage containers
  Image         Manage images
  network       Manage networks
  node          Manage Swarm nodes
  plugin        Manage plugins
  secret        Manage Docker secrets
  service       Manage services
  stack         Manage Docker stacks
  swarm         Manage Swarm
  system        Manage Docker
  volume        Manage volumes

Commands:
  attach        Attach to a running container
  build         Build an image from a Dockerfile
  commit        Create a new image from a container's changes
  cp            Copy files/folders between a container and the local filesystem
  create        Create a new container
  deploy        Deploy a new stack or update an existing stack
  diff          Inspect changes to files or directories on a container's filesystem
  events        Get real time events from the server
  exec          Run a command in a running container
  export        Export a container's filesystem as a tar archive
```

Figure 6.8 *Docker commands available to you*

Installing Docker on Windows

These installation instructions assume you are working on a 64-bit Windows 10 Pro Enterprise or Education edition. The Hyper-V package must also be enabled to properly install Docker. If it is not, refer to Docker Help (https://docs.Docker.com/Docker-for-windows/install/#download-Docker-for-windows) before proceeding. We will download and work with Docker version 17.03.0, the latest release at the time of writing:

1. Enter the following URL in your browser: https://docs.docker.com/docker-for-windows/install/#download-docker-for-windows. Click **Get Docker for Windows (Stable)**. This should start downloading the Docker toolbox in your Downloads folder.

2. Double-click on the package to open it. You should see the license agreement screen, shown in Figure 6.9.

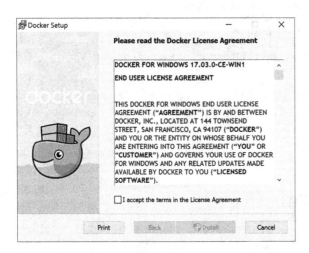

Figure 6.9 *Docker license agreement*

3. Accept the terms and conditions by checking the checkbox at the bottom of the screen, and then click **Install** to install Docker on your Windows machine.

4. After it installs, you should see a small "Docker is starting" pop-up at the bottom right of the screen. Once it starts, you will see the pop-up shown in Figure 6.10, and you're all set!

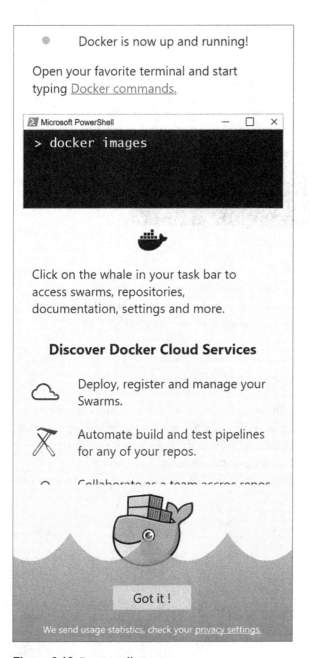

Figure 6.10 *Post-installation pop-up*

That's it—your installation of the Docker tools is complete.

We will learn Docker commands in the next chapter, but let's use some basic ones. Let's verify the Docker version we installed and play with Docker Terminal.

Open a terminal window. Execute `docker --version` to confirm the version of Docker installed on your machine, as shown in Figure 6.11.

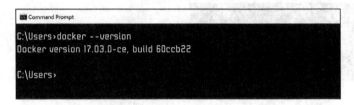

Figure 6.11 *Docker version confirmation*

You are all set with Docker version 17.03.0

To list the commands, execute `docker --help`. You should see all the commands available to you, similar to what was shown earlier in Figure 6.11.

Installing Docker on Ubuntu Linux

We will download and work with Docker version 17.2.3, the latest release at the time of writing. For up-to-date information on the most recent release, see https://docs.Docker.com/engine/installation/linux/ubuntu/#install-using-the-repository. Also refer to this URL if you are working with a different flavor of Linux.

These installation instructions assume your Ubuntu installation is a 64-bit version and one of the following versions:

- Trusty 14.04
- Yakkety 16.10
- Xenial 16.04

You can check the version by executing the following command, as shown Figure 6.12:

```
$ lsb_release -a
```

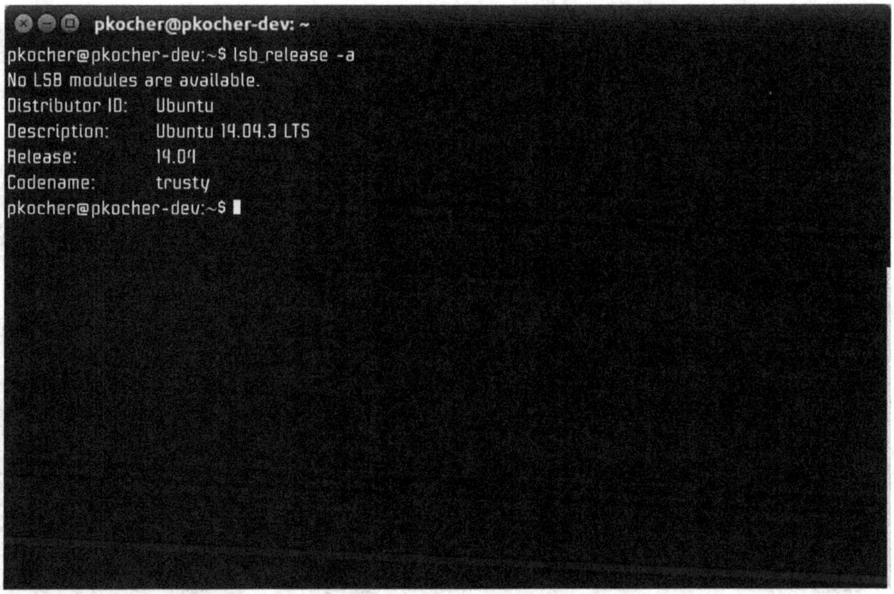

Figure 6.12 *Ubuntu version check*

The steps also assume it is a fresh install of Docker on your Linux box. While we have used Trusty 14.04, these instructions are applicable to the other two versions as well.

If you are working with Trusty 14.04, it is recommended that you install linux-image-extra -* packages if they are not already installed. These packages allow Docker to use the AUFS storage drivers. AUFS is the default storage backend for Docker installed on Ubuntu. (Device Mapper is the default on other flavors.) To install the packages, run the following command:

```
$ sudo apt-get update
```

The preceding command pulls all the latest packages, as shown in Figure 6.13, and now you are ready to install these updates. Execute the following command:

```
$ sudo apt-get install \
   linux-image-extra-$(uname -r) \
   linux-image-extra-virtual
```

```
● ● ●   pkocher@pkocher-dev: ~
pkocher@pkocher-dev:~$ sudo apt-get update
Ign http://us.archive.ubuntu.com trusty InRelease
Ign http://extras.ubuntu.com trusty InRelease
Get: 1 http//us.archive.ubuntu.com trusty-updates InRelease [65.9 kB]
Get: 2 http//extras.ubuntu.com trusty Release.gpg [72 B]
Ign http://dl.google.com stable InRelease
Get: 3 http://security.ubuntu.com trusty-security InRelease [65.9 kB]
Hit http://extras.ubuntu.com trusty Release
Get: 4 http://dl.google.com stable Release.gpg [916 B]
Get: 5 http//us.archive.ubuntu.com trusty-backports InRelease [65.9 kB]
Hit http://extras.ubuntu.com trusty/main Sources
Get: 6 http://security.ubuntu.com trusty-security/multiverse amd64 Packages [4,139 B]
Get: 7 http://dl.google.com stable Release [1,189 B]
Hit http://extras.ubuntu.com trusty/main amd64 Packages
Hit http://us.archive.ubuntu.com trusty Release.gpg
Hit http://extras.ubuntu.com trusty/main i386 Packages
Get: 8 http://dl.google.com stable/main amd64 Packages [1,427 B]
Get: 9 http://us.archive.ubuntu.com trusty-updates/main Sources [393 kB]
Get: 10 http://security.ubuntu.com trusty-security/universe amd64 Packages [154 kB]
Get: 11 http://us.archive.ubuntu.com trusty-updates/restricted Sources [5,911 B]
Get: 12 http://security.ubuntu.com trusty-security/main amd64 Packages [593 kB]
```

Figure 6.13 *Installing additional packages*

This command installs the updates, and now you can install Docker on your Linux system. There are two different editions available: Docker CE (Community Edition) and Docker EE (Enterprise Edition). We will work with CE edition:

1. You need to install the Docker repository, from which you can then pull the Docker install. Install the package by executing this command to allow apt-get to use the repository over HTTPS:

   ```
   $ sudo apt-get install \
     apt-transport-https \
     ca-certificates \
     curl \ software-properties-common
   ```

2. Add the GPG key for the official Docker repository to the system:

   ```
   $ curl -fsSL https://download.Docker.com/linux/ubuntu/gpg |
   sudo apt-key add
   ```

3. Validate that the key fingerprint is 9DC8 5822 9FC7 DD38 854A E2D8 8D81 803C 0EBF CD88 (see Figure 6.14):

   ```
   $ sudo apt-key fingerprint 0EBFCD88
   ```

```
pub     4096R/0EBFC088 2017-02-22
        Key fingerprint = 9DC8 5822 9FC7 D038 854A E208 8D81 803C 0EBF C088
uid                     Docker Release [CE deb] <docker@docker.com>
sub     4096R/F273FC08 2017-02-22
pkocher@pkocher-dev:~$ ▮
```

Figure 6.14 *Key fingerprint validation*

4. Add the Docker repository to APT (Advanced Packaging Tool) sources:

```
$ sudo add-apt-repository "deb [arch=amd64] <-DOCKER-EE-URL> \
    $(lsb_release -cs) \ stable-"
```

5. Update the package index with the Docker packages from the newly added repository:

```
$ sudo apt-get update
```

6. Install the latest version of Docker (see Figure 6.15):

```
$ sudo apt-get install Docker-ce
```

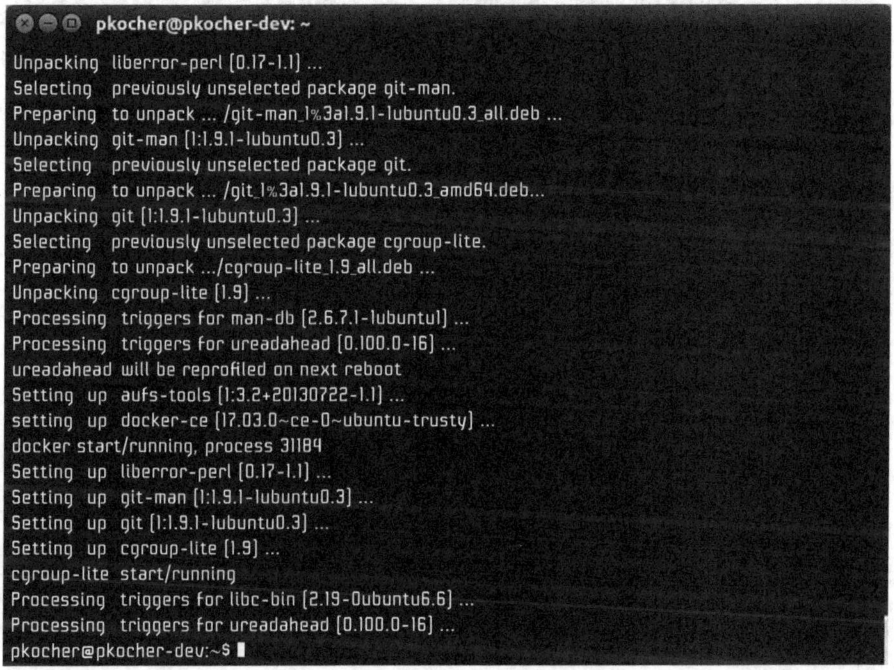

```
⊗⊖⊡  pkocher@pkocher-dev: ~
Unpacking  liberror-perl [0.17-1.1] ...
Selecting  previously unselected package git-man.
Preparing  to unpack ... /git-man_1%3a1.9.1-1ubuntu0.3_all.deb ...
Unpacking  git-man [1:1.9.1-1ubuntu0.3] ...
Selecting  previously unselected package git.
Preparing  to unpack ... /git_1%3a1.9.1-1ubuntu0.3_amd64.deb...
Unpacking  git [1:1.9.1-1ubuntu0.3] ...
Selecting  previously unselected package cgroup-lite.
Preparing  to unpack .../cgroup-lite_1.9_all.deb ...
Unpacking  cgroup-lite [1.9] ...
Processing  triggers for man-db [2.6.7.1-1ubuntu1] ...
Processing  triggers for ureadahead [0.100.0-16] ...
ureadahead will be reprofiled on next reboot
Setting  up aufs-tools [1:3.2+20130722-1.1] ...
setting  up docker-ce [17.03.0~ce-0~ubuntu-trusty] ...
docker start/running, process 31184
Setting  up liberror-perl [0.17-1.1] ...
Setting  up git-man [1:1.9.1-1ubuntu0.3] ...
Setting  up git [1:1.9.1-1ubuntu0.3] ...
Setting  up cgroup-lite [1.9] ...
cgroup-lite start/running
Processing  triggers for libc-bin [2.19-0ubuntu6.6] ...
Processing  triggers for ureadahead [0.100.0-16] ...
pkocher@pkocher-dev:~$ ▮
```

Figure 6.15 *Latest version of Docker being installed*

7. Confirm the version, as shown in Figure 6.16:

```
$ Docker --version
```

Figure 6.16 *Docker installation confirmation*

That's it—your installation of Docker on Ubuntu Linux is complete.

Chapter 7

Docker Interface

In Chapter 5, "Docker Containers," we talked about Dockerfile, which contains a set of commands that are executed by the Docker daemon. In this chapter, we cover the most commonly used commands. Then we create a Dockerfile using the commands and execute the file to review results.

Key Docker Commands

You can think of the following compendium of commands as the proverbial bible that must be mastered to work successfully with Docker—everything from searching and building images to creating your own Dockerfile. We review the simpler commands first and then build on them to get to some more involved ones.

Docker Search

The `docker search` command can be run on Docker CLI to search the available images in the Docker registry:

```
docker search [options] term
```

The GUI-based client also provides the search capability.

In the example shown in Figure 7.1, `docker search mysql` returns all the images that have "mysql" in the name of the image. As you can see, it returns the top 25 results. The GUI-based search provides similar results, as shown in Figure 7.2.

```
Parminders-MacBook-Pro:~ parminderkochers docker Search mysql
NAME                        DESCRIPTION                              STARS   OFFICIAL   AUTOMATED
mysql                       MySQL is a widely used, open-source relati...   1064    [OK]
mysql/mysql-server          Optimized MySQL Server Docker images. Crea...     41              [OK]
orchardup/mysql                                                              41              [OK]
centurylink/mysql           Image containing mysql. Optimized to be li...    27              [OK]
wnameless/mysql-phpmyadmin  MySQL + phpMyAdmin https://index.docker.io...    23              [OK]
sameersbn/mysql                                                              20              [OK]
google/mysql                MySQL server for Google Compute Engine           13              [OK]
loggstream/mysql            MySQL Image with Master-Slave replication         5              [OK]
appcontainers/mysql         CentOS 6.7 based Customizible MySQL 5.5 Co...     5              [OK]
marvambass/mysql            MySQL Server based on Ubuntu 14.04                3              [OK]
jdeathe/centos-ssh-mysql    CentOS-6 6.6 x86_64 / MySQL.                      2              [OK]
azukiapp/mysql              Docker image to run MySQL by Azuki - http:...     2              [OK]
frodenas/mysql              A Docker Image for MySQL                          1              [OK]
ibourgeois/mysql            MySQL image from ibourgeois/base                  1              [OK]
bahmni/mysql                Mysql container for bahmni. Contains the...       1              [OK]
phpmentors/mysql            MySQL server image                                1              [OK]
jmoati/mysql                                                                  0              [OK]
guihatano/mysql             MySQL Server on Ubuntu 14.04                      0              [OK]
lancehudson/docker-mysql    MySQL is a widely used, open-source relati...     0              [OK]
tetraweb/mysql                                                                0              [OK]
ukyil/mysql                 mysql base on alpine                              0              [OK]
wenzizone/mysql             mysql                                             0              [OK]
dockerizedrupal/mysql       docker-mysql                                      0              [OK]
javl3r/mysql                mysql                                             0              [OK]
ahmet2mir/mysql             This is a Debian based image with MySQL se...     0              [OK]
Parminders-MacBook-Pro:~ paraminderkochers ▮
```

Figure 7.1 *Docker search results for "mysql"*

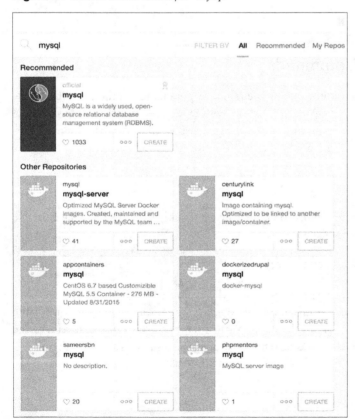

Figure 7.2 *GUI-based search results for "mysql"*

Although some of the results, such as dockerizedrupal, are unique, many are duplicates because they've been uploaded by different users who have used them for custom purposes or made integrations. Using the -s option, the search produces only the widely used files based on feedback from other users:

```
docker search -s 50 mysql
```

This command returns all the images that have "mysql" in the name of the image and at least 50 stars in feedback, as shown in Figure 7.3.

```
Parminders-MacBook-Pro:~ parminderkochers docker search -s 50 mysql
NAME          DESCRIPTION                                   STARS   OFFICIAL    AUTOMATED
mysql         MySQL is a widely used, open-source relati... 1044    [OK]
mariadb       MariaDB is a community-developed fork of M... 214     [OK]
Parminders-MacBook-Pro:~ paraminderkochers ▮
```

Figure 7.3 *Search results with "mysql" in the name of the image and at least 50 stars in feedback*

In this case, only two entries are listed, as they are the only two with more than 50 ratings.

> **Note**
>
> Docker has been evolving at a tremendous pace, so commands, options, and even features and functionality change frequently across releases. For example, as this book was written, the -s in search was deprecated; a flag called --filter must be used instead. With the filter option, the command to list all the MySQL images with star ratings of 50 or more would be
>
> ```
> docker search --filter stars=50 mysql
> ```

Docker Pull

The docker pull command downloads the requested image from the Docker registry to our local machine:

```
docker pull image:tag
```

For example, docker pull MySQL, shown in Figure 7.4, pulls the MySQL image from the registry. Unless a tag, such as version, is specified, this command appends the "latest" tag by default instead of pulling all the MySQL images available. The command is equivalent to

```
docker pull MySQL:latest
```

```
Parminders-MacBook-Pro:~ parminderkocher$ docker pull mysql
Using default tag: latest
latest: Pulling from library/mysql

ba249489d0b6: Pull complete
19de96c112fc: Pull complete
2e32b26a94ed: Pull complete
637386aea7a0: Pull complete
f40aa7fe5d68: Pull complete
ca21348f3728: Pull complete
b783bc3b44b9: Pull complete
f94304dc94e3: Pull complete
efb904a945ff: Pull complete
64ef882b700f: Pull complete
291b704c92b1: Pull complete
adfeb78ac4de: Pull complete
f27e5410cda3: Pull complete
ca4b92f905b9: Pull complete
065018fec3d7: Pull complete
6762f304c834: Pull complete
library/mysql: latest: The image you are pulling has been verified. Important: image verification is a
tech preview feature and should not be relied on to provide security

Digest: sha256:842ee1ad1b0f19561d9fee65bb7c6197b2a2b4093f069e7969acefb6355e8c1b
Status: Downloaded newer image for mysql: latest
Parminders-MacBook-Pro:~ parminderkochers ▮
```

Figure 7.4 *The docker* pull *command pulling latest MySQL image from the registry*

Docker Images

The docker images command returns the list of available top-level images on our local machine:

```
docker images [options]
```

For example, docker images -a displays a list of all the top-level images, along with their repository, tag, create date, and virtual size, as shown in Figure 7.5. It does not show the intermediate layers' images.

```
Parminders-MacBook-Pro:~ parminderkocher$ docker images -a
REPOSITORY          TAG              IMAGE ID          CREATED         VIRTUAL SIZE
ubuntu              latest           91e54dfb1179      4 weeks ago     188.4 MB
<none>              <none>           d74508fb6632      4 weeks ago     188.4 MB
<none>              <none>           c22013c84729      4 weeks ago     188.4 MB
<none>              <none>           d3a1f33e8a5a      4 weeks ago     188.2 MB
Parminders-MacBook-Pro:~ parminderkochers ▮
```

Figure 7.5 *The docker* images *command displaying list of all top-level images, along with their repository, tag, create date, and virtual size*

One important thing to keep in mind is that when we create or build Docker images on our local machine, various intermediate layers are created. For example, if we use a Dockerfile that may have multiple commands to build the image, each command executed will result in one image layer. This is one of the key aspects of Docker that make the containers lightweight and perfect for reuse.

Docker RMI

The docker rmi command removes the requested image(s) from our local machine:

```
docker rmi [options] image [image, image...]
```

For example, the docker rmi MySQL command, shown in Figure 7.6, removes the MySQL image, including all the layers that were installed, from the host.

```
Parminders-MacBook-Pro:~ parminderkochers docker rmi mysql
Untagged: mysql:latest
Deleted: 6762f304c83428bf1945e9ab0aa05119a8a758d33d93eca50ba03665a89b5d97
Deleted: 065018fec3d7c28754f0d40a3c1d56f103996a49f2995fde8c79ed1bd524a9d0
Deleted: ca4b92f905b922ee6d5faf8f21592a4e8fb16a56fce47447c58c0c9356243384
Deleted: f27e5410cda3728deb33a884fda066d826c0b9bd0268ea9990ab6754f979ac3a
Deleted: adfeb78ac4de9f11124e4585a62bb9a5bfbb7e1686b4f2977106dff8626806c9
Deleted: 291b704c92b15a350ac3be00279a251b7038826cf9253047b594bfc1c50bd82b
Deleted: 64ef882b700fb8ad04e843e28ea56552265519925f3ceafb1a187c49cf27e2df
Deleted: efb904a945ffleb48b1a03f5052a0d0ef3365e38436f0f3dd581d4c77854e1a3
Deleted: f94304dc94e325bb13db375898780bec04fc83362381d6b8476ab288287e5d9a
Deleted: b783bc3b44b9b8cd7b781bc86183ad490e3b7b1dca740a4df3e365843cbe5a5a
Deleted: ca21348f372879b0b48ccc5a7e7ce8c97da42f1339b86ec8932231c15bd548be
Deleted: f40aa7fe5d68f46e6ae72ffla2808c95411f773d140d986506f352b90e412171
Deleted: 637386aea7a0d378aef7c4213300cab50d0ccbbe8ddb0bad18620f5ce73d0c53
Deleted: 2e32b26a94eda87d141712d27037a22abc0fa0cbc5b924e4f6870d5dc207f0d3
Deleted: 19de96c112fcca5b6de1661ldc0a359b0b977c551921ca79ac5cf4a8bfff9351
Deleted: ba249489d0b6512128b60a4910e78fa2000c785d59e0599188a6802bd01155f2
Parminders-MacBook-Pro:~ parminderkochers
Parminders-MacBook-Pro:~ parminderkochers
Parminders-MacBook-Pro:~ parminderkochers docker images
REPOSITORY            TAG            IMAGE ID        CREATED        VIRTUAL SIZE
Parminders-MacBook-Pro:~ parminderkochers ▮
```

Figure 7.6 *MySQL image removed via* docker rmi *command*

Docker Run

Once we download (pull) an image, the next logical step is to execute (run) the image, and that's what the docker run command does:

```
docker run [options] image: tag [command, args]
```

This command spins up a container with its own file system, ports, and IP address. We can also pass some options along with the run commands with one or more arguments. Following are some common options:

- i switches to interactive mode with STDIN open.
- t allocates a pseudo-tty console terminal.

Many other options are available for the docker run command, such as for starting the process in the detached (-d) state (background)—that is, the container will start but not listen to the command line. We can also specify commands to override the default command that is part of the image we are running. We can also specify runtime constraints on CPU and memory.

As an example, let's pull the Ubuntu image and execute the run command (see Figure 7.7):

```
docker pull ubuntu:latest
```

```
Parminders-MacBook-Pro:~ parminderkocher$ docker pull ubuntu: latest
latest: Pulling from library/ubuntu

d3a1f33e8a5a : Pull complete
c22013c84729 : Pull complete
d74508fb6632: Pull complete
91e54dfb1179  : Pull complete
library/ubuntu: latest: The image you are pulling has been verified. Important: image verification is a tech preview feature and
should not be relied on to provide security.

Digest: sha256:73fbe2308f5f5cb6e343425831b8ab44f10bbd77070ecdfbe408ldaa4dbe3ed1
Status: Downloaded newer image for ubuntu: latest
Parminders-MacBook-Pro:~ parminderkochers ∎
```

Figure 7.7 *Downloading Ubuntu image from Docker Hub repository*

That command pulls the latest image of Ubuntu on the local host, as shown in Figure 7.8.

```
Parminders-MacBook-Pro:~ parminderkochers docker images -a
```

REPOSITORY	TAG	IMAGE ID	CREATED	VIRTUAL SIZE
ubuntu	latest	91e54dfb1179	4 weeks ago	188.4 MB
<none>	<none>	d74508fb6632	4 weeks ago	188.4 MB
<none>	<none>	c22013c84729	4 weeks ago	188.4 MB
<none>	<none>	d3a1f33e8a5a	4 weeks ago	188.2 MB

```
Parminders-MacBook-Pro:~ parminderkochers ∎
```

Figure 7.8 *Latest Ubuntu image pulled*

Now let's run Ubuntu on the local host with options i and t. Let's also specify that we want to run the shell process:

```
docker run -it ubuntu sh
```

We are now running the Ubuntu container on our local machine with an entry to the shell prompt. From here, we can run any shell command we desire. Figure 7.9 shows a few simple ones, such as

- echo 'Learning Docker'

- ls

- cd bin (to view the contents of the bin directory)

```
Parminders-MacBook-Pro:~ parminderkocher$ docker run -it ubuntu sh
# echo 'Learning Docker';
Learning Docker
# ls
bin  boot  dev  etc  home  lib  lib64  media  mnt  opt  proc  root  run  sbin  srv  sys  tmp  usr  var
# cd bin
# ls
bash            chgrp           dumpkeys    kill      mknod           openvt                      sed         true          zfgrep
bunzip2         chmod           echo        kmod      mktemp          pidof                       setfont     udevadm       zforce
bzcat           chown           egrep       less      more            ping                        setupcon    umount        zgrep
bzcmp           chvt            false       lessecho  mount           ping6                       sh          uname         zless
bzdiff          cp              fgconsole   lessfile  mountpoint      plymouth                    sh.distrib  uncompress    zmore
bzegrep         cpio            fgrep       lesskey   mt              plymouth-upstart-bridge      sleep       unicode_start znew
bzexe           dash            findmnt     lesspipe  mt-gnu          ps                          ss          vdir
bzfgrep         date            grep        ln        mv              pwd                         stty        which
bzgrep          dd              gunzip      loadkeys  nc              rbash                       su          whiptail
bzip2           df              gzexe       login     nc.openbsd      readlink                    sync        ypdomainname
bzip2recover    dir             gzip        ls        netcat          rm                          tailf       zcat
bzless          dmesg           hostname    lsblk     netstat         rmdir                       tar         zcmp
bzmore          dnsdomainname   ip          lsmod     nisdomainname   run-parts                   tempfile    zdiff
cat             domainname      kbd_mode    mkdir     open            running-in-container        touch       zegrep
#
```

Figure 7.9 *Running the interactive shell*

As you can see, the bin directory has the essential programs that the system requires to operate.

Docker ps

The docker ps command lists all the current running containers, as shown in Figure 7.10:

```
docker ps [Options]
```

Remember that each container runs one and only one process. In this case, we don't have any running container, hence the empty list.

```
Parminders-MacBook-Pro:~ parminderkochers docker ps
CONTAINER  ID        IMAGE          COMMAND        CREATED      STATUS        PORTS        NAMES
Parminders-MacBook-Pro :~ parminderkochers ▌
```

Figure 7.10 *The* docker ps *command revealing all currently running containers*

Let's run the ps command again with the -a option, as shown in Figure 7.11, to see all the containers, even the ones that aren't running.

```
Parminders-MacBook-Pro:~ parminderkochers docker ps -a
CONTAINER ID        IMAGE          COMMAND        CREATED        STATUS              PORTS
  NAMES
c8b9770c88e9        ubuntu         "sh"           5 minutes ago  Exited [0] 3 minutes ago
  admiring_albattani
Parminders-MacBook-Pro:~ parminderkochers docker restart c8b9770c88e9
c8b9770c88e9
```

Figure 7.11 *The* –a *option adding inactive containers to the mix*

As we can see, since we exited the shell prompt, our Ubuntu container is not running or active anymore. It is not deleted, though, just inactive. We can restart the container if we like, as we will learn soon.

Docker Logs

The docker logs command provides the given container's log files, which contain the standard (stdout and stderr) output of the container:

```
docker logs [Options] Container
```

This command is available only for containers with a JSON File logging driver. As an example, let's run the following command to run the shell process:

```
docker run -it ubuntu sh
```

Run a couple of shell commands, such as ls, -a, and cd bin, as shown in Figure 7.12:

```
PKOCHER-M-343X:~ parminderkochers docker run -it ubuntu sh
# ls
bin     dev   home  lib64   mnt   proc  run   srv  tmp  var
boot    etc   lib   media   opt   root  sbin  sys  usr
# cd bin
# ls -a
.                   false           more          stty                           uname
..                  fgrep           mount         su                             uncompress
bash                findmnt         mountpoint    sync                           vdir
cat                 grep            mv            systemctl                      wdctl
chgrp               gunzip          networkctl    systemd                        which
chmod               gzexe           nisdomainname systemd-ask-password           ypdomainname
chown               gzip            pidof         systemd-escape                 zcat
cp                  hostname        ps            systemd-inhibit                zcmp
dash                journalctl      pwd           systemd-machine-id-setup       zdiff
date                kill            rbash         systemd-notify                 zegrep
dd                  ln              readlink      systemd-tmpfiles               zfgrep
df                  login           rm            systemd-tty-ask-password-agent zforce
dir                 loginctl        rmdir         tailf                          zgrep
dmesg               ls              run-parts     tar                            zless
dnsdomainname       lsblk           sed           tempfile                       zmore
domainname          mkdir           sh            touch                          znew
echo                mknod           sh.destrib    true
egrep               mktemp          sleep         umount
```

Figure 7.12 *Some examples of shell commands*

Open another terminal window and find the container ID for the Ubuntu container we just started by running the following command (see Figure 7.13):

```
docker ps -a
```

```
PKOCHER-M-343X:~ parminderkochers docker ps -a
CONTAINER ID    IMAGE              COMMAND        CREATED          STATUS
      PORTS                 NAMES
eded3539719c    ubuntu             "sh"           6 minutes ago    Up 6 minutes
                              flamboyant_edison
6a3f4a2d3694    ubuntu             "sh"           7 minutes ago    Exited (0) 7 minutes ago
                              friendly_wilson
PKOCHER-M-343X:~ parminderkochers ▮
```

Figure 7.13 *Finding the container ID for the Ubuntu container we just started*

Copy the container ID for the running Ubuntu container. Now we can execute the log commands to review the log for this particular container (see Figure 7.14):

```
docker log eded3539719c
```

We can see the content of the log—in this case, the history of commands that have been executed.

```
PKOCHER-M-343X:~ parminderkochers docker logs eded3539719c
# ls
bin    dev  home  lib64   mnt   proc  run   srv  tmp  var
boot   etc  lib   media   opt   root  sbin  sys  usr
# cd bin
# ls -a
.                false        more          stty                        uname
..               fgrep        mount         su                          uncompress
bash             findmnt      mountpoint    sync                        vdir
cat              grep         mv            systemctl                   wdctl
chgrp            gunzip       networkctl    systemd                     which
chmod            gzexe        nisdomainname systemd-ask-password        ypdomainname
chown            gzip         pidof         systemd-escape              zcat
cp               hostname     ps            systemd-inhibit             zcmp
dash             journalctl   pwd           systemd-machine-id-setup    zdiff
date             kill         rbash         systemd-notify              zegrep
dd               ln           readlink      systemd-tmpfiles            zfgrep
df               login        rm            systemd-tty-ask-password-agent  zforce
dir              loginctl     rmdir         tailf                       zgrep
dmesg            ls           run-parts     tar                         zless
dnsdomainname    lsblk        sed           tempfile                    zmore
domainname       mkdir        sh            touch                       znew
echo             mknod        sh.distrib    true
egrep            mktemp       steep         umount
#
#
#
#
#
#
PKOCHER-H-343X:~ parminderkochers ▮
```

Figure 7.14 *Executing the log commands to review this container's log*

Let's take another, more complex example. Let's download and create a MySQL container.

First, pull the latest MySQL image (see Figure 7.15):

```
docker pull MySQL: latest
```

```
Parminders-MacBook-Pro:~ parminderkochers docker pull mysql
Using default tag: latest
latest: Pulling from library/mysql

ba249489d0b6: Pull complete
19de96c112fc : Pull complete
2e32b26a94ed: Pull complete
637386aea7a0: Pull complete
f40aa7fe5d68 : Pull complete
ca21348f3728 : Pull complete
b783bc3b44b9: Pull complete
f94304dc94e3 : Pull complete
efb904a945ff : Pull complete
64ef882b700f : Pull complete
291b704c92b1 : Pull complete
adfeb78ac4de : Pull complete
f27e5410cda3 : Pull complete
ca4b92f905b9 : Pull complete
065018fec3d7 : Pull complete
6762f304c834 : Pull complete
library/mysql: latest: The image you are pulling has been verified. Important : image verification is a tech preview feature and
should not be relied on to provide security.

Digest: sha256:842eeladlb0f19561d9fee65bb7c6197b2a2b4093f069e7969acefb6355e8c1b
Status: Downloaded newer image for mysql:latest
Parminders-MacBook-Pro:~ parminderkochers ▮
```

Figure 7.15 *Latest MySQL image pulled*

Next, use the `run` command to build the MySQL container (see Figure 7.16) and note the container ID:

```
docker run --name myDatabase \
> -e MySQL_ROOT_PASSWORD=myPassword \
> -d MySQL:latest
```

Here, `name` is the name of the database, `e` is the flag for environment variable specifying the database password, and `d` is the option for the `docker run` command to start the process in detached mode.

```
Parminders-MacBook-Pro:~ parminderkochers docker run --name myDatabase -e MYSQL_ROOT_PASSWORD=myPassword -d mysql:latest
fcb85434597bc8abf5e97acdf985a3315027aa9836eeef4af9b66669493d2c39
Parminders-MacBook-Pro:~ parminderkochers ▮
```

Figure 7.16 *Running the MySQL container*

Next, verify the container process:

```
docker ps
```

Notice the container is up and running, as shown in Figure 7.17.

```
Parminders-MacBook-Pro:~ parminderkochers docker ps
CONTAINER ID    IMAGE          COMMAND               CREATED         STATUS          PORTS       NAMES
fcb85434597b    mysql:latest   "/entrypoint.sh mysql" 25 seconds ago  Up 24 seconds   3306/tcp    myDatabase
Parminders-MacBook-Pro:~ parminderkochers ▮
```

Figure 7.17 *Verifying the container process*

Now that the container is up and running, we need to connect to it. First we need to know is the port. We know the default, but let's check in the log file by running the `logs` command:

```
docker logs fcb85434597b
```

Here, `fcb85434597b` is the container ID we previously started (see Figure 7.18). As shown in Figure 7.19, we see the version and the port where MySQL is listening. Please note again that the Docker logs show the `stdout` and `stderr` information for the container. Don't confuse this with standard log file for MySQL.

```
Parminders-MacBook-Pro:~ parminderkochers docker ps
CONTAINER ID      IMAGE           COMMAND             CREATED          STATUS          PORTS       NAMES
fcb85434597b      mysql:latest    "/entrypoint.sh mysql" 25 seconds ago  Up 24 seconds   3306/tcp    myDatabase
Parminders-MacBook-Pro:~ parminderkochers
Parminders-MacBook-Pro:~ parminderkochers
Parminders-MacBook-Pro:~ parminderkochers docker logs fcb85434597b
Running mysql_install_db
2015-10-14 03:32:52 0 [Note] /usr/sbin/mysqld [mysqld 5.6.27] starting as process 15 ...
2015-10-14 03:32:52 15 [Note] InnoDB: Using atomics to ref count buffer pool pages
2015-10-14 03:32:52 15 [Note] InnoDB: The InnoDB memory heap is disabled
2015-10-14 03:32:52 15 [Note] InnoDB: Mutexes and rw_locks use GCC atomic builtins
2015-10-14 03:32:52 15 [Note] InnoDB: Memory barrier is not used
2015-10-14 03:32:52 15 [Note] InnoDB: Compressed tables use zlib 1.2.8
2015-10-14 03:32:52 15 [Note] InnoDB: Using Linux native AIO
2015-10-14 03:32:52 15 [Note] InnoDB: Using CPU crc32 instructions
2015-10-14 03:32:52 15 [Note] InnoDB: Initializing buffer pool, size= 128.0M
2015-10-14 03:32:52 15 [Note] InnoDB: Completed initialization of buffer pool
2015-10-14 03:32:52 15 [Note] InnoDB: The first specified data file ./ibdata1 did not exist: a new database to be created!
2015-10-14 03:32:52 15 [Note] InnoDB: Setting file ./ibdata1 size to 12 MB
2015-10-14 03:32:52 15 [Note] InnoDB: Database physically writes the file full: wait ...
2015-10-14 03:32:52 15 [Note] InnoDB: Setting log file ./ib_logfile101 size to 48 MB
2015-10-14 03:32:52 15 [Note] InnoDB: Setting log file ./ib_logfile1 size to 48 MB
2015-10-14 03:32:52 15 [Note] InnoDB: Renaming log file ./ib_logfile101 to ./ib_logfile0
2015-10-14 03:32:52 15 [Warning] InnoDB: New log files created, LSN=45781
2015-10-14 03:32:52 15 [Note] InnoDB: Doublewrite buffer not found: creating new
2015-10-14 03:32:52 15 [Note] InnoDB: Doublewrite buffer created
2015-10-14 03:32:52 15 [Note] InnoDB: 128 rollback segment(s) are active.
2015-10-14 03:32:52 15 [Warning] InnoDB: Creating foreign key constraint system tables.
2015-10-14 03:32:52 15 [Note] InnoDB: Foreign key constraint system tables created
2015-10-14 03:32:52 15 [Note] InnoDB: Creating tablespace and datafile system tables.
2015-10-14 03:32:52 15 [Note] InnoDB: Tablespace and datafile system tables created.
2015-10-14 03:32:52 15 [Note] InnoDB: Waiting for purge to start
2015-10-14 03:32:52 15 [Note] InnoDB: 5.6.27 started; log sequence number 0
2015-10-14 03:32:53 15 [Note] Binlog end
2015-10-14 03:32:53 15 [Note] InnoDB: FTS optimize thread exiting.
2015-10-14 03:32:53 15 [Note] InnoDB: Starting shutdown ...
2015-10-14 03:32:54 15 [Note] InnoDB: Shutdown completed; log sequence number 1625977
```

Figure 7.18 *Running the* logs *command*

```
MySQL init process done. Ready for start up.

2015-10-14 03:33:00 0 [Note] mysqld [mysqld 5.6.27] starting as process 1 ...
2015-10-14 03:33:00 1 [Note] Plugin 'FEDERATED' is disabled.
2015-10-14 03:33:00 1 [Note] InnoDB: Using atomics to ref count buffer pool pages
2015-10-14 03:33:00 1 [Note] InnoDB: The InnoDB memory heap is disabled
2015-10-14 03:33:00 1 [Note] InnoDB: Mutexes and rw_locks use GCC atomic builtins
2015-10-14 03:33:00 1 [Note] InnoDB: Memory barrier is not used
2015-10-14 03:33:00 1 [Note] InnoDB: Compressed tables use zlib 1.2.8
2015-10-14 03:33:00 1 [Note] InnoDB: Using Linux native AIO
2015-10-14 03:33:00 1 [Note] InnoDB: Using CPU crc32 instructions
2015-10-14 03:33:00 1 [Note] InnoDB: Initializing buffer pool, size= 128.0M
2015-10-14 03:33:00 1 [Note] InnoDB: Completed initialization of buffer pool
2015-10-14 03:33:00 1 [Note] InnoDB: Highest supported file format is Barracuda.
2015-10-14 03:33:00 1 [Note] InnoDB: 128 rollback segment(s) are active.
2015-10-14 03:33:00 1 [Note] InnoDB: Waiting for purge to start
2015-10-14 03:33:00 1 [Note] InnoDB: 5.6.27 started; log sequence number 1625997
2015-10-14 03:33:00 1 [Note] Server hostname [bind-address]: '*'; port: 3306
2015-10-14 03:33:00 1 [Note] IPv6 is available.
2015-10-14 03:33:00 1 [Note]    - '::' resolves to '::' ;
2015-10-14 03:33:00 1 [Note] Server socket created on IP: '::'.
2015-10-14 03:33:00 1 [Warning] 'proxies_priv' entry '@ root@fcb85434597b' ignored in --skip-name-resolve mode.
2015-10-14 03:33:00 1 [Note] Event Scheduler: Loaded 0 events
2015-10-14 03:33:00 1 [Note] mysqld: ready for connections.
Version: '5.6.27' socket: '/var/run/mysqld/mysqld.sock' port: 3306 MySQL Community Server [GPL]
Parminders-MacBook-Pro:~ parminderkochers █
```

Figure 7.19 *The version and port where MySQL is listening*

> **Note**
>
> Another way to check what port(s) a container is listening on is to check the docker ps output. If you notice, from Figure 7.18, there's a PORTS column that says 3306/tcp, which indicates that MySQL will be listening on port 3306.

Docker Restart

The docker restart command restarts the specified container:

```
docker restart [Options] Container ID (s)
```

Let's restart our Ubuntu container by specifying the container ID, which is c8b9770c88e9 from our earlier example. See Figure 7.20.

```
Parminders-MacBook-Pro:~ parminderkocher$ docker ps -a
CONTAINER ID     IMAGE        COMMAND        CREATED         STATUS               PORTS
  NAMES
c8b9770c88e9     ubuntu       "sh"           5 minutes ago   Exited (0) 3 minutes ago
  admiring_albattani
Parminders-MacBook-Pro:~ parminderkocher$ docker restart c8b9770c88e9
C8b9770c88e9
```

Figure 7.20 *Restarting our Ubuntu container*

If we run the ps command again, we should see an active container, as shown in Figure 7.21.

```
Parminders-MacBook-Pro:~ parminderkocher$ docker restart c8b9770c88e9
C8b9770c88e9
Parminders-MacBook-Pro:~ parminderkocher$ docker ps
CONTAINER ID     IMAGE        COMMAND        CREATED         STATUS         PORTS          NAMES
c8b9770c88e9     ubuntu       "sh"           2 weeks ago     Up 6 seconds                  admiring_albattani
Parminders-MacBook-Pro:~ parminderkocher ▌
```

Figure 7.21 *The ps command revealing an active container*

As you can see, we did not get the shell prompt. We can fix that by running the docker attach command, which is discussed next.

Docker Attach

The docker attach command allows the user to attach to a specified running container to control it interactively or to see the ongoing output:

```
docker attach [Options] Container ID
```

Let's run this command to attach to our Ubuntu container, c8b9770c88e9, to interact with the shell prompt. See Figure 7.22.

```
Parminders-MacBook-Pro:~ parminderkochers docker ps -a
CONTAINER ID     IMAGE        COMMAND        CREATED         STATUS                  PORTS      NAMES
c8b9770c88e9     ubuntu       "sh"           8 minutes ago   Exited [0] 24 seconds ago          admiring_albattani
Parminders-MacBook-Pro:~ parminderkochers docker restart c8b9770c88e9
c8b9770c88e9
Parminders-MacBook-Pro:~ parminderkochers docker ps
CONTAINER ID     IMAGE        COMMAND        CREATED         STATUS                  PORTS      NAMES
c8b9770c88e9     ubuntu       "sh"           8 minutes ago   Up 5 seconds                       admiring_albattani
Parminders-MacBook-Pro:~ parminderkochers docker attach c8b9770c88e
■ ▮
```

Figure 7.22 *Interacting with the shell prompt via* docker attach *command*

Notice we have the command prompt back and we can carry on. Another important aspect is that we will always get to the shell prompt when we restart this container—every time, no matter what. We cannot change its behavior because that's how we spun up the container initially using –it in our run command. But certainly we can run the same Ubuntu image again with different options, parameters, and commands. That's the beauty of Docker.

Docker Remove

The Docker remove, or rm, command removes one or more specified containers:

```
docker rm [Options] Container(s)
```

As an example, let's try to remove the Ubuntu container. We must stop the container before we can remove it or use - f (force) option to directly remove it, which actually sends a SIGKILL to the process running inside the container, and then container will be removed:

```
docker stop [Options] Container(s)
```

Figure 7.23 shows the status of our Ubuntu container. The Ubuntu container is in running state and has been up for the last 38 hours, as shown under status attribute.

```
Parminders-MacBook-Pro:~ parminderkochers docker ps -a
CONTAINER ID     IMAGE        COMMAND        CREATED         STATUS          PORTS      NAMES
c8b9770c88e9     ubuntu       "sh"           2 weeks ago     Up 38 hours                admiring_albattani
Parminders-MacBook-Pro:~ parminderkochers ■
```

Figure 7.23 *Status of Ubuntu container*

Let's run the stop command and execute ps - a again. See Figure 7.24.

```
Parminders-MacBook-Pro:~ parminderkocher$ docker stop c8b9770c88e9

c8b9770c88e9
Parminders-MacBook-Pro:~ parminderkocher$
Parminders-MacBook-Pro:~ parminderkocher$ docker ps -a
CONTAINER ID   IMAGE    COMMAND     CREATED       STATUS                    PORTS      NAMES
c8b9770c88e9   ubuntu   "sh"        2 weeks ago   Exited [137] 18 seconds ago          admiring_albattani
```

Figure 7.24 *Running the stop command and executing ps - a*

As you can see, the container is no longer running, and the status is exited with code 137, which means the container received the SIGKILL command. The stop command sends a SIGTERM and then SIGKILL after a grace period. We can adjust the grace period by specifying the number of seconds with the - t option. The time option may be very important in instances where we want a process to complete the outstanding requests, as in the case of HTTP.

We can also use the docker kill command, which directly sends the SIGKILL; it does not give the container process an opportunity to exit gracefully. However, it also provides options that let us send something other than SIGKILL to the container process.

Now that the container has been stopped, let's remove the container and do ps - a again. See Figure 7.25.

```
Parminders-MacBook-Pro:~ parminderkocher$ docker rm c8b9770c88e9
c8b9770c88e9
Parminders-MacBook-Pro:~ parminderkocher$
Parminders-MacBook-Pro:~ parminderkocher$ docker ps -a
CONTAINER ID   IMAGE    COMMAND     CREATED       STATUS       PORTS      NAMES
Parminders-Mac Book-Pro:~ parminderkocher$ ▮
```

Figure 7.25 *Container removed*

Notice that the container has been completely removed with no trace in the ps - a command.

Docker Inspect

The docker inspect command provides in-depth, low-level information on the container or image:

```
docker inspect [Options] Container ID/Image
```

Let's run this command on our MySQL container, as shown in Figure 7.26; recall that fcb85434597b is the container ID from previous examples:

```
docker inspect fcb85434597b
```

```
Parminders-MacBook-Pro:~ parminderkochers docker inspect fcb85434597b
[
{
    "Id": "fcb85434597bc8abf5e97acdf985a3315027aa9836eeef4af9b66669493d2c39",
    "Created": "2015-10-14T03:32:52.567916916Z",
    "Path": "/entrypoint.sh",
    "Args": [
        "mysqld"
    ],
    "State": {
        "Running": true,
        "Paused": false,
        "Restarting": false,
        "OOMKilled": false,
        "Dead": false,
        "Pid": 501,
        "ExitCode": 0,
        "Error": "",
        "StartedAt": "2015-10-14T03:32:52.640686535Z",
        "FinishedAt": "0001-01-01T00:00:00Z"
    },
    "Image": "9726f738a97ab74feb22704dc6d0f64a409b952fe41ba4dd7d28fc3d0149f718",
    "NetworkSettings": {
        "Bridge": "",
        "EndpointID": "8bell7ced4e0716b522fd0b16d2d52ef8cd587ced4d277ab98430299ff8e7eb7",
        "Gateway": "172.17.42.1",
        "GlobalIPv6Address": "",
        "GlobalIPv6PrefixLen": 0,
        "HairpinMode": false,
        "IPAddress": "172.17.0.6",
        "IPPrefixLen": 16,
        "IPv6Gateway": "",
        "LinkLocalIPv6Address": "",
        "LinkLocalIPv6PrefixLen": 0,
        "MacAddress": "02:42:ac:11:00:06",
        "NetworkID": "476d36a59ec3c998ff0e8b8c87e1b64ad095719190695a8cdd55b99263c556ff",
        "PortMapping": null,
        "Ports": {
            "3306/tcp": null
        },
        "SandboxKey": "/var/run/docker/netns/fcb85434597b",
        "SecondaryIPAddresses": null,
        "SecondaryIPv6Addresses": null
    },
    "ResolvConfPath": "/mnt/sda1/var/lib/docker/containers/fcb85434597bc8abf5e97acdf985a3315027aa9836eeef4af9b66669493d2c39/resolv.conf",
    "HostnamePath": "/mnt/sda1/var/lib/docker/containers/fcb85434597bc8abf5e97acdf985a3315027aa9836eeef4af9b66669493d2c39/hostname",
    "HostsPath": "/mnt/sda1/var/lib/docker/containers/fcb85434597bc8abf5e97acdf985a3315027aa9836eeef4af9b66669493d2c39/hosts",
    "LogPath": "/mnt/sda1/var/lib/docker/containers/fcb85434597bc8abf5e97acdf985a3315027aa9836eeef4af9b66669493d2c39/fcb85434597bc8abf5e97acdf985a33
    15027aa9836eeef4af9b66669493d2c39-json.log",
    "Name": "/myDatabase",
    "RestartCount": 0,
    "Driver": "aufs",
```

Figure 7.26 *Results of Docker inspect*

Notice it returns the complete JSON array with all the information. We can specify another format or query for some specific information, such as database name, IP address, and port information.

This command returns the database name:

```
docker inspect -format='{{.Name}}' fcb85434597b
```

This command returns the IP address of the MySQL container:

```
docker inspect \
> -format='{{.NetworkSettings.IPAddress}}' fcb85434597b
```

Docker Exec

The `docker exec` command enables you to remotely run a command in an already running container:

```
docker exec [Options] Container ID Command [Arg...]
```

Let's run this command on our Ubuntu container, as shown in Figure 7.27; recall that c8b9770c88e9 is the container ID from previous examples:

```
docker exec c8b9770c88e9 ls -a
```

```
PKOCHER-M-343K:~ parminderkocher$ docker exec e510f8e769fc ls -a
.
..
.dockerenv
bin
boot
dev
etc
home
lib
lib64
media
mnt
opt
proc
root
run
sbin
srv
sys
tmp
usr
var
PKOCHER-M-343K:~ parminderkocher$
PKOCHER-M-343K:~ parminderkocher$
```

Figure 7.27 *The docker exec command enabling the running of a command in an already running container*

Docker Rename

Are you tired of copying and pasting the container ID yet? We can give our containers meaningful names that we can more easily remember and categorize. The docker rename command enables us to rename an already running container:

```
Usage: docker rename Container ID new_name
```

Let's rename our Ubuntu container. Let's find the existing name first.

```
docker ps -a
```

Notice in Figure 7.28 that the current name of our container is jolly_gates.

```
PKOCHER-M-343X:~ parminderkochers docker ps -a
CONTAINER ID   IMAGE    COMMAND    CREATED         STATUS                  PORTS    NAMES
e510f8e769fc   ubuntu   "sh"       8 minutes ago   Up 8 minutes                     jolly_gates
eded3539719c   ubuntu   "sh"       26 minutes ago  Exited (0) 8 minutes ago         flamboyant_edison
6a3f4a2d3694   ubuntu   "sh"       28 minutes ago  Exited (0) 27 minutes ago        friendly_wilson
PKOCHER-M-343X:~ parminderkochers docker ▌
```

Figure 7.28 *Results of* docker rename

Let's execute the rename command:

```
docker rename e510f8e769fc Parminder
```

Notice in Figure 7.29 that executing the rename command changed the name of our container.

```
PKOCHER-M-343X:~ parminderkochers docker ps -a
CONTAINER ID   IMAGE    COMMAND    CREATED         STATUS                  PORTS    NAMES
e510f8e769fc   ubuntu   "sh"       8 minutes ago   Up 8 minutes                     jolly_gates
eded3539719c   ubuntu   "sh"       26 minutes ago  Exited (0) 8 minutes ago         flamboyant_edison
6a3f4a2d3694   ubuntu   "sh"       28 minutes ago  Exited (0) 27 minutes ago        friendly_wilson
PKOCHER-M-343X:~ parminderkochers docker rename e510f8e769fc Parminder
PKOCHER-M-343X:~ parminderkochers
PKOCHER-M-343X:~ parminderkochers
PKOCHER-M-343X:~ parminderkochers
PKOCHER-M-343X:~ parminderkochers docker ps -a
CONTAINER ID   IMAGE    COMMAND    CREATED         STATUS                  PORTS    NAMES
e510f8e769fc   ubuntu   "sh"       10 minutes ago  Up 10 minutes                    Parminder
eded3539719c   ubuntu   "sh"       28 minutes ago  Exited (0) 10 minutes ago        flamboyant_edison
6a3f4a2d3694   ubuntu   "sh"       29 minutes ago  Exited (0) 28 minutes ago        friendly_wilson
PKOCHER-M-343X:~ parminderkochers ▌
```

Figure 7.29 *Container renamed successfully*

Now we can use this new name to run various other commands instead of using HexID. See Figure 7.30.

```
PKOCHER-M-343X:~ parminderkochers docker tags Parminder
# ls
bin boot dev etc home lib lib64 media mnt opt proc root run sbin srv sys tmp usr var
PKOCHER-M-343X:~ parminderkochers ▮
```

Figure 7.30 *New name all set to run other commands*

Docker Copy

The docker cp command enables us to copy files between a container and the machine on which the container is running. The following pattern copies a file from the container to the local machine:

```
docker cp [OPTIONS] CONTAINER:SRC_PATH DEST_PATH
```

The following pattern copies a file from the local machine to the specified container:

```
docker cp [OPTIONS] SRC_PATH|- CONTAINER:DEST_PATH
```

Let's run the first command on our Ubuntu container. Figure 7.31 shows the sample.txt file we'll use for this example.

```
# pwd
/var
# ls -a
... backups cache lib local lock log mail opt run sample.txt spool tmp
# ▮
```

Figure 7.31 *sample.txt file we will use*

Parminder is the container name from the previous example, so following is the command to copy the file (see Figure 7.32):

```
docker cp Parminder:/var/sample.txt .
```

```
PKOCHER-M-343X:~ parminderkochers docker cp Parminder:/var/sampte.txt .
PKOCHER-M-343X:~ parminderkochers ls
Applications                                Downloads              Public
Box Sync                                    IdeaProjects           Root
Cloudera-Admin-test-VM                      Learning Scala         VirtualBox VMs
Cloudera-Admin-test-VM.zip                  Library                Whiteboard.ucf
Cloudera-Training-Get2EC2-VM-1.1-vmware-1.1 Movies                 eclipse
Cloudera-Training-Get2EC2-VM-1.1-vmware-1.1.zip  Music             myGitProject
Desktop                                     MyDocker               sample.txt
Dockerfile                                  MyJabberFiles          target
Documents                                   Pictures
PKOCHER-M-343X:~ parminderkochers ▮
```

Figure 7.32 *Copying a file from the Parminder container to the local machine*

Now let's try the command for copying from the machine to the container. Here we use an example file called Myfile.txt on the local machine, as shown in Figure 7.33.

```
PKOCHER-M-343X:~ parminderkochers touch MyFile.txt
PKOCHER-M-343X:~ parminderkochers ls
Applications                        Downloads               Pictures
Box Sync                            IdeaProjects            Public
Cloudera-Admin-test-VM              Learning Scala          Root
Cloudera-Admin-test-VM.zip          Library                 VirtualBox VMs
Cloudera-Training-Get2EC2-VM-1.1-vmware-1.1       Movies    Whiteboard.ucf
Cloudera-Training-Get2EC2-VM-1.1-vmware-1.1.zip   Music     eclipse
Desktop                             MyDocker                myGitProject
Dockerfile                          MyFile.txt              sample.txt
Documents                           MyJabberFiles           target
PKOCHER-M-343X:~ parminderkochers ▮
```

Figure 7.33 *Copying Myfile.tx from the machine to the container*

The following command copies this file to the container called Parminder and in the /var directory, as shown in Figure 7.34; recall that Parminder is the container ID from the previous example:

```
docker cp MyFile.txt Parminder:/var
```

```
# pwd
/var
# ls -a
.  ..  MyFile.txt backups cache lib local lock log mail opt run sample.txt spool tmp
# ▮
```

Figure 7.34 *Copying Myfile.tx from the local machine to /var directory inside container named Parminder*

Docker Pause/Unpause

The docker pause command suspends all processes in the specified containers:

```
docker pause CONTAINER [CONTAINER...]
```

On Linux, this command uses the cgroups freezer. The docker unpause command gets the container running again:

```
docker unpause CONTAINER [CONTAINER...]
```

Let's run the pause command on our Ubuntu container, as shown in Figure 7.35; recall that Parminder is the container name from previous examples:

```
docker pause Parminder
```

```
PKOCHER-M-343K:~ parminderkochers docker pause Parminder
Parminder
PKOCHER-M-343K:~ parminderkochers docker ps -a
CONTAINER ID    IMAGE     COMMAND    CREATED          STATUS                    PORTS    NAMES
e02085c7ba70    ubuntu    "sh"       19 minutes ago   Exited (0) 18 minutes ago          vibrant_saha
e510f8e769fc    ubuntu    "sh"       23 hours ago     Up 16 minutes [Paused]             Parminder
eded3539719c    ubuntu    "sh"       23 hours ago     Exited (0) 23 hours ago            flamboyant_edison
6a3f4a2d3694    ubuntu    "sh"       23 hours ago     Exited (0) 23 hours ago            friendly_wilson
PKOCHER-M-343K:~ parminderkochers █
```

Figure 7.35 *Running the docker pause command on our Ubuntu container*

We have just paused the container, effectively pausing all the processes within. Try running a command inside the container, and you'll see something like Figure 7.36.

```
# ls
█
```

Figure 7.36 *Attempting to run a command inside a paused container*

Let's unpause it, as shown in Figure 7.37:

```
docker unpause Parminder
```

```
PKOCHER-M-343K:~ parminderkochers docker unpause Parminder
Parminder
PKOCHER-M-343K:~ parminderkochers docker ps -a
CONTAINER ID    IMAGE     COMMAND    CREATED          STATUS                    PORTS    NAMES
e02085c7ba70    ubuntu    "sh"       22 minutes ago   Exited (0) 21 minutes ago          vibrant_saha
e510f8e769fc    ubuntu    "sh"       23 hours ago     Up 19 minutes                      Parminder
eded3539719c    ubuntu    "sh"       23 hours ago     Exited (0) 23 hours ago            flamboyant_edison
6a3f4a2d3694    ubuntu    "sh"       23 hours ago     Exited (0) 23 hours ago            friendly_wilson
PKOCHER-M-343K:~ parminderkochers █
```

Figure 7.37 *Unpaused container*

We have just unpaused the container, so all the process are again running. Our hung ls command that was in the wait state also finished executing, as shown in Figure 7.38.

```
# ls
MyFile.txt  backups  cache  lib  local  lock  log  mail  opt  run  sample.txt  spool  tmp
# █
```

Figure 7.38 *Hung ls command, previously in wait state, now got executed*

Docker Create

The `docker create` command creates a new writeable container layer over the specified image and prepares it for running the specified command:

```
docker create [OPTIONS] IMAGE [COMMAND] [ARG...]
```

The container ID is then printed as a result. This command is a little different from running `docker run -d` in that the container is never started. You can then use the `docker start` command to start the container. The ability to create a container but delay starting it is handy when your IT team wants to set up a container configuration in advance so that it is ready to start when you are ready to go live.

Let's create a new container, as shown in Figure 7.39:

```
docker create -t -i fedora bash
```

```
PKOCHER-M-343X:~ parminderkochers docker create -t -i fedora bash
Unable to find image 'fedora:latest' locally
latest: Pulling from library/fedora
1b39978eabd9: Pull complete
Digest: sha256:8d3f642aa4d3fa8f9dc52ab0e3bbbe8bc2494843dc6ebb26c4a6958db888e5a2
Status: Downloaded newer image for fedora:latest
239cae10b3cf6d35d3f8621f8eab5a7bcdf9bcd363e4e21971de7e7b2365654f
PKOCHER-M-343X:~ parminderkochers docker ps -a
CONTAINER ID    IMAGE     COMMAND     CREATED         STATUS                   PORTS      NAMES
239cae10b3cf    fedora    "bash"      18 seconds ago  Created                             sleepy_euclid
e02085c7ba70    ubuntu    "sh"        31 minutes ago  Exited (0) 30 minutes ago           vibrant_saha
e510f8e769fc    ubuntu    "sh"        23 hours ago    Exited (0) 42 seconds ago           Parminder
eded3539719c    ubuntu    "sh"        23 hours ago    Exited (0) 23 hours ago             flamboyant_edison
6a3f4a2d3694    ubuntu    "sh"        23 hours ago    Exited (0) 23 hours ago             friendly_wilson
PKOCHER-M-343X:~ parminderkochers ▮
```

Figure 7.39 *New container created*

Notice the container is created but not started.

Docker Commit

The `docker commit` command is straightforward but important—it allows you to create a new image from the container's changes:

```
docker commit{Options] Container [Repository:Tag]
```

As you make changes to your container and want to ship it as a new image to, say, another development or test team, this command creates a new image for you from the running container.

Docker Diff

The docker diff command is self-explanatory, but it's another important command—it lists the changed files and directories in a container file system:

```
docker diff Container ID
```

Over time, as you make changes to your container, this command highlights the file system differences relative to the base image.

Dockerfile

Let's build the same MySQL container we used in the previous examples on top of Ubuntu OS using a Dockerfile. As we discussed earlier, the Dockerfile is basically a set of instructions or commands that Docker can execute to build an image. It is similar to a text file and can be created without any programming language knowledge. It has simple commands that you can use with very simple syntax.

There is a simple format that you need to learn here:

- The Dockerfile must always start with the FROM instruction that specifies the base image to start with. Use # in the beginning of the line for comments. FROM instructions do support variables, and for that reason, the only instruction that can precede FROM instruction is the ARG instruction. Here's an example:

```
ARG OS_VERSION=14.04
FROM Ubuntu:${OS_VERSION}
```

- The syntax is Instruction Arguments.
- Every instruction is executed sequentially from top to bottom.
- The Dockerfile and the associated files in this directory are sent to the Docker daemon. For that reason, and to keep the size of your image light, do not store nonessential files in this directory.

Here are some of the simple instructions you can use in a Dockerfile:

- ADD copies the file(s) from the specified source on the host system or a URL to the specified destination within the container.

- CMD executes the specified command when the container is instantiated. There can be only one CMD inside a Dockerfile. If there's more than one CMD instruction, then the last appearing CMD instruction in the DOCKERFILE will be executed.

- ENTRYPOINT specifies the default executable that should be run when the container is started. This is a must if you want your image to be runnable or you use CMD.

- ENV sets the environment variables in the Dockerfile, which then can be used as part of the instructions—for example, ENV   MySQL_ROOT_PASSWORD mypassword.

- EXPOSE specifies the port number where the container will listen.

- FROM specifies the base image to use to start the build image. This is the very first command, and a mandatory one in the Dockerfile.

- MAINTAINER sets the author information in the generated images—for example, MAINTAINER pkocher@domain.com.

- RUN executes the specified command(s) and creates a layer for every RUN instruction. The next layer will be built on the previous committed layer.

- USER sets the user name or user ID to be used when running the image or various instructions such as RUN, CMD, and ENTRYPOINT.

- VOLUME specifies one or more shared volumes on the host machine that can be accessed from the containers.

- WORKDIR sets the working directory for any RUN, CMD, ENTRYPOINT, COPY, or ADD instruction.

MySQL Dockerfile

Now that we understand the Dockerfile, let's build one for a MySQL container on top of Ubuntu OS. Use the editor of your choice (Vi, Pico, etc.) and create a new file called Dockerfile. Add the following instructions:

```
From ubuntu:14.04
Maintainer pkocher@domain.com
Run  apt -get update
Run  apt -get -y install MySQL-server
EXPOSE 3306
CMD ["/usr/bin/MySQLd_safe"]
```

Save the file and exit. Notice we are starting from the base image of Ubuntu version 14.04. The RUN command apt -get -y install downloads the MySQL package and dependencies and installs it. The EXPOSE command exposes port 3306 where the container will listen.

Finally, the docker build command starts the MySQL process in the same mode:

```
docker build [Options] Path/URL
```

This command builds an image from the specified Dockerfile and the context. Context means the specific location for other resource files. Context can be specified by a path directory or a URL to the GitHub repository.

You should always pass the -t option with docker build to tag the image so it is easily identifiable. A simple, easily readable tag will help you manage the images.

Let's build the MYSQL image using the Dockerfile we created, as shown in Figure 7.40—make sure you name the file Dockerfile; there is nothing else in the same directory:

```
docker build -t pkocher/MySQL .
```

```
Parminders-MacBook-Pro:MyDocker parminderkochers docker build -t pkocher/mysql .
Sending build context to Docker daemon 3.072 kB
Step 0 : FROM ubuntu
 ---> 91e54dfb1179
Step 1 : MAINTAINER pkocher@gmail.com
 ---> Running in ff60156730fd
 ---> 0dd9db6f7989
Removing intermediate container ff60156730fd
Step 2 : RUN apt-get -y install mysql-server
 ---> Running in fe6f48d526af
Reading package lists ...
Building dependency tree ...
Reading state information ...
The following extra packages will be installed:
    libaio1 libdbd-mysql-perl libdbi-perl libhtml-template-perl libmysqlclient18
    libterm-readkey-perl libwrap0 mysql-client-5.5 mysql-client-core-5.5
    mysql-common mysql-server-5.5 mysql-server-core-5.5 psmisc tcpd
Suggested packages:
    libclone-perl libmldbm-perl libnet-daemon-perl libplrpc-perl
    libsql-statement-perl libipc-sharedcache-perl tinyca mailx
The following NEW packages will be installed:
    libaio1 libdbd-mysql-perl libdbi-perl libhtml-template-perl libmysqlclient18
    libterm-readkey-perl libwrap0 mysql-client-5.5 mysql-client-core-5.5
    mysql-common mysql-server mysql-server-5.5 mysql-server-core-5.5 psmisc tcpd
0 upgraded, 15 newly installed, 0 to remove and 0 not upgraded.
Need to get 9159 kB of archives.
After this operation, 97.0 MB of additional disk space will be used.
Get: 1 http://archive.ubuntu.com/ubuntu/ trusty/main libaio1 amd64 0.3.109-4 [6364 B]
Get: 2 http://archive.ubuntu.com/ubuntu/ trusty/main mysql-common all 5.5.35+dfsg-1ubuntu1 [14.1 kB]
```

Figure 7.40 *Building the MYSQL image*

Notice in Figure 7.41 that Docker builds starting from the first instructions and goes sequentially. Each instruction is built once and cached.

```
Setting up libhtml-template-perl (2.95-1) ...
Setting up tcpd (7.6.q-25) ...
Processing triggers for ureadahead (0.100.0-16) ...
Setting up mysql-server (5.5.35+dfsg-1ubuntu1) ...
Processing triggers for libc-bin (2.19-0ubuntu6.6) ...
 ---> 08e9a7c04c4f
Removing intermediate container fe6f48d526af
Step 3 : EXPOSE 3306
 ---> Running in 1ae5e57c81ce
 ---> 2e9d44165b70
Removing intermediate container 1ae5e57c81ce
Step 4 : CMD /usr/bin/mysqld_safe
 ---> Running in a09f3a5bc93e
 ---> ae267abf008c
Removing intermediate container a09f3a5bc93e
Successfully built ae267abf008c
Parminders-MacBook-Pro:MyDocker parminderkochers ▮
```

Figure 7.41 *Docker instructions built sequentially and cached*

You can try rebuilding the same Dockerfile again, and basically nothing will be rebuilt, since nothing changed. Try it by executing the same command.

Once the build is complete, you have created the image that you can check into your repository. Let's confirm:

```
docker images
```

As you can see in Figure 7.42, the pkocher/MySQL image is ready.

```
Parminders-MacBook-Pro:MyDocker parminderkochers docker images
REPOSITORY           TAG          IMAGE ID          CREATED            VIRTUAL SIZE
pkocher/mysql        latest       8ef5ceb3439e      About a minute ago  318.1 MB
mysql                latest       9726f738a97a      2 weeks ago         324.3 MB
ubuntu               latest       91e54dfb1179      8 weeks ago         188.4 MB
Parminders-MacBook-Pro:MyDocker parminderkochers ▮
```

Figure 7.42 *The pkocher/MySQL image now ready*

Now, let's run this image and validate that it does what it is supposed to do, as shown in Figure 7.43:

```
docker run -d -p 3306:3306 pkocher/MySQL
```

```
Parminders-MacBook-Pro:MyDocker parminderkocher$ docker run -d -p 3306:3306 pkocher/mysql
5063c4bed669ef217b65b870c126c908e522e122e992b65447ed1ae22898b419
Parminders-MacBook-Pro:MyDocker parminderkocher$ ▮
```

Figure 7.43 *Running the pkocher/MySQL image*

Recall that in our Dockerfile we have one CMD that is supposed to bring up the MySQL server. Let's confirm:

```
docker ps
```

As you can see in Figure 7.44, our image is up and running.

```
Parminders-MacBook-Pro:MyDocker parminderkocher$ docker ps
CONTAINER ID   IMAGE          COMMAND              CREATED         STATUS         PORTS                    NAMES
5063c4bed669   pkocher/mysql  "/usr/bin/mysqld_safe" 36 seconds ago  Up 35 seconds  0.0.0.0:3306->3306/tcp   modest_euclid
Parminders-MacBook-Pro:MyDocker parminderkocher$ ▮
```

Figure 7.44 *Image up and running*

Let's go a little deeper to confirm more accuracy by running some queries. First, we'll use the exec command to execute bash on this container, as shown in Figure 7.45; notice that 5063c4bed669 is the container ID from the previous commands:

```
docker exec -it 5063c4bed669 bash
```

```
Parminders-MacBook-Pro:MyDocker parminderkocher$ docker exec -it 5063c4bed669 bash
root@5063c4bed669:/# ▮
```

Figure 7.45 *Using docker exec command to execute bash*

Let's get inside MySQL and run some queries to confirm further that everything is up and running, as shown in Figure 7.46:

```
Command: mysql
show databases;
connect information_schema
show tables
```

```
root@5063c4bed669:/# mysql
Welcome to the MySQL monitor. Commands end with ; or \g.
Your MySQL connection id is 2
Server version: 5.5.35-1ubuntu1 (Ubuntu)

Copyright (c) 2000, 2013, Oracle and/or its affiliates. All rights reserved.

Oracle is a registered trademark of Oracle Corporation and/or its
affiliates. Other names may be trademarks of their respective
owners.

Type 'help;' or '\h' for help. Type '\c' to clear the current input statement.

mysql> show databases;
+--------------------+
| Database           |
+--------------------+
| information_schema |
| mysql              |
| performance_schema |
+--------------------+
3 rows in set [0 .00 sec]

mysql> connect information_schema
Reading table information for completion of table and column names
You can turn off this feature to get a quicker startup with -A

Connection id:    3
Current database: information_schema

mysql> show tables
    ->;
+---------------------------------------+
| Tables_in_information_schema          |
+---------------------------------------+
| CHARACTER_SETS                        |
| COLLATIONS                            |
| COLLATION_CHARACTER_SET_APPLICABILITY |
| COLUMNS                               |
| COLUMN_PRIVILEGES                     |
| ENGINES                               |
| EVENTS                                |
| FILES                                 |
| GLOBAL_STATUS                         |
| GLOBAL_VARIABLES                      |
| KEY_COLUMN_USAGE                      |
| PARAMETERS                            |
| PARTITIONS                            |
| PLUGINS                               |
```

Figure 7.46 *Confirming that everything is up and running properly*

Docker Compose

Applications using Docker are typically multicontainer applications. That is, they have components (e.g., app, web, database) that are deployed in multiple Docker containers. To simplify the definition of multicontainer applications, as well as to run them in an easy way, Docker introduced Docker Compose.

Let's assume we want to spin up an application that consists of Tomcat and a MySQL database. Here's how we can capture these two services in a docker-compose.yml file.

```
version: '2'
services:
```

```
tomcat:
  image: 'tomcat:7'
  container_name: appserver
  ports:
    - '8080:80'
  depends_on:
    - db
db:
  image: 'mysql:5.7'
  container_name: dbserver
  ports:
    - '3306:3306'
  environment:
    - MYSQL_ROOT_PASSWORD=sample
    - MYSQL_DATABASE=helpdesk
    - MYSQL_USER=helpdesk
    - MYSQL_PASSWORD=helpdesk
```

Docker Compose uses YAML (YAML Ain't Markup Language) file. (You can read up about YAML at http://www.yaml.org.) Docker Compose uses it for configuration, but YAML can be used in many other types of applications as well.

In the docker-compose.yml file, we have defined two services: Tomcat and MySQL. Services configuration options are self-explanatory at this stage. One of the key things to note is that Tomcat service has an option called depends_on in its configuration, and it has db as a dependency. This instructs Docker to start the database service first and Tomcat second. Docker Compose has many more options that you can explore yourself from Docker online documentation.

Having defined the docker-compose.yml file, the way to start the services is to use the following command.

Command: `docker-compose up -d`

This command inspects the compose file, then finds out the services defined in the configuration file, builds a dependency graph on the order in which services need to be started, and finally starts them in that order. If the image configured in the services section is not located in the local machine, then it fetches the image from the Docker registry as usual. Figure 7.47 shows the output from running the command.

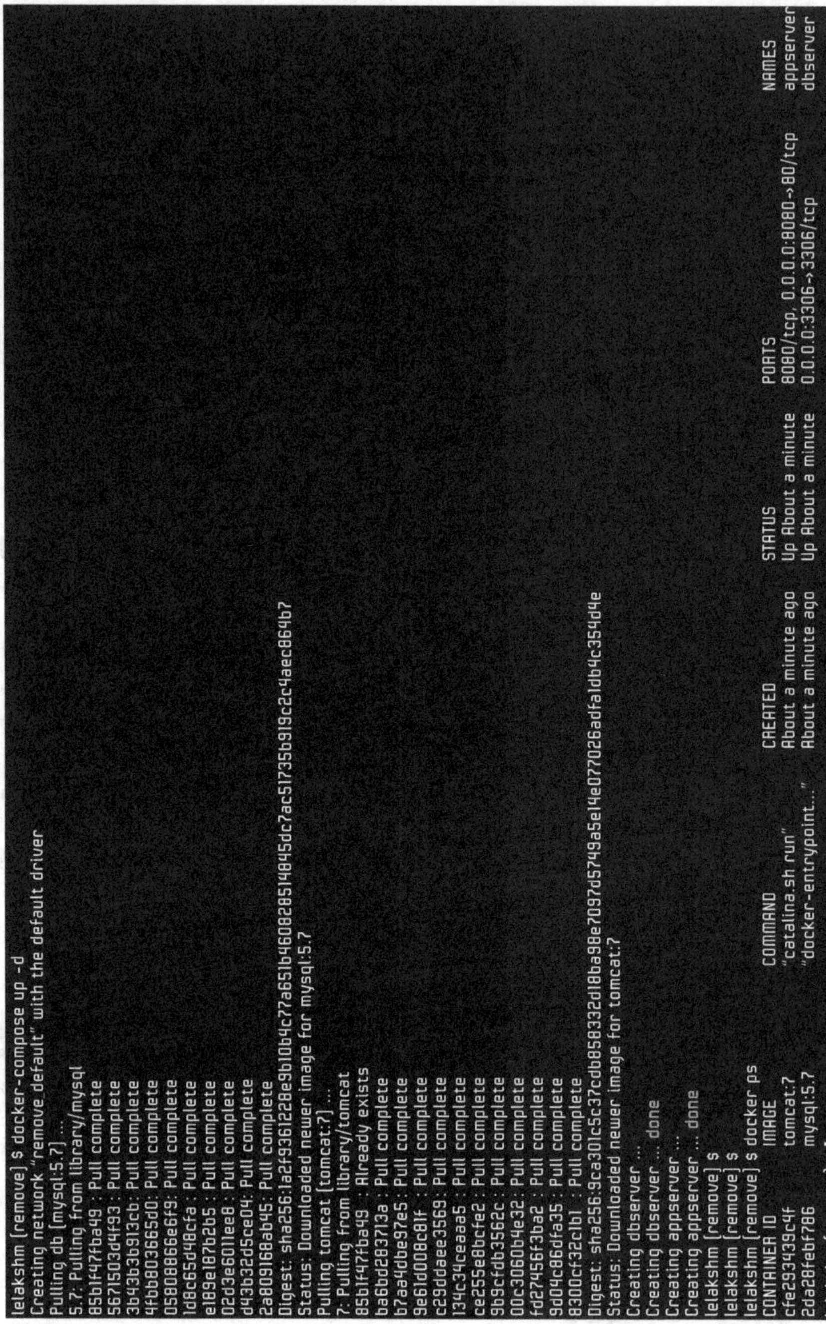

```
[elakshm [remove] $ docker-compose up -d
Creating network "remove default" with the default driver
Pulling db (mysql:5.7) ...
5.7: Pulling from library/mysql
85b1f47rba49 : Pull complete
5671503d4f93 : Pull complete
3b43b3b913cb: Pull complete
4f6b803665d0: Pull complete
0580b866e6f9: Pull complete
1d8c65d48cfa : Pull complete
e189e1b7b2b5 : Pull complete
02d3e601lee8 : Pull complete
d4b3a2d5ce04: Pull complete
2a809160ab45: Pull complete
Digest: sha256:1a2f93612a28e9b10b4c77a651b4608285148d5dc7ac51735b919c2c4aec864b7
Status: Downloaded newer image for mysql:5.7
Pulling tomcat (tomcat:7) ...
7: Pulling from library/tomcat
85b1f47rba49 : Already exists
ba6bd28371a : Pull complete
b7aa4dbe97e5 : Pull complete
9e61d008c81f : Pull complete
c29ddaee3569: Pull complete
134c34ceaaa5 : Pull complete
ce55e8bcfe2: Pull complete
9b5cfdb35b2c: Pull complete
00c30600b4e32: Pull complete
fd274563f3ba2: Pull complete
9d04c86fdfa35: Pull complete
8300cf32c1b1 : Pull complete
Digest: sha256:9ca301c5c37cdb858332d18ba98e70976574a9a5e14e077026adfa1db4c354d4e
Status: Downloaded newer image for tomcat:7
Creating dbserver ... done
Creating dbserver ... done
Creating appserver ... done
Creating appserver ... done
[elakshm [remove] $
[elakshm [remove] $
[elakshm [remove] $ docker ps
CONTAINER ID   IMAGE       COMMAND                CREATED          STATUS           PORTS                      NAMES
cfe239439c4f   tomcat:7    "catalina.sh run"      About a minute ago   Up About a minute   8080/tcp, 0.0.0.0:8080->80/tcp   appserver
2da28febf7b6   mysql:5.7   "docker-entrypoint..."  About a minute ago   Up About a minute   0.0.0.0:3306->3306/tcp          dbserver
[elakshm [remove] $
```

Figure 7.47 *Running Docker Compose*

As you can see in the figure, since the Tomcat and MySQL images are not available locally, they were pulled from the repository before they were started. Another key thing to note is that, since MySQL is marked as a dependency for Tomcat, MySQL was downloaded and subsequently started first before the Tomcat service was started.

This concludes our discussion on Docker commands. These commands will continue to evolve, so keep yourself up to date by reviewing Docker online documentation.

Chapter 8

Containers Networking

In the previous three chapters, we learned the basics of containers and how Docker takes containers to the next level. But simply standing up containers does not serve a purpose: the containers need to talk to each other, and connectivity with the external world must be designed as part of your deployment. In this chapter, we discuss and learn about networking options in the world of containers. First, let's refresh our knowledge of some basic concepts in Linux that will assist our discussion of containers networking.

Key Linux Concepts

Containers, as we know, are self-contained and isolated virtual environments. They can run an entire application or part of an application. In either case, one of the key needs is connectivity.

We have been using a client to connect to our containers, but what we need is global connectivity. We need connectivity between containers within a host, within multiple hosts, and between multiple data centers—that is, we need the ability to create our own network. Docker uses the Linux networking and kernel features to provide such capabilities.

We don't go into much detail on Linux basics, but you must understand some key Linux networking concepts to understand Docker networking:

- **Linux network namespace.** Usually, a Linux installation provides a standard set of network interfaces and routing table entries. This set is used by the entire operating system to make the routing and networking possible. Think of network namespace as a network stack with its own network interfaces and respective routing table entries operating in isolation. Docker uses this feature of network namespace to isolate containers and provide the security. You can have multiple network namespaces, giving you the ability to run each container in isolation, rendering each one unable to communicate with other containers on the same host until configured by the admin. The host has its own namespace that contains host interfaces and routing tables.

- **Linux bridge.** This is part of the Linux kernel module and enables Linux networking. Think of it as a layer 2 virtual switch that also does filtering. It makes forwarding decisions based on a MAC address table that it learns dynamically through the traffic inspection.

- **Linux virtual Ethernet devices.** Also known as veth (*virtual Eth*ernet) devices, these are interfaces that connect the network namespaces. We can create multiple entries on the network namespace stack, and we configure the veth to establish the connectivity. Think of these as pipes that can connect network namespaces to each other and to the external network.

- **Linux iptables.** iptables is part of the Linux kernel that provides the packet filtering and firewall capabilities to the operating system. You can define policies and a chain of policies to allow or block traffic. Docker utilizes this capability to segment traffic between containers, implement port mapping where you can bind the container port to the host port, and more.

Now that we've outlined Linux networking capabilities, let's discuss connection types in containers, starting with the simplest: linking.

Linking

Before Docker released advanced networking features (which we discuss shortly), the simplest way of connecting two or more containers was to "link" the containers. The --link flag, now a deprecated legacy feature of Docker, allows containers to discover and secure a connection for transfer of information between containers. This technique is more of a generic way to achieve connectivity than a true ports-based networking approach. It is done through sharing environment variables and /etc/ hosts file entries, which are automatically created for us by the Docker engine to connect the containers.

As an example, let's bring up the Tomcat application server and a MySQL database and establish connectivity between them. These two should be able to interact with each other. Let's get the latest Tomcat image, shown in Figure 8.1, by executing the following command:

```
docker pull tomcat
```

```
[ANUJSIN-M-T2H9:pkocher anujsin$ docker pull tomcat
Using default tag: latest
latest: Pulling from library/tomcat
9f0706ba7422 : Pull complete
d3942a742d22: Pull complete
2b95a7bc6bf9 : Pull complete
7bd307c6c6e7 : Pull complete
ba7da8b01135 : Pull complete
74169d04cf0d : Pull complete
08cc0e294332: Pull complete
d2f5746bc4d3 : Pull complete
eb109ae04806 : Pull complete
99ac3ea73cee: Pull complete
24772bc65b49 : Pull complete
03774cef060c : Pull complete
8673b4967afd : Pull complete
3a49ad4798f1 : Pull complete
Digest: sha256:c55c84d34b82d794298bb7ee8c70f52f9dfcd1bd34106394b2bc99ed60216f16
Status: Downloaded newer image for tomcat:latest
ANUJSIN-M-T2H9:pkocher anujsin$ ▮
```

Figure 8.1 *Latest Tomcat image pulled*

Next, we start our Tomcat container; we'll call it tomcatContainer:

```
docker run -d -- name tomcatContainer tomcat
```

To make sure our container is up and running, we use

```
docker ps
```

Figure 8.2 shows that it is running!

```
[ANUJSIN-M-T2H9:pkocher anujsin$ docker ps
CONTAINER ID   IMAGE           COMMAND             CREATED         STATUS        PORTS      NAMES
90d4a06e190e   tomcat:latest   "catalina.sh run"   4 minutes ago   Up 4 minutes  8080/tcp   tomcatContainer
ANUJSIN-M-T2H9:pkocher anujsin$ ▮
```

Figure 8.2 *Tomcat container is running*

Now let's bring up our MySQL container and link it with our Tomcat container using the --link flag:

```
docker run --link tomcatContainer:tomcat --name sqlcontainer \
> -e MYSQL_ROOT_PASSWORD=password -d mysql
```

It should pull the MySQL if it's not available locally, as shown in Figure 8.3.

```
ANUJSIN-M-T2H9:prometheus anujsins docker run --link tomcatContainer:tomcat --name sqlcontainer -e MYSQL
_ROOT_PASSWORD=password -d mysql
Unable to find image 'mysql: latest' locally
latest: Pulling from library/mysql
9f0706ba7422 : Already exists
2290e155d2d0 : Pull complete
547981b8269f : Pull complete
2c9d42ed2f48 : Pull complete
55e3122f1297 : Pull complete
abc10bd84060 : Pull complete
c0a5ce64f2b0 : Pull complete
c4595eab8e90 : Pull complete
098988cead35 : Pull complete
300ca5fa5eea : Pull complete
43fdc4e3e690 : Pull complete
Digest: sha256:d178dffba8d81afedc251498e227607934636e06228ac63d58b72f9e9ec271a6
```

Figure 8.3 *MySQL pulled*

Let's confirm these two containers are linked as specified. First, log into the MySQL container by executing the following command:

```
docker exec -it sqlcontainer /bin/bash
```

Next, check the hosts file located at /etc/hosts:

```
cat /etc/hosts
```

Notice in Figure 8.4 that we do have an application server container entry along with its IP address of 172.17.0.2.

```
[root@f864f6e4150f:/#
[root@f864f6e4150f:/#
[root@f864f6e4150f:/# cat /etc/hosts
127.0.0.1           localhost
::1          localhost ip6-localhost ip6-loopback
fe00::0 ip6-localnet
ff00::0 ip6-mcastprefix
ff02::1 ip6-allnodes
ff02::2 ip6-allrouters
172.17.0.2   tomcat 90d4a06e190e tomcatContainer
172.17.0.3   f864f6e4150f
root@f864f6e4150f:/# ■
```

Figure 8.4 *App server entry and IP address displayed*

Let's validate the IP address of the Tomcat container by opening another terminal, as shown in Figure 8.5:

```
docker inspect TomcatContainer | grep IP
```

```
ANUJSIN-M-T2H9:~ anujsin$
ANUJSIN-M-T2H9:~ anujsin$ docker inspect tomcatContainer |grep IP
            "LinkLocalIPv6Address": "",
            "LinkLocalIPv6PrefixLen": 0,
            "SecondaryIPAddresses": null,
            "SecondaryIPv6Addresses": null,
            "GlobalIPv6Address":"",
            "GlobalIPv6Prefixlen": 0,
            "IPAddress": "172.17.0.2"
            "IPPrefixlen": 16,
            "IPv6Gateway": "",
                    "IPAMConfig": null,
                    "IPAddress": "172.17.0.2",
                    "IPPrefixLen": 16,
                    "IPv6Gateway": "",
                    "GlobalIPv6Address": "",
                    "GlobalIPv6PrefixLen": 0,
ANUJSIN-M-T2H9:~ anujsin$ ▮
```

Figure 8.5 *Tomcat's IP address*

Note that the IP addresses 172.17.0.2 matches with what we found in the host file, which means everything is in place to establish connectivity. Let's test that by pinging the Tomcat container from the MySQL container. Go back to your previous terminal and issue this command:

```
ping 172.17.0.2
```

Figure 8.6 shows us the connectivity was a success!

```
[root@f864f6e4150f:/#
[root@f864f6e4150f:/# ping 172.17.0.2
PING 172.17.0.2 [172.17.0.2]: 56 data bytes
64 bytes from 172.17.0.2: icmp_seq=0 ttl=64 time=0.190 ms
64 bytes from 172.17.0.2: icmp_seq=1 ttl=64 time=0.109 ms
64 bytes from 172.17.0.2: icmp_seq=2 ttl=64 time=0.114 ms
64 bytes from 172.17.0.2: icmp_seq=3 ttl=64 time=0.089 ms
64 bytes from 172.17.0.2: icmp_seq=4 ttl=64 time=0.125 ms
64 bytes from 172.17.0.2: icmp_seq=5 ttl=64 time=0.103 ms
64 bytes from 172.17.0.2: icmp_seq=6 ttl=64 time=0.105 ms
^C--- 172.17.0.2 ping statistics ---
7 packets transmitted, 7 packets received, 0% packet loss
round-trip min/avg/max/stddev = 0.089/0.119/0.190/0.031 ms
```

Figure 8.6 *Connectivity success*

Default Options

Because the --link flag has been deprecated and may eventually be removed, its use should be avoided. In place of --link, Docker provides three default connection options, which are all created automatically during installation: none, host, and bridge. Run the following command to list these networks:

```
docker network ls
```

You should see the output shown in Figure 8.7.

```
[ANUJSIN-M-T2H9:~ anujsin$ docker network ls
NETWORK ID          NAME               DRIVER        SCOPE
fe3118460998        bridge             bridge        local
4a8e216f9a47        host               host          local
1bb6d94233c0        none               null          local
ANUJSIN-M-T2H9:~ anujsin$ ▌
```

Figure 8.7 *Network list*

Let's look into each of these networks.

None

This networking option is the simplest of all and basically means no networking. It does receive a container-specific stack and namespace, but it lacks a network interface. Consequently, no IP address is configured for this container, and cannot connect with other containers or an external network. It does have a loopback address assigned.

As an example, let's use our Tomcat image again by specifying the network option none:

```
docker run -it --network=none tomcat /bin/bash
```

Let's check out the IP address of the container:

```
docker inspect 43c10fe289b3| grep IP
```

As expected, no IP address is assigned, as shown in Figure 8.8.

```
ANUJSIN-M-T2H9:~ anujsins
ANUJSIN-M-T2H9:~ anujsins
ANUJSIN-M-T2H9:~ anujsins docker inspect 43c10fe289b3 |grep IP
            "LinkLocalIPv6Address": "",
            "LinkLocalIPv6PrefixLen": 0,
            "SecondaryIPAddresses": null,
            "SecondaryIPv6Addresses": null,
            "GlobalIPv6Address":"",
            "GlobalIPv6PrefixLen": 0,
            "IPAddress": "",
            "IPPrefixLen": 0,
            "IPv6Gateway": "",
                "IPAMConfig": null,
                "IPAddress": "",
                "IPPrefixLen": 0,
                "IPv6Gateway": "",
                "GlobalIPv6Address": "",
                "GlobalIPv6PrefixLen": 0,
ANUJSIN-M-T2H9:~ anujsins ▌
```

Figure 8.8 *No IP address assigned*

As you can see, this particular container is completely isolated from other containers and the host network. This kind of configuration is used for testing purposes in isolated environments, special custom networking, or instances where no connectivity is intended.

Host

As the name suggests, the host option adds the container to the host's network namespace, so the host and the container share the same network namespace we discussed earlier. This is the second simplest of the networking options: the added container can use all the interfaces on the host stack. In this case, there is one-to-one port mapping between the container and the host machine—that is, if you run the container on an application server on port 8080, the application server will be available on port 8080 of the host.

There are two key things to note here: you will still need to do network configurations, and in this mode you cannot use port mapping. The reason is that the container and the host share the same network namespace. If another service wants to use port 8080, you are stuck. This may not be the case with the bridge option, which we discuss in the next section.

Let's run a new CentOS image by specifying the network option host:

```
docker run --network=host -d centOS
```

Next, we validate that the container is running, and we log into it, as shown in Figure 8.9.

```
docker ps
docker exec -it kickass_minsky /bin/bash
```

```
[[root@cm1 ~]# docker ps
CONTAINER ID    IMAGE       COMMAND         CREATED         STATUS          PORTS       NAMES
9fa5e216d856    centos      "/bin/bash"     50 seconds ago  Up 49 seconds               kickass_minsky
[[root@cm1 ~]# docker exec -it kickass_minsky /bin/bash
[root@cm1 /]# ▮
```

Figure 8.9 *Logging into our CentOS container*

Looks good so far. Let's find the IP address of our CentOS container:

```
ifconfig | grep inet
```

Notice in Figure 8.10 that the IP address of our container is 10.88.30.156.

```
[[root@cm1 ~]# ifconfig |grep inet
        inet 10.88.30.156 netmask 255.255.255.128  broadcast 10.88.30.255
        inet6 2001:420:1402:2033:21d:9ff:fe6d:5aea  prefixlen 64  scopeid 0x0<global>
        inet6 fe80::21d:9ff:fe6d:5aea  prefixlen 64  scopeid 0x20<link>
        inet 172.17.0.1 netmask 255.255.0.0  broadcast 0.0.0.0
        inet6 fe80::42:bcff:fe24:ee1b  prefixlen 64  scopeid 0x20<link>
        inet 127.0.0.1 netmask 255.0.0.0
        inet6 ::1 prefixlen 128  scopeid 0x10<host>
[root@cm1 ~]# ▮
```

Figure 8.10 *Check for containers' IP address*

Now we open another terminal and find our host machine's IP address:

```
Command: ifconfig | grep inet
```

The result, shown in Figure 8.11, is what we would have expected: the container has the same IP address as the host: 10.88.30.156.

```
[root@cm1 /]#
[root@cm1 /]# ifconfig |grep inet
        inet 10.88.30.156  netmask 255.255.255.128  broadcast 10.88.30.255
        inet6 2001:420:1402:2033:21d:9ff:fe6d:5aea  prefixlen 64  scopeid 0x0<global>
        inet6 fe80::21d:9ff:fe6d:5aea  prefixlen 64  scopeid 0x20<link>
        inet 172.17.0.1 netmask 255.255.0.0  broadcast 0.0.0.0
        inet6 fe80::42:bcff:fe24:ee1b  prefixlen 64  scopeid 0x20<link>
        inet 127.0.0.1 netmask 255.0.0.0
        inet6 ::1 prefixlen 128  scopeid 0x10<host>
[root@cm1 /]# ▮
```

Figure 8.11 *Checking for our machine's IP address*

Basically, this particular container networking behaves just as if it were a physi-cal server, which actually gives it the key benefit: performance—that is, near-metal speed. Figure 8.12 shows how it looks.

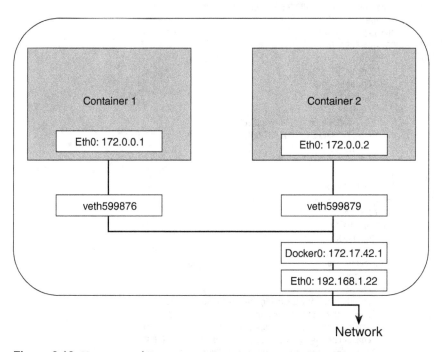

Figure 8.12 *Host networking*

Bridge

Bridge, also known as *docker0*, is the default networking option if you don't specify any parameter (none or host) with your run command. Don't confuse this with Linux bridge, which we discussed earlier, though Docker uses it to provide this bridge networking functionality.

As you probably guessed from the name, bridge creates an internal private net-work for containers to communicate with each other. Note that the IP addresses assigned in this case are not accessible from outside the host. You must expose the ports to provide the external access. To understand more, let's run the following command:

```
docker network inspect bridge
```

As you can see in Figure 8.13, the containers section is empty, since we have no containers running.

```
ANUJSIN-M-T2H9:~ anujsin$ docker network inspect bridge
[
    {
        "Name": "bridge",
        "ID": "fe31184609981ba9602670fe4de2f48458fb057b6ff786be92590c5ad79f5bbb",
        "Created": "2017-07-08T19:08:03.016505706Z",
        "Scope": "local",
        "Driver": "bridge",
        "EnableIPv6": false,
        "IPAM": {
            "Driver": "default",
            "Options": null,
            "Config": [
                {
                    "Subnet": "172.17.0.0/16",
                    "Gateway": "172.17.0.1",
                }
            ]
        },
        "Internal": false,
        "Attachable": false,
        "Ingress": false,
        "ConfigFrom": {
            "Network": ""
        },
        "ConfigOnly": false,
        "Containers": {},
        "Options": {
            "com.docker.network.bridge.default_bridge": "true",
            "com.docker.network.bridge.enable_icc": "true",
            "com.docker.network.bridge.enable_ip_masquerade": "true",
            "com.docker.network.bridge.host_binding_ipv4": "0.0.0.0",
            "com.docker.network.bridge.name": "docker0",
            "com.docker.network.driver.mtu": "1500"
        },
        "Labels": {}
    }
]
```

Figure 8.13 *Containers section empty*

Let's start a few containers by specifying a `bridge` parameter in one and leaving the other default:

```
docker run -d --network=bridge mysql
docker run -d --network=default tomcat
```

Now let's run the `inspect` command again and notice the difference:

```
docker network inspect bridge
```

As you can see in Figure 8.14, both containers are connected through the same bridge and communicate with each other by IP addresses.

```
[
    {
        "Name" : "bridge",
        "Id" : "fe31184609981ba9602670fe4de2f48458fb057b6ff786be92590c5ad79f5bbb",
        "Created" : "2017-07-08T19:08:03.016505706Z",
        "Scope" : "local",
        "Driver" : "bridge",
        "EnableIPv6" : false,
        "IPAM" : {
            "Driver" : "default",
            "Options" : null,
            "Config" : [
                {
                    "Subnet" : "172.17.0.0/16",
                    "Gateway" : "172.17.0.1"
                }
            ]
        },
        "Internal" : false,
        "Attachable" : false,
        "Ingress" : false,
        "ConfigFrom" : {
            "Network" : ""
        },
        "ConfigOnly" : false,
        "Containers" : {
            "04c7ae5a7e73b249b729b2927244122b82e114d45e63291a260847ca8634ad48" : {
                "Name" : "wonderful_kalam",
                "EndpointID" :
"30ad3accb403119dc09ae38207fdb1aa44e9f13647df980ce349181e2d2b01f7",
                "MacAddress" : "02:42:ac:11:00:03",
                "IPv4Address" : "172.17.0.3/16",
                "IPv6Address" : ""
            },
            "3c056870b9a7db53de33914a12edb65415e5e14fd26c8916d629d8439e47d928" : {
                "Name" : "blissful_babbage",
                "EndpointID" :
"1d365a32d1aea32e3e00d35e4d074f1cf8d293006dd88b3320010272920c5ae0",
                "MacAddress" : "02:42:ac:11:00:02" ,
                "IPv4Address" : "172.17.0.2/16",
                "IPv6Address" : ""
            }
        },
        "Options" : {
            "com.docker.network.bridge.default_bridge" : "true",
            "com.docker.network.bridge.enable_icc" : "true" ,
            "com.docker.network.bridge.enable_ip_masquerade" : "true",
            "com.docker.network.bridge.host_binding_ipv4" : "0.0.0.0",
            "com.docker.network.bridge.name" : "docker0",
            "com.docker.network.driver.mtu" : "1500"
        },
        "Labels" : {}
    }
]
```

Figure 8.14 *Containers connected through the same bridge, communicating with each other by IP addresses*

You can attach to each of these containers and see what the network looks like from inside the containers by running the `attach` command and then `ifconfig`, as we did earlier (see Figure 8.11). You can ping Container 2 from within Container 1 to test the connectivity. So the question is, what is happening in the backend to enable this bridge and connectivity?

Well, Docker is using the basic Linux networking to do this magic. All the containers created through the `bridge` parameter or without any networking parameters are all connected to this bridge (docker0) and are therefore able to talk to each other. Docker puts all the necessary entries in the /etc/hosts/ file (iptables and the like) to make this work. Figure 8.15 shows how it all looks:

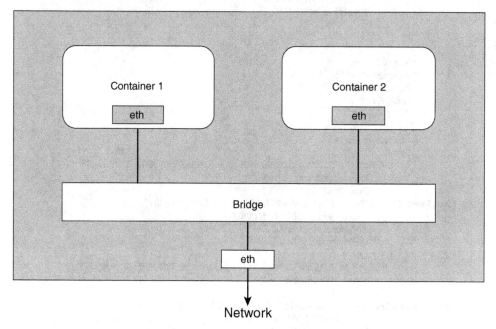

Figure 8.15 *Bridge networking*

Custom Networks

In addition to the three default networks included when you install Docker, you can define custom networks to control connectivity. Docker provides network drivers that you can utilize to create these custom networks. Creating a custom network gives you full control and flexibility, as you will learn in this section. We discuss the following three most commonly used custom networks: custom bridge network driver, overlays network driver, and underlays (MACVLAN) network driver.

Custom Bridge Network Driver

The custom bridge driver is very similar to docker0, which we discussed earlier, but has more features, such as IPAM (IP address management) and service discovery. It also provides more flexibility.

To create a custom bridge network, we use the following command:

```
docker network create [OPTIONS] NETWORK
```

We can specify an IP address and subnet in the command if required, or Docker will assign the next subnet available in the private IP space. Let's execute this command:

```
docker network create --driver bridge pkNetwork
```

Let's use ls again to verify:

```
docker network ls
```

The pkNetwork we just created is shown in Figure 8.16.

```
ANUJSIN-M-T2H9:~ anujsins
ANUJSIN-M-T2H9:~ anujsins
ANUJSIN-M-T2H9:~ anujsins docker network ls
NETWORK ID          NAME                    DRIVER       SCOPE
fe3118460998        bridge                  bridge       local
133b7c28f2be        docker_gwbridge         bridge       local
d163ca8f2882        dockerservices_default  bridge       local
4a8e216f9a47        host                    host         local
vf5dr217stoa        ingress                 overlay      swarm
1bb6d94233c0        none                    null         local
33edf6b8d0de        pkNetwork               bridge       local
ANUJSIN-M-T2H9:~ anujsins
```

Figure 8.16 *List networks*

Just as we did with docker0, let's inspect this new network:

```
docker network inspect pkNetwork
```

Look at Figure 8.17 and note the driver we used, bridge. This is our custom bridge network.

```
ANUJSIN-M-T2H9:~ anujsin$ docker network inspect pkNetwork
[
    {
        "Name": "pkNetwork",
        "Id": "33edf6b8d0de1493a2d7dfde6762c1664ce59ae8b38aa7cae0a5726552d8edd9",
        "Created": "2017-07-08T21:59:15.8214098562",
        "Scope": "local",
        "Driver": "bridge",
        "EnableIPv6": false,
        "IPAM": {
            "Driver": "default",
            "Options": { },
            "Config": [
                {
                    "Subnet": "172.20.0.0/16",
                    "Gateway": "172.20.0.1"
                }
            ]
        },
        "Internal": false,
        "Attachable": false,
        "Ingress": false,
        "ConfigFrom": {
            "Network": ""
        },
        "ConfigOnly": false,
        "Containers": { },
        "Options": { },
        "Labels": { }
    }
]
```

Figure 8.17 *Custom bridge network*

Currently, there are no containers built into this network. As in the bridge/docker0 example, we can create a few containers by specifying the network as `pkBridge` and then inspect the network to see the association. Behind the scenes, Docker creates the necessary configuration in the underlying Linux to make this work.

Port Mapping

With Docker, as we discussed earlier, containers on the same network can communicate with each other. Of course, that is the purpose of the putting the container on the same network. But the external access is firewalled—that is, containers cannot be accessed from the outside world unless access is explicitly granted to make the external connectivity possible. This is achieved by internal port mapping whereby we bind the container port to the host port within the Docker run command. We can also use a combination of the exposing and publishing commands to first expose and then publish all the exposed ports to the host interfaces.

Consider the following example:

```
docker run -d --network pkBridge -p 8000:80 --name tomcatPK -d
tomcat
```

We can access the Tomcat server externally from the browser, as shown in Figure 8.18.

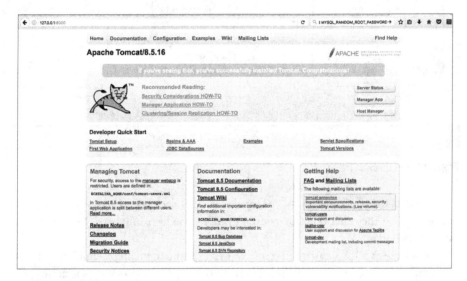

Figure 8.18 *Accessing Tomcat server externally via the browser*

So, what is happening here? On the backend, the Docker engine adds a NAT (network address translation) rule in the Linux iptables. Take a look at the underlying iptables. You should see the mapping entry in the list.

As you may have noticed, the bridge driver is a local scope—that is, it is limited to a single host. The other two network drivers, overlay and underlay, address the multihost scope.

Overlay Network Driver

The overlay driver is utilized to achieve the containers' connectivity across multiple hosts. It does this by decoupling the container network from the underlying physical layer and creating a tunnel across the hosts to enable communication. Think of it as one network spread across multiple hosts, and all the containers on this particular network are able to communicate just like within a single host. Figure 8.19 shows the network.

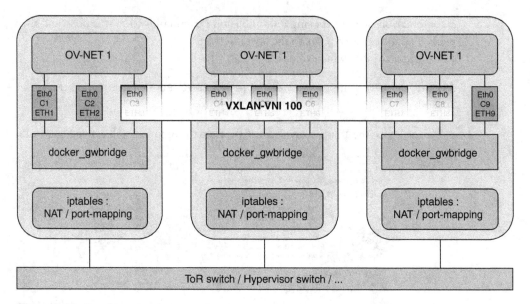

Figure 8.19 *Overlay network*

Note that the container on this particular overlay network won't be able to communicate with the other containers even on the same host unless they are on same overlay network.

Docker uses VXLAN (virtual extensible LAN) as the tunneling technology. Just as we created the bridge network, we can create the overlay network by specifying the subnet. Docker automatically instantiates the required settings (Linux bridge between hosts along with associated VXLAN interfaces) for connectivity on each host.

Docker is smart enough to create these settings only on hosts where this container connectivity is required. This prevents the existence of each overlay network on all the host machines, a key feature of Docker containers that addresses microservices' distributed deployment and connectivity needs.

Docker Swarm

In practice, you will have a cluster of Docker engine nodes running your application services. Docker Swarm provides cluster management and orchestration. Each Docker engine running on a node runs in the swarm mode. One of the key features is multihosting networking, which Docker Swarm provides through the overlay network driver we just discussed. When a service is created that uses an overlay network, the manager node of the swarm automatically extends the network to other nodes that are part of this service.

Docker Swarm is not the only way to manage clusters. Several other open source technologies, such as Kubernetes and Mesos, are available. In such cases, the overlay network requires a valid key-value store service to store necessary information such as discovery, endpoints, IP addresses, and the like. Support key-value stores include Consul, Zookeeper, and etcd, among others.

Underlay Network Driver or Macvlan

A media access control virtual local area network, or Macvlan, is another built-in network driver that is very lightweight and is simpler than other drivers. It does not use the built-in Linux bridging and port mappings; instead it connects the container's interface directly to the host interfaces (eth0 or a sub-interface).

Basically, these are all virtual interfaces behind one host's single physical interface. With this approach, each virtual interface has unique MAC and IP addresses. This enables the containers to communicate directly with external resources without the need for NATing and port-mapping, which makes this driver more efficient than other alternatives.

Like overlay networks, Macvlan networks are segmented from other networks. Containers that live on the same host but not on this network cannot talk to each other. Figure 8.20 shows this underlay network.

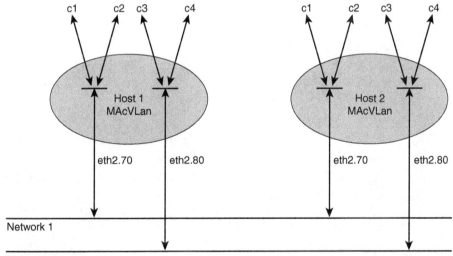

Figure 8.20 *Macvlan network*

As you can see, Docker is pretty flexible when it comes to networking. If your needs are more complex and cannot be addressed by the options we discussed, you can write your own network driver plugin or use readily available plugins such as Weave Net or Flannel.

Chapter 9

Container Orchestration

Managing a handful of containers is completely different from managing production-scale containers, which may number in from hundreds to thousands. To support container management, we need an easy way of deploying and handling these containers at scale. This is what is called *container orchestration*. In this chapter, we look into a few of the options available in the industry and cover the basics of how each inherently works. Container orchestration is a fast-changing area, so look at the provided links for the latest developments once you understand how these technologies work and the key differences between them.

The good news is that there are many options in the container orchestration space. The flip side, of course, is that determining which tool is the best fit for your environment will not be an easy decision. Here are several of the popular options that are being used extensively in the industry:

- Kubernetes
- Mesos + Marathon
- Docker Swarm

We cover these options throughout the next several sections.

Kubernetes

Kubernetes is an open source project led by Google. Google has extensive experience in managing and deploying containers at scale. Kubernetes is one of the orchestration engines that helps you run your containerized applications where and when you want by providing the resources and capabilities they need, as shown in Figure 9.1.

Let's look at the major components of this orchestration engine.

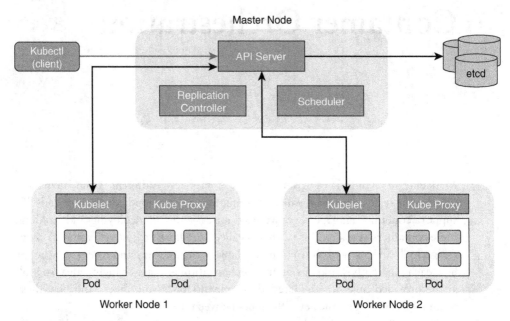

Figure 9.1 *Kubernetes's major components*

Kubectl

Kubernetes has a command-line interface called kubectl. It is used for running commands and interacting with Kubernetes clusters.

Master Node

The master is the brain of Kubernetes. It coordinates the cluster activities with the help of some supporting services. It has an API server, a scheduler, and a replication controller. They manage all activities—scheduling and maintaining applications' desired state, scaling up and down, and so on.

API Server

The API server is responsible for exposing Representational State Transfer (REST) APIs to interact with the Kubernetes cluster. All external communications that happen between the client (kubectl) and the Kubernetes cluster is handled by the API server. Additionally, cluster-wide communications between worker nodes and the master is also handled by the API server. This is also the only component that talks to the distributed key-value store (etcd) to store the state of the objects.

In Kubernetes terminology, we use objects to describe what we want from the cluster or what state we want the cluster to be in. For example, an object could be the applications you want to run in the cluster, how many instances of the application you want in the cluster at any given time, or how you want your applications to communicate with each other.

Let's take an example of how the API server handles requests. Say we issue a command to run a Tomcat container and have three instances of Tomcat running in the cluster:

```
kubectl run myTomcat --image=Tomcat --replicas=3
```

What happens behind the scenes is that kubectl submits our "intent," or request, to run three instances of Tomcat server in the cluster to the API server. The API server then works with the scheduler and replication controller components to execute our request and brings the cluster to the desired state.

Scheduler

Kubernetes scheduler is a component that is responsible for placing (scheduling to run) the containers in the cluster nodes. It does this by creating *pods*, the basic units of scheduling in Kubernetes. You can imagine a pod as a logical host with separate namespace where one or more containers live. All the containers live inside a pod and share a pod's namespace.

When a request is submitted to the Kubernetes API server, the API server works with the scheduler to place the pods in the cluster nodes. Before placing a pod on a worker node, the scheduler checks various criteria:

- Which nodes have sufficient resources, such as CPU and memory, to run the containers in the pod
- Whether the node has sufficient ports open, as requested by the pod
- Where to place the pod such that it is close enough in the cluster to avoid latency issues (node affinity)
- Whether the pods are distributed in the cluster to support high availability

As you can see, the scheduler has to make a smart, informed decision about where to place the pods in the cluster. And that is one of the Kubernetes scheduler's key responsibilities. It reads data from the pods that describe the pod's policies (required amount of CPU, memory, high availability needs, node affinity, etc.) and runs its own algorithms to arrive at a best possible node to place the pod.

Here's a typical process that the Kubernetes scheduler goes through before making a decision on where to place a given pod:

1. Scheduler reads the pod's needs in terms of resources, node affinity, and so on, and inspects the list of available nodes by pulling the information from the etcd database. It carefully filters out any node(s) that does not meet the pod's policies / requirements at that time.

   For instance, let's say a node has 12G memory and is running a pod that is already using 8G RAM. The leftover memory in this node is 4G. If the scheduler is looking for a node that has at least 8G RAM to schedule a pod to run, then this node will be excluded, as it does not have the required amount of RAM to run the given pod.

2. Nodes that got past step 1 are analyzed carefully by Kubernetes. It follows a set of criteria to choose the best one from a list of qualifying nodes. For example, if an application has two pods, A and B, you don't want both to be scheduled to run on the same node because if that node goes down, then it may affect the application availability, especially in the case of microservices.

   Another example would be replication. Here you don't want pod replicas to be scheduled on the same node for the same reason (impacts availability). Many such policies are taken into account before Kubernetes comes up with the best possible node on which a given pod should be scheduled to run.

3. Once the best node is selected, the scheduler schedules the pod to run on the chosen node.

Kubernetes is a very pluggable architecture. If you need a better scheduler to fit your business or organizational needs, you can plug in your own scheduler.

Replication Controller (Controller Manager)

The replication controller's job is to ensure that the intended or desired number of pod replicas are running in the cluster at any given time. Let's say we request Kubernetes to run three instances of the Tomcat container in the cluster. Kubernetes creates three pods and schedules it to run in the cluster. It goes through the scheduling process and picks up the best nodes to run those three pods. Now suppose one of the nodes that runs the Tomcat pod dies for some reason. This introduces a delta between the desired number of pods we want running in the cluster and the actual number of pods running. Given this delta, the replication controller will kick in and request the Kubernetes scheduler to spin up another instance of the Tomcat pod somewhere in the cluster along with all the other pods running on that machine.

Additionally, let's say you don't need three instances of the Tomcat pod running in the cluster. Maybe your application's time has passed and you want to cut down on the resources because you are expecting less traffic. You may run the same command with an adjusted number of pods replicas:

```
kubectl run myTomcat --image=tomcat --replicas=2
```

The replication controller will again kick in and kill the excess pods, one in this case, running in the cluster to maintain the desired state.

Worker Nodes

Worker nodes are where the pods are scheduled to run. An agent called kubelet runs inside each worker node. Kubelet serves as the single point of contact for each worker node. It is responsible to get "work" from the master node and execute the work in the worker node. Work here is the pod or pods that need to be executed in the worker node. Typically, the scheduler component in the master node uses an API server to provide pod details to kubelet. After receiving the work from the master node, it ensures that the pods are successfully launched in the nodes.

Kubelet is also responsible for reporting both the status of the node—its health, resource availability, and so on—and the status of each pod running in the node. Kubelet stores these statistics in the etcd database via the API server. This data, available in the etcd database, serves as the source for the scheduler to decide which nodes are available (as well as what resources are available in each node) for scheduling a pod. This data is also leveraged by the replication controller to decide whether the desired number of replicas for a service are running in the cluster. If the desired number of replicas are not running the cluster, then it steps in to match the desired state.

Pods

Kubernetes pods are dynamic. In other words, they are created as needed; they can be moved to another node because of a node failure, they may be scaled up by the replication controller to handle more traffic, or they can be scaled down to conserve some resources. Let's discuss this topic with a concrete example to make it clear.

Example: Kubernetes Cluster

Let's assume that we have three instances of MySQL pods running in our Kubernetes cluster as shown in Figure 9.2.

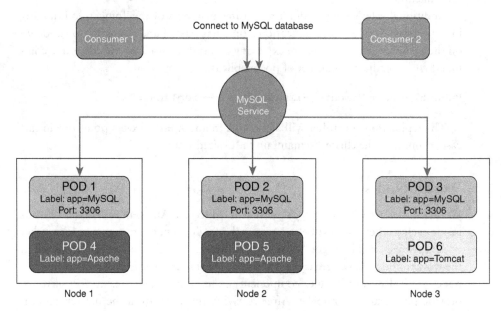

Figure 9.2 *Three MySQL pods running in our Kubernetes cluster*

Pods can have metadata to describe itself. In the figure, you can see that the MySQL pods have a label, app=MySQL, and a port, 3306. You see that Pods 1, 2, and 3 are all tagged or labeled exactly the same way. By doing this, we are creating a logical set of "related" pods that offer a service collectively in a cluster. In this case, those three pods are offering a database service to its consumers.

Let's run through a traditional three-tier application use case in which an application server such as Apache Tomcat (Consumer 1) is trying to pull data from the MySQL database. The consumer's challenge with a microservices architecture is knowing where the MySQL pod is. The nodes on which the MySQL pod live are not static, as we saw earlier. The challenge, then, is locating these pods reliably and being able to communicate with them. That's where Kubernetes Services comes into the picture.

Kubernetes Services form an abstraction layer that provides a single point of entry for client requests through a related set of pods. In other words, we could say that a service front ends a bunch of related backend pods. This is a very powerful abstraction, because now the location of the backend pods becomes irrelevant to the consumers. Consumers can simply reach out to the service, and each service has a virtual IP address and a port that does not change for the lifetime of the service. In short,

Kubernetes Services enable communication to a collection of related pods by keeping track of what pods make up a service.

Plenty of documentation is available to help you install and configure Kubernetes: https://Kubernetes.io. The purpose of covering these topics here is to explain the concepts. You should always refer to the latest online documentation for installation and configuration.

Apache Mesos and Marathon

Apache Mesos is an open source containers orchestration framework that is proven to work well in large-scale production environments. Mesos is like an operating system kernel that manages resources in a cluster of machines. It works in a master/slave-based architecture. By itself, Mesos manages only the cluster resources; it's the job of the frameworks, which sit atop Mesos, to schedule tasks in the cluster. There are many frameworks available, the best known of which include Marathon, Hadoop, and Chronos. We focus on Marathon in this chapter.

The Mesos architecture consists of masters, slaves (or *agents*), and frameworks, as shown in Figure 9.3. Let's look at the major components that make up Mesos.

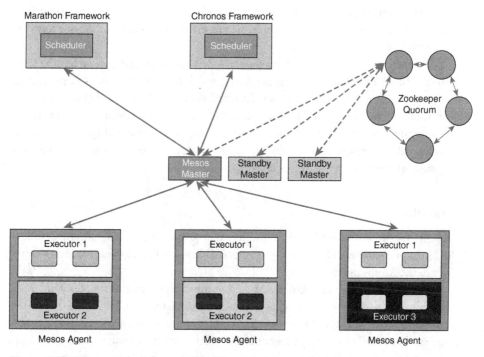

Figure 9.3 *Mesos architecture*

Mesos Master

The Mesos master daemon runs on a master node. This daemon is responsible for managing the agent daemons running on each cluster node; that is, the master daemon is the one that provides work (tasks) to the agent daemons. The master daemon is also responsible for serving frameworks that consume services (computing power such as CPU, memory, network, disk resources) from the Mesos cluster. Any number of frameworks can run on top of the same Mesos cluster. Frameworks are the entities that bring in tasks to be run in the Mesos cluster. Tasks the frameworks want to run in the cluster get to the agent nodes through the master and get executed on the agent nodes.

The job of the Mesos master is to enable sharing of cluster resources such as CPU and memory to the frameworks that are waiting to run their tasks. It does this by sharing the cluster resources in what are called *offers* in the Mesos world. Offers contain details such as amount of RAM and number of CPU cycles available to execute a task. The offers are sent to the registered frameworks, and the frameworks have complete freedom to accept or reject them.

Offers are nothing but a way for a Mesos master to let the registered frameworks know of available resources in the cluster. As an example, an offer can include details such as "12G memory, 8 core CPU cycles are available to be used." A framework that receives an offer inspects the offer received and the tasks in hand to be executed. If the task can be executed by using the offer received, then the framework accepts it; otherwise, the offer is rejected.

The fact that any number of frameworks can consume resources from the same Mesos cluster introduces challenges such as which framework gets what percentage of resources from the cluster. Mesos handles resource allocation elegantly by making it completely configurable through policies that can be defined. It's up to the cluster administrator to define how many resources are allocated to a given framework based on organizational priorities and/or the criticality of the tasks that a given framework may run in the Mesos cluster.

Agents

Agents are the worker nodes where the actual tasks run. A slave daemon runs on each of the worker nodes. This daemon is responsible for collecting and reporting statistics to the Mesos master.

Say your machine has 8GB RAM and 4 core CPU cycles available. This information will be sent from the agent to the Mesos master, which forwards the offers upstream to the registered frameworks. Tasks that the frameworks request actually run in these worker nodes. Agents get the work (task to execute) from the Mesos master. Once they receive the task, they launch the task inside an *executor*.

An executor is simply a process or a container that can execute shell commands or Docker containers and other processes. Mesos provides simple executors that can execute shell commands and Docker containers; however, most frameworks, such as Marathon, ship with their own executors, which offer more capabilities than the ones that come with the default Mesos executor.

Frameworks

Frameworks are the consumers of cluster resources. As we saw earlier, Mesos by itself only manages the cluster's resources; it is the frameworks that run the tasks in the cluster. Frameworks have two major components: the scheduler, which registers itself with the Mesos master and is responsible for looking at an incoming offer and making a decision whether to accept or reject it; and the executor, which actually runs the tasks in the agents. If the frameworks choose not to provide their own executor, they can use the default executor that comes with Mesos.

Example: Marathon Framework

Let's say we want to deploy three instances of a catalog microservice. Here is how we would describe this requirement and hand it off to Marathon:

```
{
 "id": "catalog-svc",
 "cpus": 0.5,
 "mem": 8.0,
 "instances": 3,
 "container": {
 "type": "DOCKER",
 "Docker": {
 "image": "helpdesk/catalog-svc",
 "network": "BRIDGE",
 "portMappings": [
 {"containerPort": 80, "hostPort": 80, "protocol": "tcp"}
 ]
 }
 }
}
```

Notice your Docker networking knowledge coming in handy here. According to this JSON, we need three instances of the catalog microservice running in the cluster. The container section explains what type of container we need—in this case, the Docker container. That section also explains what image will be used inside the

Docker container as well as the ports that need to be exposed. In addition to all of these details, this file also explains how much memory and CPU are required for each container instance.

Here's how we can submit this JSON file to Marathon, assuming this JSON file is saved as application.json:

```
curl -X POST http://hostip:port/v2/apps \
-d @application.JSON \
-H "Content-type: application/JSON"
```

When we hand this off to Marathon, Marathon waits for offers from the Mesos master (note that Marathon does not store offer history). As soon as it receives an offer that fulfills the request, it hands off the request to Mesos so that the executor process inside the agent can launch these containers. Recall that we instructed Marathon to launch three instances of the catalog microservice. If for any reason that cluster does not have three instances of the catalog microservice, Marathon will work with Mesos to spin up additional containers to ensure three instances are always running in this cluster.

It is easy to scale up or scale down the instances running in the cluster. It is a matter of submitting a new JSON file with the required number of instances. For details on installation and configuration, refer to the Mesos project online at https://mesosphere.com.

Docker Swarm

Docker Swarm is a native container orchestration engine from Docker itself. Swarm is simply a group of machines (Docker engines) running Docker containers with swarm mode turned on. Swarm effectively manages the cluster by instructing the cluster nodes to run containers. Let's look at the main concepts.

Nodes

A node, in simple terms, is a Docker engine that's part of the Swarm cluster. The cluster has worker nodes as well as Swarm manager nodes. Swarm manager nodes are the brain of the Swarm cluster. They are responsible for managing the Swarm cluster by instructing the worker nodes to execute containers.

The manager is not deployed as a single node; rather, multiple nodes are typically deployed in odd numbers such as three, five, and seven to avoid being a single point of failure. Manager nodes run what's called a *raft consensus algorithm* to "elect" a single leader. In the event a leader goes down, one of the followers will be elected as a new leader, thus avoiding disruption or any kind of a system failure.

Services

A service is simply a definition of what needs to be executed in the cluster nodes. A service definition consists of the following:

- Image to run in the container
- Any commands that need to be run inside the container
- Replicas or number of instances of the running container

Task

Task is the basic unit of scheduling in Swarm. It contains the Docker container and the commands that need to be run in the container. When the Swarm manager gets a request to spin up a service, the service simply indicates which container is to be launched and the number of instances that need to run in the cluster. The manager node then assigns the task (container to launch and commands to run in the container) to the worker nodes and lets the worker nodes launch those containers. It also ensures that the desired number of replicas (instances) are launched in the cluster.

As end users, we simply mention our intent or the desired state of an application, and it's the job of the Swarm manager to ensure the desired state of the application is achieved and maintained.

Example: Swarm Cluster

Let's get our hands dirty and take a look at how to create a simple Swarm cluster. The good news is that there's no additional software setup required for Swarm as long as you have Docker installed. As of this writing, Docker's latest version is 17.06, and that's what we'll use to explore Swarm.

Swarm Cluster Setup

In this example, we set up a two-node Swarm cluster (one manager, one worker). On the node that we want as Swarm manager, we run the following command to initialize a Swarm cluster:

```
docker swarm init --listen-addr 10.88.237.217:2377
```

In this command, 10.88.237.217 is the interface IP address of the machine where the command is executed, and 2377 is the default port on which the node listens for Swarm manager traffic.

As you can see in Figure 9.4, the command has initialized a Swarm cluster.

```
[root@swarm-master ~]# docker swarm init --listen-addr 10.88.237.217:2377
Swarm initialized: current node (ckmtounajpf06pglhv8jerlou) is now a manager.

To add a worker to this swarm, run the following command:

    docker swarm join \
    --token SWMTKN-1-60v0219bqi48oeimlhbby39huseueu9redz94obklzzceazw43-6hlck485hgtifuw2u7lu3j2dy \
    10.88.237.217:2377

To add a manager to this swarm, run 'docker swarm join-token manager' and follow the instructions.
```

Figure 9.4 *Swarm cluster initialized*

At this stage, there are no worker nodes in the Swarm cluster. All we have is the Swarm manager. Let's list the nodes in the Swarm cluster to quickly see what nodes are there:

```
docker node ls
```

As you can see in Figure 9.5, the Swarm master is the only node in the cluster.

```
[root@swarm-master ~]# docker node ls
ID                          HOSTNAME        STATUS    AVAILABILITY    MANAGER STATUS
ckmtounajpf06pglhv8jerlou * swarm-master    Ready     Active          Leader
```

Figure 9.5 *Swarm master is only node in the cluster*

To add a worker node to this Swarm cluster, we go to a node that has Docker running and run a `swarm join` command to participate in the Swarm cluster:

```
docker swarm join --token <tokenID> 10.88.237.217:2377
```

As you can see, to make a node a worker node, all you have to do is run the `swarm join` command to provide the master's IP and port details, as shown in Figure 9.6.

```
[root@swarm-worker1]# docker swarm join \
>   --token SWMTKN-1-60v0219bqi48oeimlhbby39huseueu9redz94obklzzceazw43-6hlck485hgtifuw2u7lu3j2dy \
>   10.88.237.217:2377
This node joined a swarm as a worker.
```

Figure 9.6 *The* `swarm join` *command providing master's IP and port details*

Now let's look at the nodes participating in the cluster:

```
docker node ls
```

You should now see one manager and one worker node in the Swarm cluster, as shown in Figure 9.7.

```
[root@swarm-master ~]# docker node ls
ID                          HOSTNAME              STATUS      AVAILABILITY      MANAGER STATUS
ckmtounajpfO6pglhvBjerlou *  swarm-master          Ready       Active            Leader
p8c4lftcu9gOugicxf7g5cnff   linux-dev.localdomain  Ready       Active
```

Figure 9.7 *One manager and one worker node in Swarm cluster*

Service Creation

To create a Tomcat service in Swarm and deploy it in the cluster, all we have to do is first establish what image should be used in the container and then how many instances (replicas) are needed to run in the cluster.

In Figure 9.8, you can see that we start with a clean slate with *no* running containers (indicated by `docker ps -a` returning 0 entries in the first line). We then create a service by passing in the Docker image (`tomcat : 7.0`, which is already in the repository) and asking Swarm manager to create just one instance (indicated by `--replicas 1`).

```
[root@swarm-master ~]# docker ps -a
CONTAINER ID     IMAGE           COMMAND           CREATED         STATUS        PORTS        NAMES
[root@swarm-master ~]#
[root@swarm-master ~]# docker images
REPOSITORY       TAG             IMAGE ID          CREATED         SIZE
tomcat           7.0             f8e399bdd39b      6 days ago      357MB
[root@swarm-master ~]#
[root@swarm-master ~]# docker service create --name TomcatService --replicas 1 tomcat:7.0
s7g73pnm2iko?njdmnlfnwpBo
Since --detach=false was not specified, tasks will be created in the background.
In a future release, --detach=false will become the default.
[root@swarm-master ~]#
[root@swarm-master ~]#
[root@swarm-master ~]# docker ps -a
CONTAINER ID     IMAGE           COMMAND           CREATED         STATUS        PORTS        NAMES
1525a4bd2b17     tomcat:7.0      "catalina.sh run"  5 seconds ago Up 3 seconds    8080/tcp     TomcatService.1.tlwr
pk878feb53r7wsh2ikbvw
[root@swarm-master ~]#
[root@swarm-master ~]# docker service ls
ID               NAME            MODE              REPLICAS        IMAGE         PORTS
s7g73pnm2iko     TomcatService   replicated        1/1             tomcat:7.0
```

Figure 9.8 *Starting with a clean slate*

Once we pass in these parameters, we have the Tomcat instance spun up in the cluster (indicated by `docker ps -a` following the service creation command). Finally, running `docker service ls` is a quick way to list the service that we just launched, which indicates that the service called TomcatService is up and running and that the desired number of replicas are met.

Scale Up and Scale Down

First, scale up the service by asking Swarm manager to increase the number of Tomcat replicas:

```
docker service scale service TomcatService=2
```

It'll take a bit of time to launch the additional container in the cluster, as shown in Figure 9.9.

```
[root@swarm-master ~]# docker service scale TomcatService=2
TomcatService scaled to 2
[root@swarm-master ~]#
[root@swarm-master ~]# docker service ls
ID              NAME            MODE            REPLICAS        IMAGE           PORTS
s7q73pnm2lko    TomcatService   replicated      1/2             tomcat:7.0
[root@swarm-master ~]#
[root@swarm-master ~]#
[root@swarm-master ~]#
[root@swarm-master ~]# docker service ls
ID              NAME            MODE            REPLICAS        IMAGE           PORTS
s7q73pnm2lko    TomcatService   replicated      2/2             tomcat:7.0
```

Figure 9.9 *Scaling up the service by asking Swarm manager to increase the number of Tomcat replicas*

Scaling down the service is as simple as running this command:

```
docker service scale TomcatService=1
```

For more details and latest configuration options, visit the online project page: https://docs.docker.com.

Service Discovery

We have talked a lot about service discovery, but let's take a step back and understand what it is and why it's critical. Simply put, service discovery is about locating where a particular service is running—for example, "Where is service X?" where X may be a database server, cache server, or any other application server.

In the good old days, when we had physical machines to deploy our applications, services running on machines used to be named appropriately to represent the services running on them. For example, a database server for the helpdesk application running on a physical machine would possibly be named "helpdesk-db.domain.com." Now when the client—say, an application server such as Tomcat—wants to consume the database, it typically gets configured using properties or configuration files on the database server.

Yet when the need for quickly spinning up machines on the fly became widespread, virtual machines (VMs) emerged. With VMs, what was once difficult to do with physical machines, such as dynamically adding nodes to handle additional load, became easy and very approachable. As a result, cloud technologies became popular. Now, when we have multiple servers offering a single service (e.g., a database cluster), how do the clients know which server to talk to? They use a load balancer such as NGINX or HAProxy and configuring the load balancer with the nodes representing a given service.

For example, let's say we have a load balancer configured to balance the load between two Tomcat servers. As the traffic increases, a new Tomcat VM may be spun up; using scripts/automation, the load balancer will be updated to reflect that a new Tomcat VM was added. With this new configuration in place, the load balancer knows that an additional server representing a Tomcat service is in place, and it can direct traffic to that instance. Client applications don't need to know that a new VM has been added to the Tomcat service, nor do they care about details such as where that VM is running, its IP address, and so on. Client applications continue to talk to the load balancer, which in turn abstracts the changes in the Tomcat service (e.g., adding or removing nodes).

Fast-forward to today. We live in the era of containers and microservices. With containers, the problem of discovering where a given service is located is going to be more difficult than other cases. Containers can be both launched and killed extremely quickly, and their location is not static, making it difficult for the clients to know where a given service is located in the cluster. The good news is that there are a good number of tools in the service discovery space that can be leveraged according to our needs.

Before we look at the many tools available for service discovery, let's understand a couple of service discovery patterns. There are at least two ways to do service discovery, depending on where it occurs:

- **Client-side service discovery.** Service registry is a tool or a database that contains the list of all services, details about where those services reside (IP address, port), and so on, as shown in Figure 9.10. The locations of the actual services gets registered with the registry when these services come up. Likewise, the entries in the registry are removed as these services are terminated. Outside a service start or stop, some kind of a heartbeat mechanism must be in place to ensure that the registered services are up and healthy.

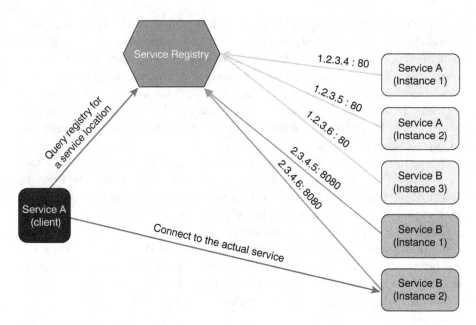

Figure 9.10 *Client-side service discovery*

The major drawback of this approach is that the client has to know about the service registry, which puts the responsibility on the client applications to discover the services before they can communicate with the service.

- **Server-side service discovery.** In the case of server-side service discovery, the client can directly send a request to an API gateway or a load balancer and not worry about connecting to the right service. The load balancer does the heavy lifting of managing the service registry, querying the registry to get the location of services to handle incoming requests, and performing a load-balancing operation across multiple instances of the service, as shown in Figure 9.11. A classic example of this pattern is the popular Amazon ELB (elastic load balancers).

With Amazon Web Services, let's say we set up a four-node EC2 (Amazon Elastic Compute Cloud) cluster for an application tier (Tomcat). In order to split the traffic between these four EC2 Tomcat instances, we have to add/register these instances to an ELB by providing details such as the instance name, port on which the service is running, mechanism to be used to ensure these services are healthy (ELB should be used for heartbeat/health checks), and frequency at which the health check should happen. Once the configuration is done in the ELB, the ELB does the heavy lifting of handling the incoming requests and routing the requests to the appropriate Tomcat instance.

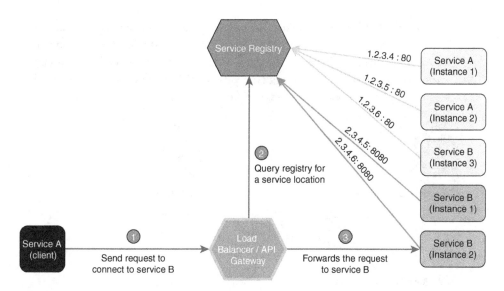

Figure 9.11 *Server-side service discovery*

Microservices and service discovery go hand in hand. In fact, there are many open source tools for service discovery, including Consul (HashiCorp), Zookeeper (Apache), etcd, SmartStack (AirBnB), Eureka (Netflix), and SkyDNS. These tools have a lot of capabilities in common. They are mainly differentiated in terms of the footprint (light versus heavy) and protocols supported to query services (DNS, HTTP/TCP, etc.).

Service Registry

Service registry is like a Yellow Pages for the microservices running in the environment. It has details about where a given microservice is running in the cluster (e.g., host and port). As we know, microservices can come up (new instances may be spun up for scaling) or go down in the event of failure and eventually may be restarted in another node. What this means is that their location is not static—it may change. There are at least two different ways to communicate the location of a given microservice to service registry:

- **Self-registration.** This a process by which a given microservice itself sends its location information to service registry, as shown in Figure 9.12. For example, Consul is a popular choice for service registry, and it exposes an API to interact with it. With self-registration, each microservice will have to interact with the

Consul API to send its whereabouts. According to microservices' patterns and best practices, each microservice should focus on a single concern—one piece of functionality. However, forcing the microservices to send their location information to the service registry violates the single-concern-responsibility pattern. For this reason, self-registration is not a widely used option.

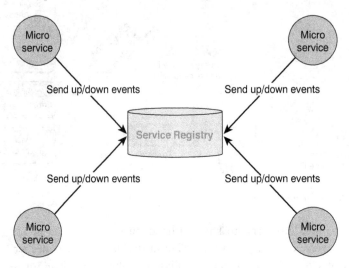

Figure 9.12 *Service registry self-registration*

- **External tools, or third-party registration.** Leveraging external tools for service registry is the best choice for a simple reason: the microservices can focus on their core responsibility and not worry about sending their location information to a service registry. It's a clear separation of concern; tomorrow, if you want to change the way the microservices need to be discovered and stored in the service registry, you can do it without touching the microservices code.

Let's see how a third-party registration would work in the same Consul example previously discussed. Registrator (https://github.com/gliderlabs/registrator) is an open source component that serves as a bridge between service registry and Docker containers. It automatically registers and deregisters services by keeping an eye on the Docker containers as they come up and go down.

As a Docker container comes up or goes down, it fires off events (notifications), and any third-party tool can subscribe to these events to take appropriate actions. Registrator simply watches for these Docker events and, like `docker inspect`, inspects those containers to see what services they provide. It then communicates with any service registry tool (e.g., Consul, etcd, SkyDNS2) and sends the information about the discovered service.

In Figure 9.13, you can see that Registrator is a component that's installed on all the worker nodes that run containers. It's configured with a service registry (which is where the actual information about the services running in in cluster is stored) to which it sends information about the discovered services. As a container is spun up or goes down in a given node, Docker fires off events, and the Registrator component living in each node picks up those events and inspects the containers to get additional information about the services.

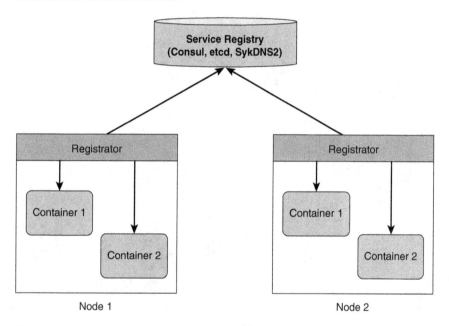

Figure 9.13 *Registrator installed on all the worker nodes that run containers*

This wraps up our deployment and discovery topics. We use this learning extensively in dockerizing our project in Part III of the book.

Chapter 10

Containers Management

Now that we understand containers orchestration, scaling, and networking, let's talk about what happens when things go wrong. You will have potentially hundreds to thousands of containers running in the production, and you need to know how to manage them effectively and efficiently. To that end, our deep dive into containers concludes by getting into the nitty gritty of container monitoring and management that includes capturing logs, collecting resource metrics, and using some cluster-wide monitoring systems. Let's first understand the overall monitoring aspect of containers and why it may be different from what already exists in the market.

Monitoring

Monitoring an environment with containers is not difficult, but the speed, quantity, and environment can make it so. Legacy-wise, the monitoring tools market to monitor and manage physical hosts, network, and virtual machines has matured. Containers are new; the marketplace is still in the process of solving the monitoring problem. Containers monitoring is different because of the following aspects and challenges:

- **Deployment environment.** An organization may run some containers directly on physical infrastructures within its own data center and some containers on virtual machines with a service provider such as AWS Managed Service Partners, which adds little more to complexity in terms of management.

- **Scalability of containers.** Whole applications can be run on a physical machine or on few virtual machines. With containers, the best practices dictate one service per container, and an application may consist of hundreds to thousands of services, which means hundreds to thousands of containers. In a microservices architecture, application scaling requires auto-shrinking and auto-expanding the number of containers on the basis of changing needs.

- **Velocity of change.** Unlike physical hosts or virtual machines, the life expectancy of a container may vary from a few seconds to several days. When a task is finished, the container goes away.

- **Various tools in use.** Although containers provide speed and efficiency, they throw simplicity out the window. Deployment, management, and discovery of the containers involves a plethora of tools. For example, you may use one of several containers orchestrators, such as Docker Swarm, Kubernetes, or Mesos. You can specify the networking configuration, number of instances of a container to spin up, and so on. The orchestrators then control the creation, deletion, and management of the containers based on resource availability within the hosts. Each time a new container is created, it gets a new IP address. With all this going on, it becomes very hard to set up the overall monitoring and collection of metrics.

- **Distributed data.** Data must be collected from the various tools and merged at one centralized place to make sense of it and find potential issues. Docker provides some capabilities to get these data and statistics to proactively monitor the containers and overall system.

There are lot of vendor-specific options, and each has its own benefits. Docker has recently launched the Ecosystem Technology Partner (ETP) program with the companies that have integrated their monitoring tools with Docker through APIs. You can search for such partners at https.www.docker.com.

Let's begin the discussion with available logging and container metrics collection. You can pull this data to your existing monitoring tools or build some dashboards.

Logging

In a production environment that supports multiple applications on multiple clusters with multiple copies of a running service, you may have a very high number of containers running. Things do go wrong, and when they do, logging becomes very important to troubleshoot the issues. For example, recall that with microservices, we are talking about hundreds to thousands of microservices as part of one typical large-scale application. Docker containers are well suited to run such a high number of microservices because they offer the many advantages we have discussed. The question is, how do we manage the logging when each container is spitting everything that comes out of `stdout` and `stderr` into the logs? How do we keep all these logs in sync and in a place that makes troubleshooting straightforward and efficient?

Docker, once again, provides drivers that simplify our job. Each driver helps us get the logging information from the containers and running services. They differ in the way they provide and format the information and how they forward it to different log processors. Example drivers include JSON, Syslog, Splunk, Amazon Cloud-Watch Logs, and the like. We discuss these options thoroughly, but for more details, refer to Docker online documentation.

At the time of writing, the following logging drivers are supported:

- **json-file.** The default logging driver for Docker daemon. Each container uses json-file unless you configure the container or daemon to use a different driver. The output log file is in well-understood JSON format.

- **None.** Turns off logging.

- **Syslog.** Sends the log messages to the syslog server installed locally or remotely. As discussed earlier, you can modify the daemon.json file on the host to set the log driver to syslog and specify options in the options section. You can also do this at the container level. Syslog brings all the messages to the same location, which helps in troubleshooting, but it is not sufficient to deal with hundreds of containers, as in the case of microservices.

- **awslogs.** Sends the log messages to Amazon CloudWatch Logs. In this case, set the log driver to awslogs and specify the required options.

- **Splunk.** Sends the log messages to Splunk using the HTTP event collector. In this case, set the log driver to Splunk. Splunk-token and splunk-url are the required options you must specify in the file or at the time of running the container.

- **Journald.** Sends the log messages to the system journal. In this case, set the log driver to journald. Log entries can be retrieved using journalctl or Docker log commands.

- **gcplogs.** Sends the log messages to Google Cloud Platform logging where you can search and analyze these messages. In this case, set the log driver to gcplogs. You can also set several options to include more details in the messages.

- **GELF.** Sends messages to Graylog Extended Log Format (GELF) endpoints such as Logstash server. In this case, set the log driver to gelf along with various options. GELF is extensively used as part of ELK (Elasticsearch, Logstash, and Kibana).

As mentioned earlier, json-file is the default driver. You can check this by running the following command:

```
docker info | grep 'Logging Driver'
```

You should see the result – `Logging Driver: json-file`.
Let's run an Ubuntu container and check the default logging:

```
docker run -it ubuntu:latest sh
```

Open another terminal, find the container ID, and copy it:

```
docker ps
```

Now run the following command to find the logging driver for our Ubuntu container:

```
docker inspect -f '{{.HostConfig.LogConfig.Type}}' ec5e917eb9b0
```

You should see the result shown in Figure 10.1.

```
[root@linux-dev pkocher]# docker inspect -f '{{.HostConfig.LogConfig.Type}}' ec5
e917eb9b0
json-file
```

Figure 10.1 *Using* `docker inspect` *to find the logging driver for our Ubuntu container*

You can change the default logging driver at the daemon level or at the container level. For the daemon level, you can modify the value of `log-driver` in the daemon.json file located in /etc/Docker on the Linux host machine. The structure looks like this:

```
"log-driver":
"log-opts":{ options like syslog server info, etc. }
```

For the container level, you can specify the logging driver during the `run` command, as we'll see in the next example.

Of course, another option is to turn logging off altogether. Let's restart our Ubuntu container with the none option and run the logs command again.

```
docker run -it --log-driver none ubuntu:latest sh
```

Let's run a couple of commands at the sh prompt to create some log data, as shown in Figure 10.2.

```
# ps
  PID TTY          TIME CMD
    1 ?        00:00:00 sh
    8 ?        00:00:00 ps
# ls
bin  boot  dev  etc  home  lib  lib64  media  mnt  opt  proc  root  run  sbin  srv  sys  tmp  usr  var
# ▇
```

Figure 10.2 *Creating log data*

Now check the logs:

```
docker ps //Copy ContainerID
docker logs 73c1b74d6091
```

You can see that there is no logging available, as it has been turned off for this particular container. The subsequent containers have no impact because we changed the setting at the container level.

Keep in mind that the container logging options we discussed do not account for application or services messages that don't pass messages through the stderr and stdout streams. Also, some of these drivers rely on services running on the host machine, which is a little risky.

Another thing to keep in mind is that as the number of containers grow within your application, you will need a very sophisticated centralized logging system that contains all the information starting from system data such as CPU and memory to last-mile application performance data. So, when building the application, you need to include proper tagging and tracking as part of your code. This centralized logging system should include capabilities such as filtering, indexing, categorizing, sorting, and searching to make application and containers troubleshooting faster and easier.

Metrics Collection

In this section, we discuss metrics collection mechanisms that use the basic utilities provided by Docker and some open source tools that you can use to solve for monitoring given the complexity of your deployment. We start with Docker Stats.

docker stats

The `docker stats` command provides you with live performance data for the containers running on your host system at the given time:

```
docker stats [Options] [Containers]
```

You can provide container IDs for the specific containers you are interested in or use the `-a` option for all containers. If you do not specify an option, Docker presents you with all running containers.

Let's execute this command:

```
docker stats
```

Figure 10.3 shows the result of the `docker stats` command, which returns the resource usage statistics.

```
CONTAINER      CPU%        MEM USAGE / LIMIT      MEM%        NET I/O      BLOCK I/O      PIDS
b4831186f0d4   0.00%       1.98 MiB / 47.08 GiB   0.00%       0 B / 0 B    2.12 MB / 0 B  1
```

Figure 10.3 *Executing the* `docker stats` *command*

Press Ctrl+C to exit the stream. You can customize the output by providing the desired format with the `--format` option. For example:

```
docker stats --format "table {{.Name }} \t {{.ID }} \t {{.CPUPerc}} \t
{{.MemUsage}}"
```

You can include the following metrics with the `--format` option:

- `.Name` returns the container name.
- `.ID` returns the container ID.
- `.CPUPrec` returns the CPU utilization percentage.
- `.MemUsage` returns the memory utilization.
- `.NetIO` returns the network I/O utilization.
- `.BlockIO` returns the block I/O utilization.
- `.MemPerc` returns the memory utilization percentage.
- `.PIDs` returns the number of PIDs.

As you can see in Figure 10.4, this provides a great way to see the performance data by host.

```
NAME                CONTAINER ID                                                        CPU %      MEM USAGE / LIMIT
nervous_bhaskara    b4831186f0d47a248caabf44a4b7cf469bf0d6e6c7c7f975b0b931954611        0.00%      1.98 MiB / 47.08 GiB
```

Figure 10.4 *Using the* --format *option to see performance data by host*

APIs

The docker stats command is a great way to pull a live stream of data. The good news is that REST APIs are available that you can utilize to build your own performance dashboards across clusters. These APIs provide similar live stream data but are more detailed than docker stats.

```
GET /containers/(ID/Name)/stats
```

The API end point to pull statistics about a running container is

```
curl --unix-socket /var/run/docker.sock -X GET
'http:/v1.24/containers/<container ID>/stats'
```

Just as the docker stats command does, the API starts streaming the data every second. It is up to you to program it in a way that does not disrupt performance. For e.g. you may want a snapshot at some defined frequency. Hopefully, this limitation will be fixed soon by including some kind of streaming flag in the API.

As we learned in previous chapters, one of the best practices to effectively monitor containers is to tag the containers in a meaningful way. You can define the tags when you build the images. This way, rather than working at a particular host or container level, you can work with tag names.

For more information on REST APIs, refer to docker.com.

cAdvisor

cAdvisor, also known as Container Advisor, is a monitoring solution developed by Google. It provides detailed data on the usage and performance metrics of containers through a graphical user interface. It comes as a container itself that you can deploy on your host machines. cAdvisor collects the data from all the containers running on the host, then aggregates and processes these data for your consumption. It also exposes this data through APIs that you can take advantage of.

So that you can quickly try out cAdvisor on your machine with Docker, there is a Docker image that includes everything you need to get started (for more information, see https://github.com/google/cadvisor). You can run a single cAdvisor to monitor the whole machine. Simply run the following code:

```
sudo docker run \
  --volume=/:/rootfs:ro \
  --volume=/var/run:/var/run:rw \
  --volume=/sys:/sys:ro \
  --volume=/var/lib/docker/:/var/lib/docker:ro \
  --publish=8080:8080 \
  --detach=true \
  --name=cadvisor \
  google/cadvisor:latest
```

cAdvisor runs in the background. You can see the GUI by going to http://localhost:8080, which brings up the built-in web UI.

The last two ways of collecting metrices we discussed are good solutions but very host-centric. They do provide APIs that you can use to centralize your monitoring system, but many off-the-shelf systems provide cluster-wide metrics and monitoring. We discuss a couple of systems next. This is a very fast-changing area, so the idea here is to provide the key concepts. You should continue to search online for the respective project pages for these solutions to get the latest information.

Cluster-wide Monitoring Tools

Let's look into some of the open source cluster-wide monitoring tools available.

Heapster

Heapster is another solution developed by Google to solve cluster-wide monitoring. It uses cAdvisor heavily to achieve its goals and is a good fit if you are using Kubernetes as your orchestration engine. However, at this book's publication, Heapster supports only Kubernetes and CoreOS.

In Kubernetes, cAdvisor is integrated into the Kubelet binary. As we discussed, cAdvisor auto-discovers all containers within the host and collects the usage, performance, and network usage statistics. Kubelet takes all these statistics from cAdvisor and exposes the aggregated resource usage statistics to Heapster through a REST

API. Heapster processes and groups this data and pushes to the configured back end for visualization. Currently supported back ends include InfluxDB and Grafana for visualization.

Refer to https://kubernetes.io/ and https://github.com/kubernetes/heapster for more details.

Prometheus

Prometheus is an open source cluster monitoring and alerting solution. It is a little different from other solutions in that it is built on a pull-based model. In this model, the monitoring agent pulls its targets on a predefined frequency to collect, store, and alert on data. The applications must expose their data rather than send it out. It also offers a flexible query language called PromQL. Before we look into how Prometheus works with Docker, let's look at its main components:

- **Prometheus server.** This component pulls/scrapes and stores the collected data and run rules to record new time series. It also can be configured to generate diagnostic alerts that can be picked up by Alertmanager.

- **Web UI.** Prometheus uses Grafana as the graphical front-end interface to build highly visual and interactive dashboards.

- **Push gateway.** This intermediate service enables you to push the metrics from short-lived services for which the data pull is not possible. The Prometheus server can then pull those metrics. Be careful when using push gateways, as they can become single points of failure for that particular source.

- **Exporters.** These are special-purpose plugins or libraries used to export metrics from certain systems in which it is not feasible to instrument them with Prometheus metrics. Following are some examples:

  - *HAProxy* is a simple server that scrapes HAProxy stats and exports them, via HTTP/JSON for Prometheus consumption at regular intervals.

  - *Memcached exporter* exports metrics from a mem-cached server for Prometheus consumption. You can create custom exporters for your third-party applications. There are many available. For the latest list of available exporters, refer to https://github.com/prometheus/docs/blob/master/content/docs/instrumenting/exporters.md.

- **Alertmanager.** Alerts sent by the Prometheus server and other applications are processed by Alertmanager as configured. The processing includes deduplication, grouping, and routing to the configured medium (e.g., email, pager).

Given all these components and their functions, it is easy to understand how Prometheus can be used to monitor Docker containers with an example. In this example, we set up the following:

- Run Prometheus and the components mentioned previously.
- Add a node exporter container that can be used to export metrics from containers and a cAdvisor container.
- Set the node exporter, cAdvisor, and Prometheus containers as our targets to be monitored by Prometheus (in this case, Prometheus will monitor itself).
- Set up and configure Grafana.
- View the stats.
- Integrate with Alertmanager to configure alerts.

Step 1: Running Prometheus

The first step is to bring up Prometheus server. We run this server as a Docker container. In order to collect Docker metrics, we configure this container as the Prometheus target so that it monitors itself too.

Let's begin with a Docker compose file, docker-compose.yml, that runs Prometheus as a container:

```
version: '2'

networks:
- pk_network:
 driver:bridge

volumes:
prometheus_data: {}

services:
prometheus:
image: prom/prometheus
container_name: pk_prometheus
volumes:
- ./prometheus/:/etc/prometheus/
- prometheus_data:/prometheus
command:
- '-config.file=/etc/prometheus/prometheus.yml'
```

```
- '-storage.local.path=/prometheus'
- '-storage.local.memory-chunks=100000'
restart: unless-stopped
expose:
- 9090
ports:
- 9090:9090
networks:
- pk_network
labels:
 org.label-schema.group: "monitoring for PK containers"
```

As you notice, we pulled the Prometheus image and ran it as pk_prometheus. We also created a bridge-based network, pk_network, to which containers are added. Next, we mapped the configuration file, prometheus.yml, that defines the scrape information, and we mapped and exposed the port.

Here is what prometheus.yml looks like:

```
global:
scrape_interval: 20s
evaluation_interval: 20s

#Attach the below label for graph view
external_labels: monitor: 'Docker-pk-monitor'

# End points for scrape
- job_name: 'pk_prometheus'
scrape_interval: 25s
static_configs:
- targets: ['localhost:9090']
```

It is quite self-explanatory. We set the scraping and evaluation intervals. The scraping interval defines how frequently to scrape the target, whereas the evaluation interval defines rules evaluation frequency. Notice we added the Prometheus container that we are about to bring up as its target so it will monitor itself.

Now, let's bring Prometheus up by running docker-compose, as shown in Figure 10.5:

```
docker-compose up -d
```

```
[ANUJSIN-M-T2H9: dockprom anujsin$
ANUJSIN-M-T2H9: dockprom anujsin$ docker-compose up -d
WARNING: The Docker Engine you're using is running in swarm mode.

Compose dose not use swarm mode to deploy services to multiple nodes in a swarm.

to deploy your application across the swarm, use `docker stack deploy`.

Pulling prometheus (prom/prometheus:lastest)...
lastest:pulling from prom/prometheus
4b0bc1c4050b : pull complete
a3ed95caeb02: pull complete
d6ab6c75ce17 : pull complete
96eeb64debe6: pull complete
1e7ee99aa461 : pull complete
8d3b35efed41 : pull complete
be179630d433 : pull complete
63e70970c133 : pull complete
83449160ff0d : pull complete
Digest: sha256:4f6d3a525f030e598016be765283c6455c3c830997a5c916b27a5d727be718e1
Status: Downloaded newer image for prom/prometheus: latest
Creating prometheus ...
Creating prometheus ... done
ANUJSIN-M-T2H9:dockprom anujsin$ ▮
```

Figure 10.5 *Creating Prometheus container*

To confirm that Prometheus is up and running, let's run docker ps, as shown in Figure 10.6.

```
ANUJSIN-M-T2H9:dockprom anujsin$ docker ps
CONTAINER ID      IMAGE             COMMAND             CREATED          STATUS
PORTS                   NAMES
48d1efc55881      prom/prometheus   "/bin/promethus -..."  54 seconds ago   up 53 seconds
  0.0.0.0:9090->9090/tcp     promethus
ANUJSIN-M-T2H9:dockprom anujsin$ ▮
```

Figure 10.6 *Prometheus up and running*

Everything looks good so far. To get to the Prometheus UI, go to http://localhost:9090/. Figure 10.7 shows what you should see.

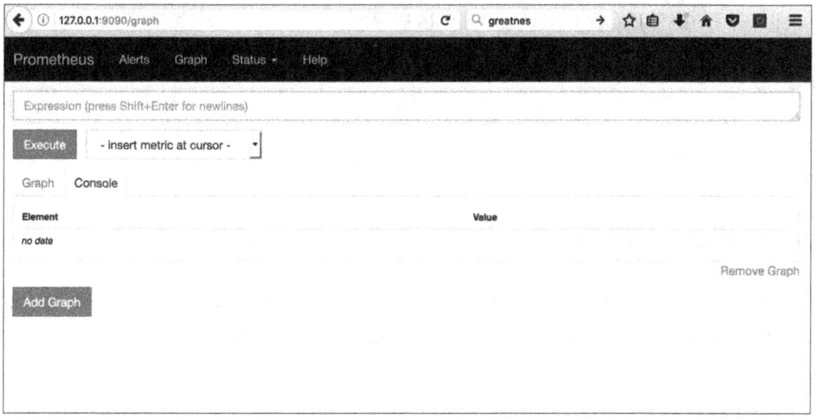

Figure 10.7 *Prometheus user interface*

Step 2: Adding Node Exporter and cAdvisor

Let's start adding other components in the same compose file and add targets. To start, we add the node exporter and cAdvisor to our existing Docker compose file so that they will also run as containers. Notice we are creating these as example place-holders to collect metrics from application containers. We will use these containers as targets for our Prometheus server in the next step.

```
nodeexporter:
image: prom/node-exporter
container_name: pk_nodeexporter
restart: unless-stopped
expose:
- 9100
networks:
- pk_network
labels:
 org.label-schema.group: "monitoring for PK containers"


cadvisor:
image: google/cadvisor:v0.26.1
container_name: pk_cadvisor
volumes:
- /:/rootfs:ro
- /var/run:/var/run:rw
- /sys:/sys:ro
```

```
- /var/lib/docker/:/var/lib/docker:ro
restart: unless-stopped
expose:
- 8080
networks:
- pk_network
labels:
 org.label-schema.group: "monitoring for PK containers"
```

What we did here is very straightforward. We spun up the node exporter and cAdvisor containers, and we exposed the ports on the same network.

Step 3: Adding Targets

The next step is to add the node exporter and cAdvisor as our Prometheus targets. Let's add them to our existing Prometheus.yml file:

```
scrape_configs:
- job_name: 'pk_nodeexporter'
scrape_interval: 15s
static_configs:
- targets: ['nodeexporter:9100']


- job_name: 'pk_cadvisor'
scrape_interval: 20s
static_configs:
- targets: ['cadvisor:8080']
```

Let's run the compose file again and make sure our new containers are up:

```
docker-compose up -d
```

As you can see in Figure 10.8, all is well so far.

```
Status: Downloaded newer image for google/cadvisor:v0.26.1
Creating prometheus ...
Creating cadvisor ...
Creating nodeexporter ...
Creating prometheus
Creating nodeexporter
Creating cadvisor ... done
```

Figure 10.8 *Running docker compose*

Step 4: Bringing Up the User Interface: Grafana

To stand up Grafana to view the metrics, we go back to our Docker compose file and update it to include Grafana:

```
...
volumes:
prometheus_data: {}
grafana_data: {}

...
grafana:
image: grafana/grafana
container_name: grafana
volumes:
- grafana_data:/var/lib/grafana
env_file:
- user.config
restart: unless-stopped
expose:
- 3000
ports:
- 3000:3000
networks:
- pk_network
labels:
 org.label-schema.group: "monitoring for PK containers"
```

Next, let's add a user configuration file to create an admin user for Grafana at the same location where our Docker compose file resides. Call this file user.config, as specified previously in `env_file`:

```
GF_ SECURITY_ADMIN_USER=admin

GF_ SECURITY_ADMIN_PASSWORD=admin

GF_ USERS_ALLOW_SIGN_UP=false
```

Now let's run bring up our Grafana and test it:

```
docker-compose up -d
```

As you can see in Figure 10.9, all our containers are up.

```
Creating  pk_prometheus ...
Creating  pk_nodeexporter ...
Creating  pk_alertmanager ...
Creating  pk_cadvisor ...
Creating  pk_grafana ...
Creating  pk_nodeexporter
Creating  pk_prometheus
Creating  pk_alertmanager
Creating  pk_cadvisor
Creating  pk_prometheus ... done
```

Figure 10.9 *Containers are up*

To check the status of Docker containers, use the docker ps command, as shown in Figure 10.10.

```
ANUJSIN-M-T2H9:dockprom anujsin$ docker ps
CONTAINER ID      IMAGE                     COMMAND               CREATED            STATUS
     PORTS                     NAMES
1c98a5683541      grafana/grafana           "/run.sh"             About a minute ago  Up 58 seconds
     0.0.0.0:3000->3000/tcp    pk_grafana
b6935f85ce88      google/cadvisor:v0.26.1   "/usr/bin/cadvisor..."  About a minute ago  Up 58 seconds
     8080/tcp                  pk_cadvisor
2e6535fda4ef      prom/alertmanager         "/bin/alertmanager..."  About a minute ago  Up 58 seconds
     0.0.0.0:9093->9093/tcp    pk_alertmanager
dba0e0aa1ce5      prom/prometheus           "/bin/prometheus -..."  About a minute ago  Up 57 seconds
     0.0.0.0:9000->9090/tcp    pk_prometheus
99703482e361      prom/node-exporter        "/bin/node_exporter"   About a minute ago  Up 58 seconds
     9100/tcp                  pk_nodeexporter
ANUJSIN-M-T2H9:dockprom anujsin$
```

Figure 10.10 *Using the* Docker ps *command to check the status*

Let's check out our apps. Go to http://localhost:9090/ to see Prometheus, as shown in Figure 10.11. Go to http://localhost:3000/ to see Grafana, as shown in Figure 10.12.

Figure 10.11 *Checking out Prometheus*

Figure 10.12 *Checking out Grafana*

As we can see, our applications are up and running.

Configuring Grafana

We need to configure Grafana to visualize the data. First, log in with the username and password from the Grafana configuration file, which we specified as admin/admin.

Now add the data sources for Grafana, as shown in Figure 10.13.

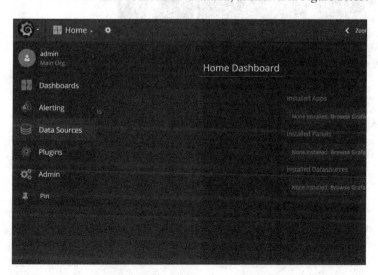

Figure 10.13 *Adding the data sources for Grafana*

Let's fill in the detailed source information such as type of source and credentials, as shown in Figure 10.14:

- Name: Prometheus
- Type: Prometheus
- URL: http://prometheus:9090
- Access: proxy

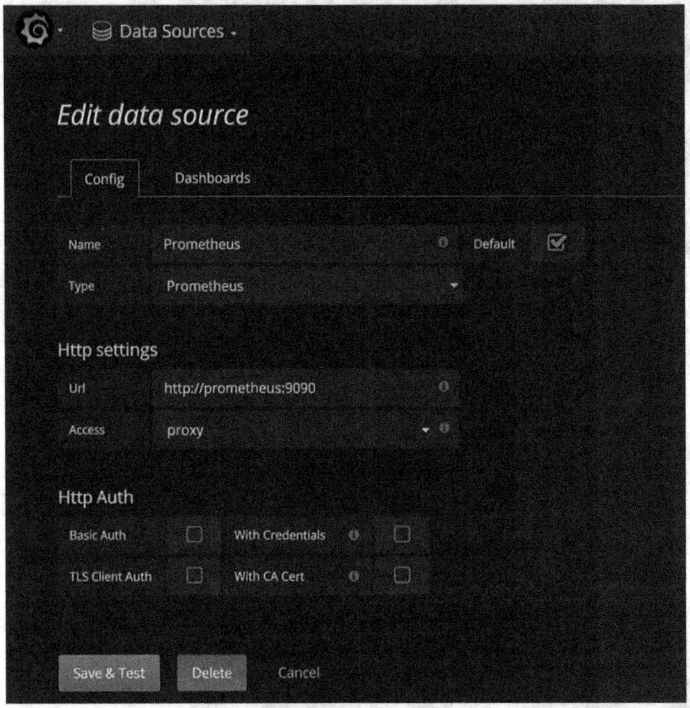

Figure 10.14 *Setting the data sources*

Click **Save & Test,** and you should see a success message. Grafana and Prometheus are now connected.

Step 5: Viewing the Stats

We are all done with the setup. Now we're ready to see the stats that Prometheus has collected from three targets: cAdvisor, node exporter, and Prometheus itself.

Bring up the Prometheus UI by going to http://localhost:9090. Click the drop-down menu next to the Execute button, and select the queries to view the collection stats; click **Execute**, as shown in Figure 10.15.

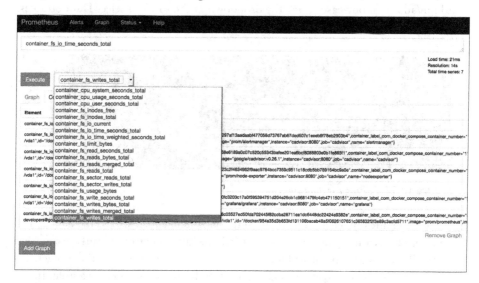

Figure 10.15 *How to view the collection stats*

In the example shown in Figure 10.16, we've selected container_cpu_system_seconds_total. The results show all the containers and total system CPU time consumed in seconds.

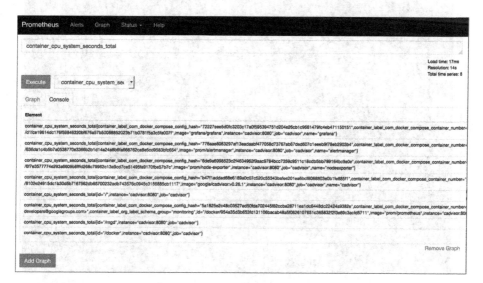

Figure 10.16 *Container results: total system CPU time consumed, in seconds*

Great stats, but the display doesn't look that great. Let's improve the aesthetics by importing Prometheus stats to Grafana. Bring up the Grafana UI by going to http://localhost:3000. Log in with your username and password, which is set to admin/admin in our case. Click the dropdown at the top and select **Data Sources**. Click on the **Dashboards** tab, as shown in Figure 10.17.

Figure 10.17 *Editing the data source*

You will already see a Prometheus Stats entry: remember, we did the data source configuration earlier (see Figure 10.14). Click the **Import** button toward the right end of the Prometheus entry. It will import all the stats and events from the Prometheus database. This step needs to be done only once; the new data will now automatically be pulled with each refresh by Grafana.

To review the sample stats from what you just imported, click **Prometheus Stats**. You should see the new, more attractive dashboards, as shown in Figure 10.18.

Figure 10.18 *Some good-looking dashboards!*

Looks good, all thanks to the power of Grafana!

Let's move another step forward and create a simple custom dashboard to show the cumulative CPU load of containers on the host. Bring up the Grafana UI, click on the top left menu, select **Dashboards,** and then click **New,** as shown in Figure 10.19.

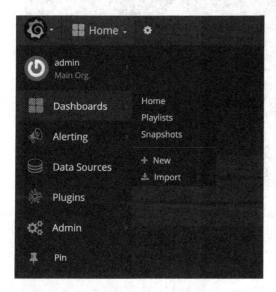

Figure 10.19 *Creating a simple custom dashboard to show the cumulative CPU load of containers on the host*

Click on **Single Stat.** Go ahead and configure it as follows:

```
sum(rate(container_cpu_user_seconds_total{image!=""}[1m])) /
count(node_cpu{mode="system"}) * 100
```

The query pulls the CPU resource utilization at a given point in time, as shown in Figure 10.20. This will be in real time.

Figure 10.20 *Pulling the CPU resource utilization*

Other such examples that can be built in the same way include memory utilization and system load graphs, as shown in Figures 10.21 and 10.22.

Figure 10.21 *Pulling the memory load*

CLUSTER-WIDE MONITORING TOOLS   165

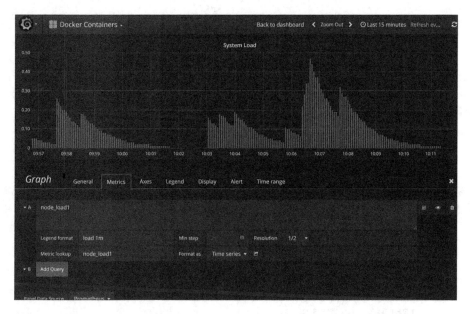

Figure 10.22 *Pulling the system load*

Step 6: Integrating the Alertmanager

To finish, let's now integrate the Alertmanager as part of this configuration. You can configure the alerts in the Alertmanager based on the data collection within Prometheus.

Let's do the following setup:

1. Open the Docker compose file and add the following:

```
alertmanager:
 image: prom/alertmanager
 container_name: alertmanager_pk
 volumes:
 - ./alertmanager/:/etc/alertmanager/
 command:
 - '-config.file=/etc/alertmanager/config.yml'
 - '-storage.path=/alertmanager'
 restart: unless-stopped
 expose:
 - 9093
 ports:
 - 9093:9093
```

```
networks:
- pk_network
labels:
  org.label-schema.group: "monitoring for PK containers"
```

2. Add the Alertmanager in the Prometheus container service within the Docker compose file:

```
prometheus:
  image: prom/prometheus
  container_name: Prometheus_pk
  volumes:
  - ./prometheus/:/etc/prometheus/
  - prometheus_data:/prometheus
  command:
  - '-config.file=/etc/prometheus/prometheus.yml'
  - '-storage.local.path=/prometheus'
  - '-alertmanager.url=http://alertmanager:9093'
  - '-storage.local.memory-chunks=100000'
  restart: unless-stopped
  expose:
  - 9090
  ports:
  - 9090:9090
  networks:
  - pk_network
  labels:
    org.label-schema.group: "monitoring for PK containers"
```

3. Create a rules file to configure alerting rules; name this file container.rules:

```
ALERT tomcat_down
  IF absent(container_memory_usage_bytes{name="tomcat"})
  FOR 10s
  LABELS { severity = "critical" }
  ANNOTATIONS {
  summary= "tomcat down",
  description= "tomcat container is down for more than
  10 seconds."
  }
```

This rule checks for the Tomcat status. It generates alerts if Tomcat goes down. It does this by checking the memory used by Tomcat; if the stats are absent, it sends out an alert.

4. Add this rule to the Prometheus.yml file:

```
# Load and evaluate rules in this file every
  'evaluation_interval' seconds.
rule_files:
 - "containers.rules"
```

5. Run the Docker compose file again:

```
docker-compose up -d
```

Bring up Prometheus by going to http://localhost:9090. Click the **Alerts** menu at the top. You can see the active alerts, as shown in Figure 10.23.

Figure 10.23 *Showing active alerts*

You can further improve this by configuring the tools of your choice for notification. For more information, check out the Prometheus site: https://prometheus.io/.

As discussed earlier, monitoring is a very important task and should be a primary concern, not an afterthought, when transitioning to containers. This is a new field, and a bit problematic thanks to the challenges highlighted in this chapter, but new solutions are hitting the market. Keep an eye out and keep learning!

## PART III

Hands-On Project—Putting Learning into Practice

Chapter 11

Case Study: Monolithic Helpdesk Application

In this chapter, we build a traditional web-based helpdesk application following industry standard practices. However, we build it without using the concepts we have learned so far; that is, we build a monolithic application. The idea here is to gain real-world experience. We build this application and then look at some real-world complexities such as application deployment, managing updates, and scalability. Once we understand the complexities of using monolithic architecture, we will see how these challenges can be solved using a combination of microservices and Dockers, which we will do in the next two chapters when we rebuild the application using microservices architecture and deploy using containers.

Helpdesk Application Overview

In today's digital world, most companies are transforming the customer support experience by providing a self-service model through mobile/web applications. Application experience, availability, performance, and search capabilities are all keys to faster issue resolution and are critical characteristics of the system to meet the aforementioned objectives.

This application provides support capabilities to help and manage customer concerns. It is important to note that the application is simplified for the purpose of explaining the concepts, architecture, and complexities of monolithic applications.

Assume that in the real world, this application provides customer support for a mobile phone vendor. This application provides the following capabilities:

- **Account management.** Provides the user account management functionality (add/modify/delete). Authentication is managed through username and password on local database to keep it simple.

- **Incident creation and management.** Provides the ability to submit new incidents along with viewing and updating existing ones.

- **Product catalog management (admin only).** Stores and manages the product catalog based on the product sold and inventory.

- **Appointment setup.** Provides ability to set up an appointment with support professional.

- **Search.** Provides capability to search for existing issues and resolutions as well as to search the product catalog.

- **Message boards.** Customer community board for customers to collaborate and help each other.

The following technologies will be used to build this application:

- **User interface:** HTML, JavaScript, and JQuery
- **Middle layer:** Java 7, Spring 3.x, Jersey 1.8, and Hibernate
- **Database:** MySQL 5.x

Refer to Appendix A to better understand the application workflows and step-by-step process. All the code and assets are available on the GitHub repository located at https://github.com/kocherMSD/Helpdesk_Monolithic.git.

You can clone the code to your local machine using the `git clone` command. We will use this code during our set up process.

Application Architecture

Now that we understand how this application is used, let's dive into the technical details of the application. Figure 11.1 shows the component-based architecture of the application.

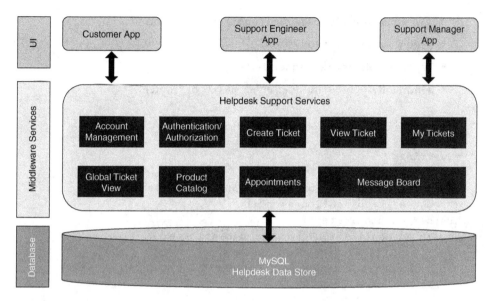

Figure 11.1 *Our helpdesk app's components and basic architecture*

As you see, it is a three-tier architecture application composed of a database, business logic/services, and a user interface. Now let's take a high-level look at the list of services that are part of the application. For implementation details, you can refer to code posted at GitHub.

Authentication, Interceptor, and Authorization

As the name indicates, this module provides services to authenticate users and authorize what level of information users are entitled to access based on their role. To make it simple, we have implemented simple authentication (database username/password) and role (database username and role)–based authorization. We have implemented spring interceptor to make sure every request is authenticated. The role and login are saved into session and are fetched from session as required.

Following is the pseudocode for authentication.

Authentication

This service is use to authenticate user using username and password from the text field of login page. The username/password pair is matched with the entry in the database.

- Context: authenticate
- Method: POST

- Consumes: `application/xml, application/json`
- Produces: `application/json`
- Input: `HttpHeaders, request`
- Output: Response status (i.e., either success or failure)

Following is the pseudocode for authentication service:

```
@Override
@POST
@Consumes({"application/xml", "application/json"})
@Produces({"application/json"})
@Path("/authenticate/")
public AuthenticationResponse authenticate(
     @Context HttpHeaders headers,
     AuthenticationRequest request)
  //To-do Implementation
}
```

Interceptor

The Interceptor intercepts all the incoming requests to the application server using `./*` pattern matching, which helps in executing the `prehandle` function. Following is the spring pseudocode for XML and Java:

```
<interceptors>
  <interceptor>
    <mapping path="/*"/>
    <beans:bean>
        class="org.spring.controller.AuthenticationInterceptor"
    <beans:bean/>
  </interceptor>
</interceptors>

@Override
public boolean preHandle(
     HttpServletRequest request,
     HttpServletResponse response,
     Object handler) throws Exception {
//To-do Implementation
}
```

Authorization

Our application has multiple roles, and when users log in, their roles are saved in the HTTP session as part of the interceptor logic. The following code snippet is used in the authorization controller to fetch the HTTP session.

```
LoginForm userData = (LoginForm)
context.getSession().getAttribute("LOGGEDIN_USER");
```

The following code snippet is for the authorization frontend JavaServer Pages (JSP):

```
<%

LoginForm loginform=(LoginForm)session.getAttribute
("LOGGEDIN_USER");
String user=loginform.getUsername();
if(session.getAttribute("ACCESS_LEVEL").equals("4"))
%>
```

Account Management

This component provides services related to managing user accounts, associated contract or entitlement details, details of purchases such as product information, serial number, and so on. For example, a customer may have bought one or more mobile phones with warranty and professional support services. These details will be made available through APIs for entitlement check and support. The following services are provided:

- `getAccount`: Gets details of an onboarded user.
- `addAccount`: Onboards a new user.
- `updateAccount`: Updates an existing onboarded user.
- `deleteAccount`: Removes existing user from the system.

Following is the signature for the service class:

```
@Component
@Path("/AccountService")
public class AccountServiceImpl implements AccountService {
```

getAccount

This service pulls the account information for the registered user if available in the system. Account information is fetched from a backend database and returned in JSON format.

- Context: `AccountService/getAccount/{customerId}`
- Method: `GET`
- Consumes: `application/xml, application/json`
- Produces: `application/json`
- Input: `HttpHeaders, customerId`
- Output: JSON of user, account information, device, and services information

Following is the pseudocode for `getAccount`:

```
@Override
@GET
@Consumes({"application/xml", "application/json"})
@Produces({"application/json"})
@Path("/getAccount/{customerId}")
public AccountViewResponse getAccount(
      @Context HttpHeaders headers,
      @PathParam("customerId")String customerId)
      throws ServiceInvocationException     {
  //To do the task and implementation of DAO
}
```

addAccount

This service adds the given account for the customer. It adds account information in the backend database. The input is constructed in JSON from text fields and persisted in respective database tables.

- Context: `AccountService/addAccount`
- Method: `POST`
- Consumes: `application/xml, application/json`
- Produces: `application/json`
- Input: `HttpHeaders`, JSON of user, account information, device, and services information
- Output: Response status (i.e., either success or failure)

Following is the pseudocode for `addAccount`:

```
@Override
@POST
@Consumes({"application/xml", "application/json"})
@Produces({"application/json"})
@Path("/addAccount/")
public AccountResponse addAccount(
      @Context HttpHeaders headers,
      AccountRequest req)
      throws ServiceInvocationException {
//To do the task and implementation of DAO
}
```

updateAccount

This service updates the account information of the given user in the system. The updated information is persisted in the backend database.

- Context: `AccountService/updateAccount`
- Method: `POST`
- Consumes: `application/xml, application/json`
- Produces: `application/json`
- Input: `HttpHeaders`, JSON of user, account information, device and services information
- Output: Response status (i.e., either success or failure)

Following is the pseudocode for `updateAccount`:

```
@Override
@POST
@Consumes({"application/xml", "application/json"})
@Produces({"application/json"})
@Path("/updateAccount/")
public AccountResponse updateAccount(
      @Context HttpHeaders headers,
      AccountRequest req)
      throws ServiceInvocationException {
//To do the task and implementation of DAO
}
```

deleteAccount

This service is used to delete an account of the given user from the application. If an account's information is available, then that account's information is removed from the database.

- Context: `AccountService/deleteAccount`
- Method: `POST`
- Consumes: `application/xml`, `application/json`
- Produces: `application/json`
- Input: `HttpHeaders`, JSON of user, account information, device and services information
- Output: Response status (i.e., either success or failure)

Following is the pseudocode for `deleteAccount`:

```
@Override
@POST
@Consumes({"application/xml", "application/json"})
@Produces({"application/json"})
@Path("/deleteAccount/")
public AccountResponse deleteAccount(
        HttpHeaders headers,
        AccountRequest req)
        throws ServiceInvocationException {
//To do the task and implementation of DAO
}
```

Ticketing

This set of services is used by a registered user to open and review support tickets on the products purchased. The following services are provided:

- `createTicket`: Creates a ticket.
- `viewTicket`: Opens a ticket to be viewed.
- `viewAllTicket`: Opens all tickets to be viewed.

Following is the service class definition:

```
@Component
@Path("/TicketService")
public class HelpDeskTicketServiceImpl
      implements HelpDeskTicketService, ApplicationContextAware {
```

createTicket

This service creates a ticket for the user. A JSON request is constructed using the content of a create ticket webpage. This JSON request is transformed as a data model and persisted in the database using hibernate so that it can be viewed later for resolution.

- Context: `TicketService/createTicket`
- Method: `POST`
- Consumes: `application/xml, application/json`
- Produces: `application/json`
- Input: `HttpHeaders`, JSON of ticket information (e.g., contract number, issue information, user ID)
- Output: Ticket number generated, response status (i.e., either success or failure)

Following is the pseudocode for `createTicket`:

```
@Override
@POST
@Consumes({ MediaType.APPLICATION_JSON,
MediaType.APPLICATION_XML })
@Produces({ MediaType.APPLICATION_JSON,
MediaType.APPLICATION_XML })
@Path("/createTicket/")
public TicketResponse createHdTicket(
      @Context HttpHeaders headers,
      TicketRequest ticketRequest)
      throws ServiceInvocationException{
//To do the task and implementation of DAO
}
```

viewTicket

This service returns the ticket details based on the given ticket number and the user role. It pulls the ticket information from the database if the ticket number provided for the customer is available. A data model is fetched using hibernate and returned as JSON.

- Context: `TicketServices/viewTicket/{userId}`
- Method: `GET`
- Consumes: `application/xml`, `application/json`
- Produces: `application/xml`, `application/json`
- Input: `HttpHeaders`
- Output: JSON of tickets information (e.g., contract number, issue information, user ID)

Following is the pseudocode for `viewTicket`:

```
@Override
    @GET
    @Consumes({"application/xml", "application/json"})
    @Produces({"application/json"})
    @Path("/viewTicket/{userId}/{ticketId}")
public ViewTicketResponse viewTicket(
        @Context HttpHeaders headers,
        @PathParam("userId")String userId,
        @PathParam("ticketId")String ticketId)
        throws ServiceInvocationException {
}
```

viewAllTicket

This service returns all the tickets available in the system that were created by a logged-in user. A data model is fetched using hibernate and returned as JSON.

- Context: `TicketServices/viewAllTicket`
- Method: `GET`
- Consumes: `application/xml`, `application/json`
- Produces: `application/xml`, `application/json`
- Input: `HttpHeaders`
- Output: JSON of tickets information (e.g., contract number, issue information, user ID)

Following is the pseudocode for `viewAllTicket`:

```
@Override
@GET
@Consumes({"application/xml", "application/json"})
@Produces({"application/json"})
@Path("/viewAllTicket/")
public ViewAllTicketResponse viewAllTicket(
     @Context HttpHeaders headers)
     throws ServiceInvocationException {
//To do the task and implementation of DAO
}
```

Following are the options that are available to the users based on the role:

- **My Tickets.** Provides a list of tickets assigned to support engineers or a list of tickets opened by users based on user roles.
- **Global Ticket View.** Enables viewing of all tickets for executive or support manager view.

Product Catalog

The product catalog service enables an administrator to manage a list of products offered by a company. It also enables users to view a list of products they purchased and on which they can open a support ticket. Following is the list of available services:

- `getCatalog`: Returns the product catalog.
- `addCatalog`: Creates a new entry in product catalog.
- `updateCatalog`: Updates the specified entry in the product catalog.
- `deleteCatalog`: Deletes an existing product catalog entry.

The service class definition is as follows:

```
@Path("/CatalogService")
public class CatalogServiceImpl implements CatalogService {
```

getCatalog

This service returns a list of products available in the system. A data model is fetched using hibernate and returned as JSON.

- Context: `CatalogService/getCatalog/{customerId}`
- Method: `GET`
- Consumes: `application/xml, application/json`
- Produces: `application/json`
- Input: `HttpHeaders, customerId` (all occurrences of `header` should be replaced with `HttpHeaders`)
- Output: JSON of product information customer has under his or her account

Following is the pseudocode for `getCatalog`:

```
@Override
@GET
@Consumes({"application/xml", "application/json"})
@Produces({"application/json"})
@Path("/getCatalog/{customerId}")
public ProductDetailsResponse getCatalog(
      @Context HttpHeaders headers,
      @PathParam("customerId") String customerId)
      throws ServiceInvocationException {
//To do the task and implementation of DAO
}
```

addCatalog

This service adds a new product to the Catalog. A JSON request is created using the input page and then transformed into a data model and saved in a database using hibernate.

- Context: `CatalogService/addCatalog`
- Method: `POST`
- Consumes: `application/xml, application/json`
- Produces: `application/json`
- Input: `HttpHeaders`, JSON of product information customer has under his or her account
- Output: Response status (i.e., either success or failure)

Following is the pseudocode for addCatalog:

```
@Override
@POST
@Consumes({"application/xml", "application/json"})
@Produces({"application/json"})
@Path("/addCatalog/")
public CatalogResponse addCatalog(
      @Context HttpHeaders headers,
      CatalogRequest req)
      throws ServiceInvocationException {
//To do the task and implementation of DAO
}
```

updateCatalog

This service updates an existing product catalog entry if the specified product is available in the system. JSON is changed in the data model, and it updates the database.

- Context: CatalogService/updateCatalog
- Method: POST
- Consumes: application/xml, application/json
- Produces: application/json
- Input: HttpHeaders, JSON of product information customer has under his or her account
- Output: Response status (i.e., either success or failure)

Following is the pseudocode for updateCatalog:

```
@Override
  @POST
  @Consumes({"application/xml", "application/json"})
  @Produces({"application/json"})
  @Path("/updateCatalog/")
  public CatalogResponse updateCatalog(
        HttpHeaders headers,
        CatalogRequest req)
        throws ServiceInvocationException {
//To do the task and implementation of DAO
}
```

deleteCatalog

This service is used to delete a product catalog entry from the catalog. The entry from the database is deleted using hibernate.

- Context: `CatalogService/deleteCatalog`
- Method: `POST`
- Consumes: `application/xml, application/json`
- Produces: `application/json`
- Input: `HttpHeaders`, JSON of product information customer has under his or her account
- Output: Response status (i.e., either success or failure)

Following is the pseudocode for `deleteCatalog`:

```
@Override
@POST
@Consumes({"application/xml", "application/json"})
@Produces({"application/json"})
@Path("/deleteCatalog/")
public CatalogResponse deleteCatalog(
     HttpHeaders headers,
     CatalogRequest req)
     throws ServiceInvocationException {
//To do the task and implementation of DAO
}
```

Appointments

The appointments service works similarly to the Apple Genius Bar. Users can reserve an appointment with support engineers to schedule a time at the store. The following services are available in appointments:

- `getAvailableTimeSlots`: Gets all available times slots for an appointment for a given date.
- `getAvailableDates`: Returns the days for which at least one slot is available.
- `saveAppointment`: Saves an appointment to the schedule.

Following is the service class definition:

```
@Component
@Path("/AppointmentService")
public class AppointmentServiceImpl {
```

getAvailableTimeSlots

This service retrieves all the available time slots for a given date in JSON format.

- Context: `AppointmentService/getAvailableTimeSlots`

- Method: `GET`

- Consumes: `application/xml, application/json`

- Produces: `application/json`

- Input: `HttpHeaders, TITLE`

- Output: Response status (i.e., either success or failure)

Following is the pseudocode for `getAvailableTimeSlots`:

```
@Override
@POST
@Consumes({"application/xml", "application/json"})
@Produces({"application/json"})
@Path("/getAvailableTimeSlots/")
public
AppointmentAvailableTimeSlotResponse getAvailableTimeSlots(
     @Context HttpHeaders headers,
     AppointmentAvailableTimeSlotRequest Request) {
//To Do}
```

getAvailableDates

This service returns all the available dates that have available one or more time slots for the appointment.

- Context: `AppointmentService/getAvailableDates`

- Method: `POST`

- Consumes: `application/xml, application/json`

- Produces: `application/json`

- Input: `HttpHeaders, TITLE`

- Output: Response status (i.e., either success or failure)

Following is the pseudocode for `getAvailableDates`:

```
@Override
@POST
@Consumes({"application/xml", "application/json"})
@Produces({"application/json"})
@Path("/getAvailableDates/")
public
AppointmentAvailableDateResponse getUnAvailableDates(
    @Context HttpHeaders headers,
    AppointmentAvailableDateRequest request) {
///to do}
```

saveAppointment

This service sets and saves the appointment for a selected available time and date.

- Context: `AppointmentService/saveAppointment`
- Method: `POST`
- Consumes: `application/xml`, `application/json`
- Produces: `application/json`
- Input: `HttpHeaders`, `TITLE`, `request`
- Output: Response status (i.e., either success or failure)

Following is the pseudocode for `saveAppointment`:

```
@Override
@POST
@Consumes({"application/xml", "application/json"})
@Produces({"application/json"})
@Path("/saveAppointment/")
//To Do}
```

Message Board

The message board service enables collaboration between the user community and support experts. The following services are available in the message board:

- `getMessage`: Retrieves a message available in the system.
- `getAllMessage`: Gets all messages based on a given time.
- `createMessage`: Saves a message, question, or answer provided by a user.

Following is the service class definition:

```
@Component
@Path("/MessageService")
public class MessageServiceImpl implements MessageService {
```

getMessage

This service pulls the messages, questions, and answers available in a system, based on the question asked by a user.

- Context: `MessageService/getMessage/{title}`
- Method: `GET`
- Consumes: `application/xml, application/json`
- Produces: `application/json`
- Input: `HttpHeaders, TITLE`
- Output: Response status (i.e., either success or failure)

Following is the pseudocode for `getMessage`:

```
@Override
@GET
@Consumes({"application/xml", "application/json"})
@Produces({"application/json"})
@Path("/getMessage/{title}")
public MessageViewResponse getMessage(
    @Context HttpHeaders headers,
    @PathParam("title")String title)
    throws ServiceInvocationException {
  //To do the task and implementation of DAO
}
```

getAllMessage

This service returns all the available messages or questions in the system based on a given time slot provided by the user and returns them in JSON format.

- Context: `MessageService/getAllMessage`
- Method: `GET`
- Consumes: `application/xml, application/json`

- Produces: `application/json`
- Input: `HttpHeaders`
- Output: Response status (i.e., either success or failure)

Following is the pseudocode for `getAllMessage`:

```
@Override
@GET
@Consumes({"application/xml", "application/json"})
@Produces({"application/json"})
@Path("/getAllMessage/")
public MessageViewAllResponse getAllMessage(
      @Context HttpHeaders headers)
      throws ServiceInvocationException {
//To do the logic
}
```

createMessage

This service saves a message, question, or answer provided by a user on the message board.

- Context: `MessageService/createMessage`
- Method: `POST`
- Consumes: `application/xml, application/json`
- Produces: `application/json`
- Input: `HttpHeaders, MessageRequest`
- Output: Response status (i.e., either success or failure)

Following is the pseudocode for `createMessage`:

```
@Override
@POST
@Consumes({"application/xml", "application/json"})
@Produces({"application/json"})
@Path("/createMessage/")
public RestResponse createMessage(
      @Context HttpHeaders headers,
```

```
            MessageRequest req)
            throws ServiceInvocationException {
//To do the logic
}
```

Search

The search service allows users to perform text-based search across the application. It looks for the text in all of the entities (database table); for example, ticketing, catalog, and message data. It matches the text if the text is contained in the data available for the application. It interacts with the backend database through DAO (data access object) layers and pulls all the related information from database tables using hibernate mapping with the text provided as input in a search field.

Following is the service class definition:

```
@Component
@Path("/Search/Service")
public class SearchServiceImpl implements SearchService {
```

- Context: `SearchService/search`

- Method: `GET`

- Consumes: `application/xml`, `application/json`

- Produces: `application/json`

- Input: `HttpHeaders`, search text

- Output: Response status (i.e., either success or failure)

Following is the pseudocode for the search service:

```
@Override
@GET
@Consumes({"application/xml", "application/json"})
@Produces({"application/json"})
@Path("/search")
public MessageViewResponse search(
        @Context HttpHeaders headers,
        @PathParam("title")String title)
        throws ServiceInvocationException {
    //To do the task and implementation of DAO
}
```

Building the Application

Now that we have covered the architecture, web services, and various dependencies of the application, let's download the code, build it, and see it in action.

Setting Up Eclipse

We have used Eclipse IDE for development; you can choose whatever IDE you are most comfortable with, but following are instructions for how to set up Eclipse on Windows (skip this step if you already have Eclipse installed):

1. Download Eclipse from https://eclipse.org/downloads/index-developer.php.

2. Unzip or Unrar, depending on your system. The prerequisite for Eclipse is JRE on your system path.

3. Double-click **eclipse.exe**, shown in Figure 11.2.

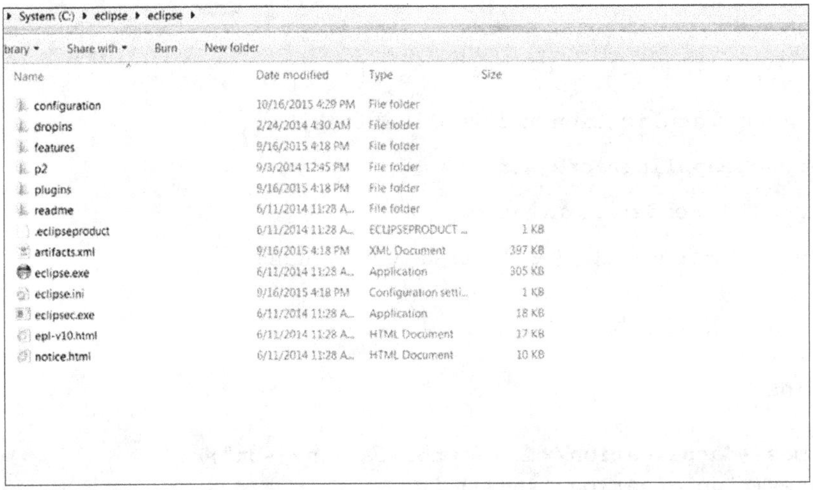

Figure 11.2 *Unzipping Eclipse*

4. Right-click on the package explorer and select **New Java Projects**. We'll name this project Helpdesk, as shown in Figure 11.3, and leave default values in the other fields.

5. Uncheck **Use default location**, browse to the directory where you have cloned the code (as discussed in the beginning of this chapter), and click **Open**. Then, click **Next**.

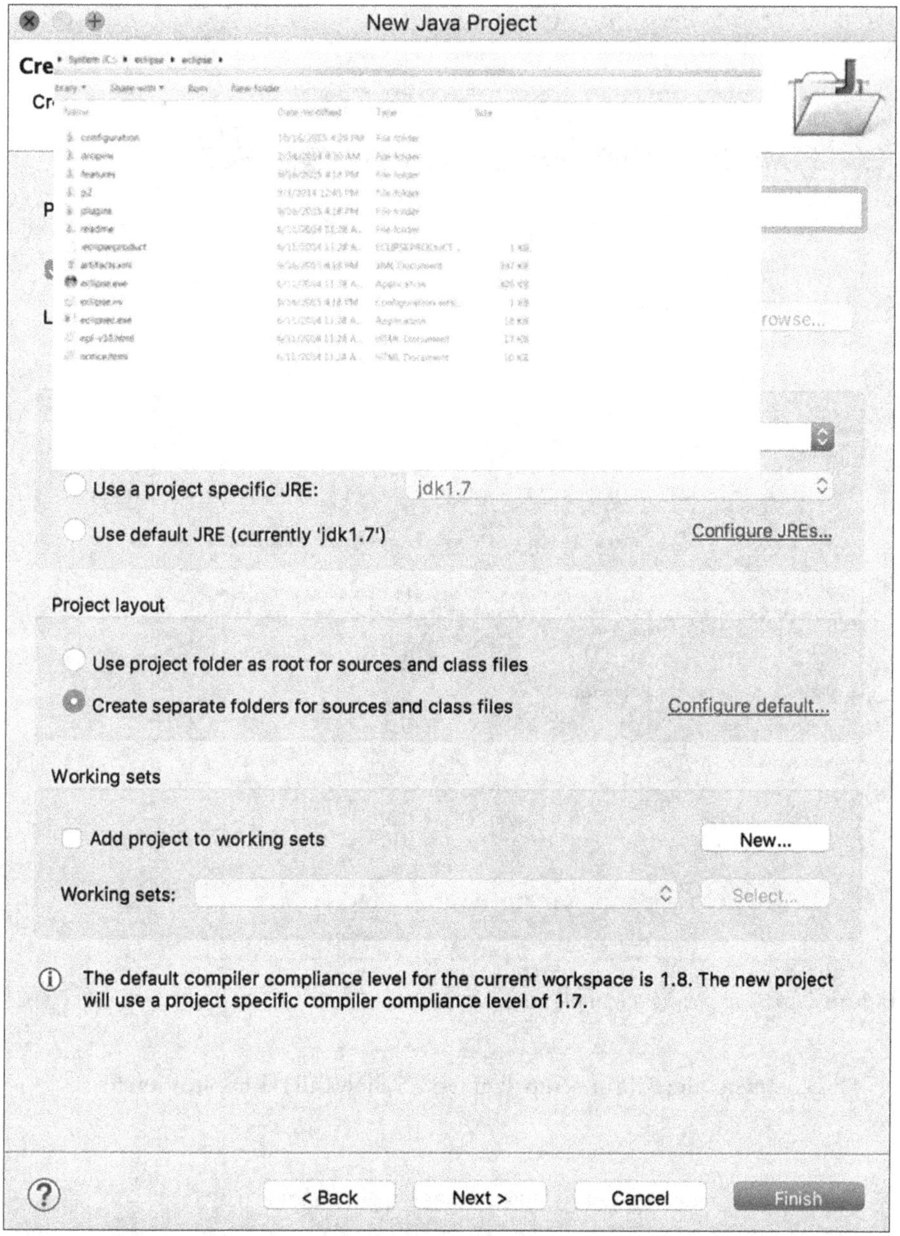

Figure 11.3 *Creating a new Java project (named Helpdesk)*

6. Click **Finish**, as shown in Figure 11.4.

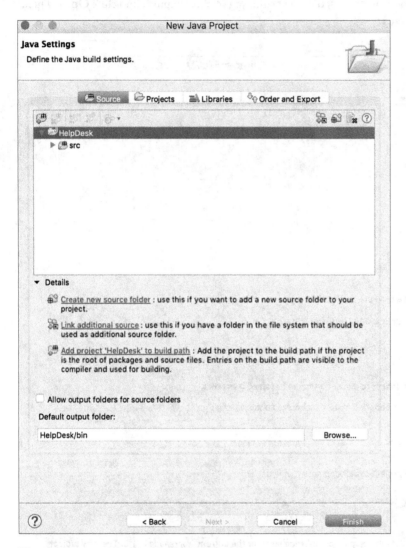

Figure 11.4 *Completing our application setup*

This completes the Eclipse setup. Figure 11.5 shows all the application files.

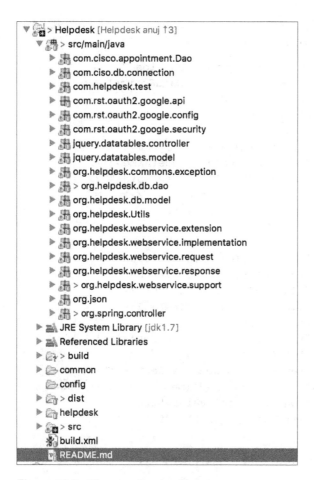

Figure 11.5 *All our application files*

Building the Application

The following instructions show you how to run the build and produce the deployable WAR file. We use plain old Apache Ant build.

1. We need to configure the database in the applicationContext.xml file of code base before building the WAR file. You can find it in Project Location/src/main/webapp/WEB-INF/ applicationContext.xml. Change the `url`, `username`, and `password` properties of the `DataSource` bean in the following code snippet.

Make sure you use these same credentials when you install and configure MySQL database, shown in later steps.

```
<bean id="DataSource" destroy-method="close"
class="org.apache.tomcat.jdbc.pool.DataSource">
  <property name="driverClassName"
            value="com.mysql.jdbc.Driver" />
  <property name="url"
            value="jdbc:mysql://<dbhost>:<dbport>/<dbname>" />
  <property name="username" value="<Username>" />
  <property name="password" value="<Password>" />
  <property name="initialSize" value="5" />
  <property name="maxActive" value="50" />
  <property name="validationQuery"
            value="select 1 from dual" />
  <property name="testWhileIdle" value="true" />
  <property name="testOnBorrow" value="true" />
  <property name="minIdle" value="020000" />
  <property name="minEvictableIdleTimeMillis"
            value="30000000" />
  <property name="timeBetweenEvictionRunsMillis"
            value="6000000" />
  <property name="removeAbandoned" value="true"/>
  <property name="removeAbandonedTimeout" value="30000" />
  <property name="logAbandoned" value="true" />
  <property name="maxWait" value="120000" />
</bean>
```

2. Create a new Build.xml file in the project root directory with the following targets:

```
<project name="projects" default="jar" basedir=".">

    <property name="src" location="src"/>
    <property name="build" location="build"/>
    <property name="dist" location="dist"/>
    <property name="jar.location" location="${dist}/lib"/>

  <dirname property="projects.basedir"
           file="${ant.file.projects}"/>
  <echo>projects.basedir=${projects.basedir}</echo>
```

```
<echo>Inside smartview project:
     smartview.basedir=${smartview.basedir}</echo>

     <path id="project.classpath">
         <fileset refid="sv.jars"/>
         <fileset refid="common.dist"/>
     </path>

<filelist id="project.build.files" dir="${projects.
basedir}">
     <file name="build.xml" />
</filelist>

<fileset id="sv.jars" dir="${projects.basedir}">
     <include name="src/main/lib/*.jar"/>
 </fileset>

<fileset id="common.jars" dir="${projects.basedir}">
 <include name="src/main/lib/*.jar"/>
</fileset>

<fileset id="common.dist" dir="${projects.basedir}">
 <include name="dist/lib/*.jar"/>
</fileset>
```

3. Compile and create the JAR file with these targets:

```
<target name="compile.individual" depends="init">
    <javac includeantruntime="false"
          debug="true"
          compiler="javac1.6"
          srcdir="${src}" destdir="${build}">
        <classpath refid="project.classpath"/>
    </javac>
    </target>

    <target name="jar.individual" depends="compile.
    individual">
    <mkdir dir="${jar.location}"/>
    <mkdir dir="${build}/META-INF"/>

    <copy todir="${build}/META-INF">
        <fileset dir="${src}/main/resource/META-INF"
                includes="*.xml"/>
    </copy>
```

```
        <jar jarfile=
            "${jar.location}/org-${ant.project.name}.jar"
            basedir="${build}"/>
    </target>

    <!-- Methods only used by the top level of JARing or
         WARing everything up -->

    <target name="jar" depends="init">
        <mkdir dir="${dist}/lib"/>
        <subant target="jar.individual">
            <filelist refid="project.build.files"/>
        </subant>
    </target>
```

4. Create the WAR file using the following targets:

```
    <target name="copy.files" depends="jar">

        <copy todir="${stage.war.lib}" flatten="true">
            <fileset dir="${projects.basedir}"
              includes="*/dist/lib/*.jar"
              excludes="*test*.jar" />
        </copy>

        <copy todir="${stage.war.lib}" flatten="true">
            <fileset dir="${projects.basedir}"
              includes="common/configproperties/*.xml" />
        </copy>

        <copy todir="${stage.war.lib}" flatten="true">
            <fileset refid="common.jars"/>
        </copy>
        <copy todir="${stage.war.lib}" flatten="true">
            <fileset refid="sv.jars"/>
        </copy>
    </target>

    <target name="war" depends="init.war,copy.files">
        <war destfile="dist/lib/helpdesk.war"
            webxml="src/main/webapp/WEB-INF/web.xml">
            <fileset dir="src/main/webapp">
                <exclude name="**/.svn"/>
            </fileset>
```

```
      <lib dir="src/main/webapp/WEB-INF/lib" />
      <classes dir="${build}/classes" />
      </war>
   </target>
```

5. Right-click the **Build.xml file** and click **Run As → Ant Build...**, as shown in Figure 11.6.

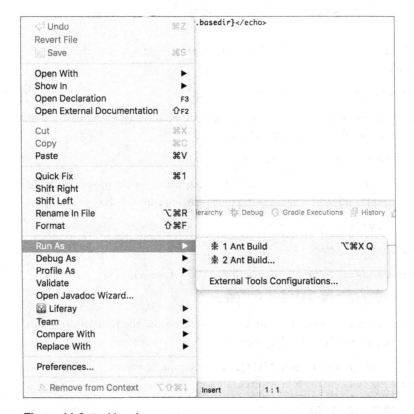

Figure 11.6 *Build.xml run options*

6. In the next screen, select all targets from the window.

Our local environment is ready, and we have generated the WAR file under <Project Location>/helpdesk/dist/lib named helpdesk.war.

Deploying and Configuring

We will host our application and all related services on Amazon Web Services (AWS) and will use a single virtual machine for deployment. You are encouraged to follow the instructions in this section to get hands-on experience. The first step is to spin up an EC2 instance on AWS. For our purposes, we'll use a medium-flavor virtual machine running an Ubuntu operating system. Tomcat 7 and MySQL should be installed as prerequisites. (Installing Tomcat 7 will also install Java and other dependencies.)

1. To install Tomcat 7 to the /var/lib/tomcat7 directory, run the following command:

   ```
   sudo apt-get install tomcat7
   ```

2. The service should be up and running. Check that Tomcat is running normally by issuing the following command:

   ```
   sudo service tomcat7 status
   ```

   The Tomcat servlet engine should be running with its own process identifier. You can start and stop Tomcat using the following commands:

   ```
   sudo service tomcat7 start

   sudo service tomcat7 stop
   ```

3. Run the following command to install the MySQL server:

   ```
   sudo apt-get install mysql-server
   ```

4. During the installation, you will be asked to provide the password for root. Enter the password to complete the installation.

5. At the end of the installation, MySQL server should be up and running. Ensure it's running by using the following command:

   ```
   sudo service mysql status
   ```

   You can start and stop MySQL using the following commands:

   ```
   sudo service mysql start

   sudo service mysql stop
   ```

6. Create a database named helpdesk:

   ```
   Create database helpdesk
   ```

7. Copy the application.properties file located at Project Location/src/main/ webapp/WEB-INF/ into the tomcat lib directory. These are the properties or key-value pair used in our project.

8. Copy the jstl.1.2.jar file located at Project Location/src/main/lib/ into the tomcat lib directory. This is the library for supporting jsp tags.

9. The Tomcat instance by default runs on 8080 port. Verify by checking http://<yourhost>:8080/console.

10. We can now deploy the web app from the Tomcat manager console. Click the **Browse** button to play the WAR file you created earlier, then click **Deploy**, as shown in Figure 11.7.

Deploy

Deploy directory or WAR file located on server

Context Path (required):	
XML Configuration file URL:	
WAR or Directory URL:	
	Deploy

WAR file to deploy

Select WAR file to upload	Browse...	helpdesk.war
	Deploy	

Figure 11.7 *Deploying the WAR file*

As you can see in Figure 11.8, your application is deployed on the Tomcat server and can be opened from http://<yourhost>:8080/helpdesk.

Figure 11.8 *Location of our app on the Tomcat server*

The whole application is now bundled into a single WAR file. At this point, the application should be up and running on your system. Figure 11.9 shows all of the dependencies across various modules.

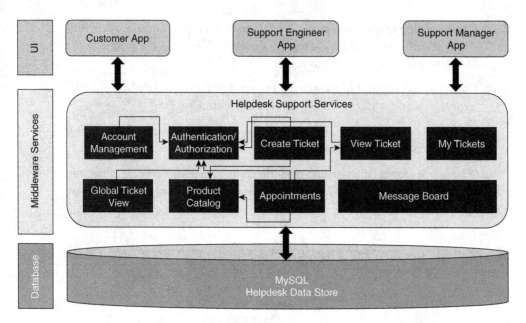

Figure 11.9 *Helpdesk application's dependencies across various modules*

New Requirements and Bug Fixes

Imagine the application is up and running and serving the customers. This starts the software maintenance lifecycle. With time, new requests to update or alter the application functionality will come in, and bugs may be uncovered by customers. All these requests will require changing code and/or rebuilding the application. Let's understand the challenges and work it entails to maintain our monolithic application.

Let's assume we need to add an extra parameter to the view ticket service that has very limited to no dependency on other components. With the following code, we change the ticket request:

```
public TicketResponse createHdTicket(
      @Context HttpHeaders headers,
      TicketRequest ticketRequest)
      throws ServiceInvocationException{
```

The following allows us to add a new property to a Plain Old Java Object, or POJO (web model):

```
@Component
  private String emailAddress;
@XmlElement
```

```
public String getEmailAddress() {
     return emailAddress;
  }
public void setEmailAddress(String emailAddress) {
     this.emailAddress = emailAddress;
  }
```

Using the following code, we can add logic to the DAO layer to get that property from the database:

```
private String saveToDatabase(TicketRequest ticketRequest){
     //added with existing one
     ticket.setEmailAddress(ticketRequest.getEmailAddress());
}
```

That's about all for the code change, which looks pretty straightforward. But what happens next? You need to do the following activities on all your environments and deploy the code:

1. Build the whole web application. This means you have to deploy the whole application again.

2. Perform regression testing of the whole application to make sure all the other capabilities are still working as expected.

3. Resolve any bugs or dependencies.

4. Deploy the code to test the environment and perform a quality assurance process.

5. Deploy the changes to production and deploy.

If the application is not deployed in a high availability (HA) mode, it means downtime will occur, as the application will be redeployed.

All these steps increase the time to release this minor change and defeat the whole agile principle. This is not accounting for ongoing changes where you may have to create a new code branch and merge and test again.

There are other issues, as well:

- **Addressing bugs.** Each bug fix will require a whole build to be deployed, which means potential downtime for the system if proper HA is not built into the deployment architecture. In addition, depending on the systems development life cycle (SDLC) methodology used, this could mean a lengthy time before the bug fix could even be introduced. For critical bugs, it usually means creating and maintain a "hot fix" branch of the code, which can complicate the code base and create problematic merges later on.

- **Replacing application components.** Here is another case where the whole application has to be potentially refactored/reimplemented. Let's assume the organization would like to use cloud services for ticket management; the way the application is written currently, it is hard to decouple the related modules from the application.

- **Replacing or adding new technology stack.** In this case, you don't have the freedom to choose the technology for new modules/capabilities unless the whole application is reimplemented. The organization is stuck with the chosen technology because of the monolithic architecture.

- **Scaling selectively.** Say you want to scale just the ticketing module to accommodate the usage patterns. In this case, it is complex because the application components are tightly integrated as a monolithic application. Separating ticketing alone, for example, requires a lot of code refactoring, integration with the standalone ticketing system, testing, new deployment architecture, and more.

- **Handling faults.** In a monolithic application, a fault in one component potentially breaks up the whole application. Let's suppose that the product catalog service is down. This will prevent the users from submitting a new work ticket. A new work ticket should indicate which product the user has a problem with for better ticket routing and faster problem resolution. However, a bug in the product catalog service should not prevent the user from creating the ticket itself—that is, it shouldn't bring down the ticketing service itself. But given the monolithic nature, if product catalog is a required field and there is a bug, the user will be stuck at this stage even though he or she could have described the issue.

While challenging for our application, these are the simple needs of today's digital world. It becomes very costly and time consuming to address them with the monolithic approach our current application uses. In the next two chapters, we discuss how these challenges go away with microservices and containers.

Chapter 12

Case Study: Migration to Microservices

In Chapter 11, "Case Study: Monolithic Helpdesk Application," we built a traditional web-based helpdesk application following industry standard practices. The purpose was to provide a close-to-real-world example and highlight the challenges that organizations are facing with such monolithic applications today. In this chapter, we modify the same helpdesk application by using our microservices knowledge, and we learn how some of the challenges we highlighted can be addressed.

In Chapter 4, "Migrating and Implementing Microservices," we discussed two possible scenarios: creating a new application with microservices and migrating a monolithic application to microservices. Since our helpdesk is an existing monolithic application, here we follow the second scenario of migrating to microservices.

Planning for Migration

Let's say that the high-level business needs for our helpdesk application were as follows when the application was first written, back in 2005:

- Support roughly 500,000 customers on the web where they can open work tickets for their issues.

- All features are equally important and should be available at all times.

- Application is horizontally scalable.

- Reduce number of tickets submitted by allowing users to search for existing solutions.

Now it is 2018. Let's review customer behavior and how this application is being utilized:

- The number of users has grown to 1.5 million and is expected to grow to 3 million over the next 2 years due to the boom in the mobile space.
- The top two features being utilized by most users are ticketing and search.
- There are very few changes in usage of features like message boards.
- Traffic especially peaks twice a year: early summer (June) and the holiday season (November and December).
- The number of times ticketing services is affected due to impact of other services, such as product catalog, has grown considerably.
- Technological advances in natural language processing means that customers no longer expect just keyword-based search. They want the system to understand plain English and be able to search the tickets and help them appropriately. In other words, they want semantic search.
- The greatest number of enhancement requests concerns ticketing functionality.

It's clear that our application is doing really well, as the number of customers has expanded and the application is still serving. Furthermore, we can assume that the application has scaled well horizontally to support the increase in users. Scaling horizontally in this case means having many instances of the application with active-active database machines with proper load balancing in place. The point to note is that we are talking about uniform scalability; that is, the whole application is scaled, not just some specific components, such as ticketing, that might be have been needed to be scaled.

Now assume you are given the task to modify the application so that it can meet the new needs and can scale and perform to support 3 million users. Also, the application should be easy to evolve (open to change components) as the technology changes.

Given what we have learned, microservices may sound like a great solution. The application we deployed in Chapter 11 is not very old. In fact, it is already using a model–view–controller (MVC) architecture and web services, so it wouldn't be a wise decision to start from scratch. Also, notice that the new needs are applicable to only a few components of the application, which further makes the case for microservices. So how do we do it? There are quite a few ways to go about it. Let's apply our learning from Chapter 4 and convert our existing project to a microservices-based application.

Applying Microservices Criteria

Recall that the microservices criteria outlined in Chapter 4 define one of the possible ways to select and prioritize the capabilities of a monolithic application that should be migrated to microservices. We looked at seven best practices, which apply in our scenario as we consider the new needs and user behavior:

- **Scale.** From the first two new requirements, it is clear we need to scale the application. The two most important and highly used components are ticketing and search, so it makes sense to convert these services to microservices.

- **Improved technology alternatives, or polyglot programming.** From the new requirements, we see that this system needs a smart search, and Apache Solr is an open source tool readily available for these purposes. It will improve the search capabilities by providing relevant, context-sensitive results.

- **Storage alternatives, or polyglot persistence.** Our monolithic application has been using the MySQL database for all the data storage needs. While it makes sense for ticketing data to be stored in a relational database, our application can be improved by storing product catalog data in an in-memory cache with a flat-file backing store for the following reasons:

  - It would allow for easier updates by simply dropping updated files.

  - Since there are no relational queries or joins, simply reading the file in-memory as a keyed list would increase speed.

- **Changes.** Given that most enhancements have been in ticketing logic, per requirements, it makes sense to convert ticketing to a microservice. By the same logic and per our new requirements, it would not make much sense to convert the message board as a microservice.

- **Deployment.** In our application, there is no deployment complexity in any given component, so we can call it not applicable.

- **Helper services.** Per the new requirements, the existing ticketing flows have been impacted due to unavailability of, or issues with, the product catalog. We must short-circuit this service, which means that even if the product catalog goes down, our ticketing should work as expected. This requirement qualifies the product catalog service to be converted to a microservice.

The only requirement we have not discussed is that of heavy seasonal traffic. Basically, this issue can be addressed easily within the current version of the application by adding application servers and databases to scale horizontally during the high-traffic seasons and then shrinking them back during normal traffic times. But based on what we know about microservices and the way we are converting the existing services, it would be more cost effective to scale the components with expected higher traffic. We cover this aspect of migration to microservices in Chapter 13, "Case Study: Containerizing a Helpdesk Application."

Conversion Summary

Per the new requirements and our microservices criteria, we conclude that the following services be converted to microservices architecture:

- Product catalog
- Ticketing
- Search

Further, we will add a Solr search engine to our application. In the current application, searches are done by database scan, which is a very crude way of implementing search functionality. This method simply matches text against available data in the database. Neither the quality of results nor the performance match the caliber of today's technologies.

Let's briefly discuss Solr. (For detailed installation and configuration instructions, refer to Appendix B.) Solr is a search engine platform based on Apache Lucene. It is written in Java and uses the Lucene library to implement indexing. It can be accessed using a variety of REST APIs, including XML and JSON. The basic capabilities include

- Advanced full-text search
- Optimized for high-volume web traffic
- Comprehensive HTML administration interfaces
- Server statistics exposed over Java Management Extensions (JMX) for monitoring
- Linearly scalable, auto-index replication, and automatic failover and recovery
- Near-real-time indexing
- Flexible and adaptable with XML configuration
- Extensible plugin architecture

For more information, visit http://lucene.apache.org/solr.

Impact on Architecture

After the product catalog, ticketing, and search services are converted to self-contained standalone microservices, the architecture will look like Figure 12.1.

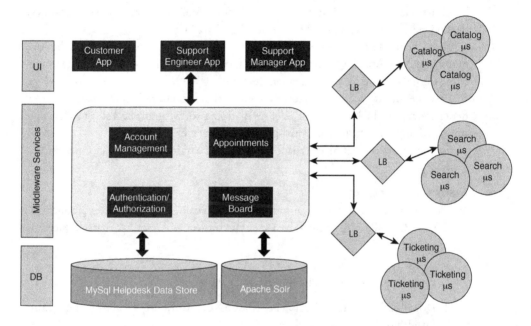

Figure 12.1 *Our new architecture, with self-contained and standalone microservices*

As you see, services such as catalog, ticketing, and search are separated out of the monolith paradigm and deployed as individual and independent microservices. These individual microservices are deployed behind a load balancer such as HAProxy for high availability and scale.

Converting to Microservices

Now that we understand the new microservices-based architecture, let's convert the identified three components of the monolithic application to independent microservices. We cover the product catalog microservice conversion in detail but leave ticketing and search for you to converted in a similar manner to get some hands-on experience. You can also refer to the code base posted on GitHub at https://github .com/kocherMSD/Helpdesk_Microservices.git.

Product Catalog

For this project, we migrate catalog service-specific code out of the monolithic help-desk application into its own build entity. This involves taking out the interfaces, service implementations, helper classes, and configuration files and creating a new build artifact. This new build artifact includes reference to only those third-party dependencies actually required by the new build artifact.

Next, we modify the catalog service to use Apache Maven instead of Apache Ant, mainly because Apache Maven is a newer, more flexible build system that has superior external dependency management features.

Last, we modify the catalog service build artifact to upgrade third-party external dependencies to the latest major release. By doing so, we gain the ability to leverage improved implementations of third-party dependencies.

Following are the detailed steps for the product catalog microservice conversion.

Steps for Conversion

We create the product catalog microservice by reusing the monolithic application code base. Basically, it is going to be a separate project and a service in itself. Here are the steps:

1. Create a new project in Eclipse named catalog-svc.

2. Download and install Apache Maven. Refer to https://maven.apache.org/install.html.

3. Create a Maven pom.xml file, and define the required dependency for the project in the root directory. You can find the details in the code posted on GitHub: https://github.com/kocherMSD/Helpdesk_Microservices/blob/master/catalog-svc/pom.xml.

4. Create the service interface, service implementation, service helper, data access object (DAO) classes, and application context XML file.

   Based on the microservice definition, we will have a single interface, service implementation, service helper, and service DAO Java class. Here is the pseudocode for our service, but you are strongly encouraged to look into this code, which is available on GitHub:

   a. Service interface pseudocode:
   ```
   public interface CatalogService extends BeanFactoryAware,
   ApplicationContextAware {
           public abstract ProductDetailsResponse getCatalog(
             @Context HttpHeaders headers,
   ```

```
            String userId)
            throws ServiceInvocationException;

    public abstract CatalogResponse addCatalog(
            @Context HttpHeaders headers,
            CatalogRequest req)
            throws ServiceInvocationException;

    public abstract CatalogResponse updateCatalog(
            @Context HttpHeaders headers,
            CatalogRequest req)
            throws ServiceInvocationException;

    public abstract CatalogResponse deleteCatalog(
            @Context HttpHeaders headers,
            CatalogRequest req)
            throws ServiceInvocationException;
        }
```

b. Service implementation pseudocode:

```
        @Component
        @Path("/CatalogService")
    public class CatalogServiceImpl implements
    CatalogService {

        @Override
        @GET
        @Consumes({"application/xml", "application/json"})
        @Produces({"application/json"})
        @Path("/getCatalog/{customerId}")
    public ProductDetailsResponse getCatalog(
            @Context HttpHeaders headers,
            @PathParam("customerId") String customerId)
            throws ServiceInvocationException  {
        //To Do Task
            }
```

c. Service helper pseudocode:

```
        public class CatalogServiceHelper {
        CatalogDao dao=null;
                //To Do
        }
```

d. DAO class pseudocode:

```
public class CatalogDao extends DataService{
//To Do
}
```

5. Modify the applicationContext.xml file for only this microservice's beans. The new project structure should look like Figure 12.2.

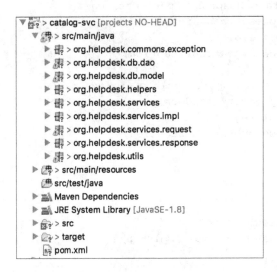

```
▼ 🗂 > catalog-svc [projects NO-HEAD]
   ▼ 🗂 > src/main/java
      ▶ 🗂 > org.helpdesk.commons.exception
      ▶ 🗂 > org.helpdesk.db.dao
      ▶ 🗂 > org.helpdesk.db.model
      ▶ 🗂 > org.helpdesk.helpers
      ▶ 🗂 > org.helpdesk.services
      ▶ 🗂 > org.helpdesk.services.impl
      ▶ 🗂 > org.helpdesk.services.request
      ▶ 🗂 > org.helpdesk.services.response
      ▶ 🗂 > org.helpdesk.utils
   ▶ 🗂 > src/main/resources
      🗂 src/test/java
   ▶ 🗂 Maven Dependencies
   ▶ 🗂 JRE System Library [JavaSE-1.8]
   ▶ 🗂 > src
   ▶ 🗂 > target
      🗂 pom.xml
```

Figure 12.2 *The new project structure*

6. Run mvn install from the pom.xml. This will create a catalog-svc WAR file.

7. Deploy the WAR file on the same monolithic application Tomcat server: http://<host>:<port>/catalog-svc/rest/catalogservice/<Rest Verb>. The web service endpoint for our standalone microservice will be changed.

8. Remember that we are still using the same database. Before building the WAR file, change the database configuration in applicationContext.xml as follows; change the url, username, and password properties of the DataSource bean according to your database credentials:

```
<bean id="DataSource" destroy-method="close"
   class="org.apache.tomcat.jdbc.pool.DataSource">
      <property name="driverClassName"
               value="com.mysql.jdbc.Driver" />
      <property name="url"
               value="jdbc:mysql://<dbhost>:
               <dbport>/<dbname>"/>
```

```
        <property name="username" value="<Username>"/>
        <property name="password" value="<Password>"/>
        <property name="initialSize" value="5"/>
        <property name="maxActive" value="50"/>
        <property name="validationQuery"
                value="select 1 from dual"/>
        <property name="testWhileIdle" value="true"/>
        <property name="testOnBorrow" value="true"/>
        <property name="minIdle" value="020000"/>
        <property name="minEvictableIdleTimeMillis"
                value="30000000"/>
        <property name="timeBetweenEvictionRunsMillis"
                value="6000000"/>
        <property name="removeAbandoned" value="true"/>
        <property name="removeAbandonedTimeout"
                value="30000"/>
        <property name="logAbandoned" value="true"/>
        <property name="maxWait" value="120000"/>
    </bean>
```

Ticketing

Similar to the product catalog, migrating the ticketing service–specific code out of the monolithic helpdesk application into its own build entity also includes taking out the interfaces, service implementations, helper classes, and configuration files and creating a new build artifact. This new build artifact includes reference to only those third-party dependencies actually required by the new build artifact.

The ticketing service will be modified to use Apache Maven instead of Ant for the same reasons we used it in the product catalog service modification.

The steps for the ticketing microservice conversion are exactly the same as for converting the product catalog service.

Search

As discussed, we have a very rudimentary database-based search service. Now we are going to add the Solr search component to provide us with advanced search capabilities. We will still perform searches the old way, but we will also perform the Solr-based search and show results from both on the user interface, indicating them as basic and advanced. For that reason, we will also modify the search view to include this enhancement.

Database-Based Search

Search service–specific code is migrated similarly to the way we migrated it for the other two services. The effort includes taking out the interface, services implementations, helper classes, and configuration files and creating a new build artifact.

Again, we will leverage Apache Maven, which will help in getting third-party external dependencies required by our service.

Solr-Based Search

The first step in adding Solr-based search is to install and configure the Solr engine. Refer to Appendix B for detailed instructions. Once it is up, we can create our microservice. We will build an advanced search service as a separate entity and also leverage Apache Maven here to build our artifacts.

Following is the Solr implementation code snippet from the same search web service:

```
@POST
@Consumes({"application/xml", "application/json"})
@Produces({"application/json"})
@Path("/solrSearch")
public QueryResponse search(
@Context HttpHeaders headers,
SearchRequest request)
```

The code to query the Solr interface follows:

```
HttpSolrServer solr = new HttpSolrServer(
                   "http://<ip of solr host>
                   :8983/solr/helpdesk");
SolrQuery query = new SolrQuery();
query.setQuery(request.getQuery());
query.setStart(0);
QueryResponse response = solr.query(query);
```

You can do a lot with the Solr, such as apply search filters, but these topics are out of this book's scope. For more information, refer to http://lucene.apache.org/solr.

Now, let's review the application build and deployment process.

Application Build and Deployment

We have converted the following three components from the monolithic application and created them as individual microservices:

- Product catalog
- Ticketing
- Search

Let's look at what changes have gone into these microservices, including how to build, configure, and deploy them.

Code Setup

The original monolithic application used Apache Ant to build the project. As the evolving project based on microservices has become increasingly modularized and must manage dependencies, the individual microservices have adopted Apache Maven as the build tool. Ant has no built-in capability for dependency management, although it can be supplemented with Ivy. This illustrates a key concept: that each microservice can have its own way of building its source code if required.

Code for these individual microservices is available at GitHub: https://github .com/kocherMSD/Helpdesk_Microservices.git.

Building the Microservices

You can build individual microservices in two ways: via the command line or automatically from an integrated development environment such as Eclipse:

- **Building via the command line.** To build a Maven project via the command line, run the `mvn` command from the command line. The command should be executed in the project directory that contains the relevant POM file. To build the individual microservices, the command to run is `mvn clean package`. This command ensures the artifacts are cleaned up and packaged into a WAR file that's ready to be deployed.

- **Building from Eclipse.** Once you have the project imported into Eclipse, right-click the project name, choose **Run As**, and select **Run configurations**. In the Run configurations window, enter **clean package** against the goals field and click **Run**. This should build the code clean and produce the WAR file, which is ready to be deployed in an application container such as Tomcat.

Deploying and Configuring

There are quite a few options for deploying microservices. Each option has its pros and cons, so let's quickly see what they are. In Chapter 13, we'll delve deeper into the deployment space along with automated deployment, scaling, and so on.

- **Multiple microservices within a single machine.** In this option, the strategy is to deploy more than one microservice within the same machine (physical or virtual). The major advantage of this approach is that the resource usage is relatively efficient because multiple services or instances are sharing the same resources (CPU, memory, I/O, etc.). The drawback is that there is little or no isolation of these services unless each service is a separate process. Also, a misbehaving service can potentially consume all of the memory or CPU of the host.

- **Single microservice per virtual machine.** The major benefit with this approach is that each service runs in complete isolation because it's wrapped inside a virtual machine. Each microservice has full access to its allocated memory, CPU, and I/O. However, the major drawback with this approach is the lack of efficient resource utilization. Virtual machines may well be underutilized, but again, this drawback can be overcome by allocating sufficient resources and putting the virtual machine on auto-scale.

- **Single microservice per container.** Deploying a microservice in a container is simply packaging the service to run inside a container. Once you have the service packaged in a container, you can launch containers at will, depending on the varying, on-demand, and real-time application needs. The benefit of this approach is that each container runs in isolation. Resources consumed by the containers can be monitored, controlled, and managed. However, unlike virtual machines, these containers are very lightweight and easy to build, package, and start. They start extremely fast because there's no operating system to bootstrap like with a virtual machine. The major disadvantage of this approach is the technological? maturity. With the advent of Docker in 2013, containers are far more accessible to mainstream teams now; however, the technology is still evolving to address issues such as security, managing containers at scale, and so on.

For simplicity, we will deploy our new microservices in the same Tomcat server where we have hosted the monolithic application. In Chapter 13, we'll take these microservices and package them in a Docker container and deploy them as individual microservices.

Following are the steps to deploy the helpdesk application with the new microservices:

1. We need to point the newly created microservices from our existing monolithic application. To do so, modify the property file, Application.properties, by changing the endpoints for our web services, as follows:

```
endPoints.serachEndPoint=
  http://host:port/search-svc/rest/SerachService/search
endPoints.getCatalog=
  http://host:port/ticketing-svc/rest/CatalogService/
  getCatalog
```

```
endPoints.createTicket=
  http://host:port/catalog-svc /rest/TicketService/
  createTicket
```

2. To change the search view, modify the search.jsp file in the monolithic application to include an advanced search button; call the Solr search web service end point from the JavaScript function:

```
function solrsearch()
{
    var solrSearchEndPoint=
       <%= props.getProperty(
          "endPoints.solrSearchEndPoint") %>';
    var searchText=document.getElementById("searchText").
    value;
    if(searchText=='')
    {
        alert('Empty text. Please provide value in text');
    }

    var dataToSend= {"query":searchText};
    $.ajax({headers: {
        'Accept': 'application/json',
        'Content-Type': 'application/json'
    },
    url: solrSearchEndPoint,
    type: 'POST',
    dataType: 'json',
    data: JSON.stringify(dataToSend)       ,
    success: function(data, textStatus, jqXHR) {

    $("#solrresults").empty();
    var docs = data.results;
    $.each(docs, function(i, item) {
            $('#solrresults').prepend($('<div>' +
            objToString(item) + '</div>'));
    });
    var total = 'Found ' + docs.length + ' results';
    $('#solrresults').prepend('<div>' + total + '</div>');
    }
    }).fail(function (jqXHR, textStatus, error) {
    // Handle error here
    alert(jqXHR.responseText);
    });
}
```

3. Create the individual microservices WAR files by building them separately, as shown in Figure 12.3. Use the Apache Maven pom.xml, as outlined earlier in this chapter.

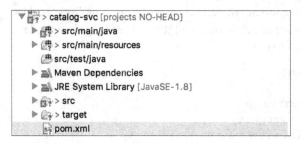

Figure 12.3 *Structure for a microservice in Eclipse*

4. Execute the Maven build, as shown in Figure 12.4.

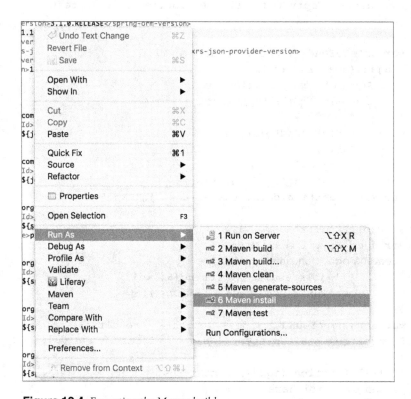

Figure 12.4 *Executing the Maven build*

You should see the message shown in Figure 12.5 if the build is successful.

```
[INFO] Processing war project
[INFO] Copying webapp resources [/opt/projects/BOOKCODE/catalog-svc/src/main/webapp]
[INFO] Webapp assembled in [1523 msecs]
[INFO] Building war: /opt/projects/BOOKCODE/catalog-svc/target/catalog-svc.war
[INFO] WEB-INF/web.xml already added, skipping
[INFO]
[INFO] --- maven-install-plugin:2.4:install (default-install) @ catalog-svc ---
[INFO] Installing /opt/projects/BOOKCODE/catalog-svc/target/catalog-svc.war to /Users/anujsin/.m2/repository/org/helpdesk/services/catalog-svc.
[INFO] Installing /opt/projects/BOOKCODE/catalog-svc/pom.xml to /Users/anujsin/.m2/repository/org/helpdesk/services/catalog-svc/1.0.0/catalog-
[INFO] ------------------------------------------------------------------------
[INFO] BUILD SUCCESS
[INFO] ------------------------------------------------------------------------
[INFO] Total time: 7.783 s
[INFO] Finished at: 2017-09-10T16:24:17-05:00
[INFO] Final Memory: 14M/210M
[INFO] ------------------------------------------------------------------------
```

Figure 12.5 *Build output*

5. Follow the previous steps for the rest of the microservices. Copy all these WAR files into the Tomcat webapp directory.

Your deployed directory structure will look like the following in Linux:

```
search-svc   catalog-svc   docs   helpdesk   host-manager
ROOT   ticketing-svc.war   search-svc.war   catalog-svc.war
examples
helpdesk.war manager   ticketing-svc
```

As you can see, along with helpdesk.war, there are three additional microservices deployed in the same Tomcat container.

New Requirements and Bug Fixes

We have successfully migrated our monolithic application architecture to microservices based on new business needs. We also know business needs will continue to evolve. Let's look at some ways to manage possible change requests with a microservices-based architecture.

Suppose we need to add to the view-ticket service an extra parameter that has limited to no dependency on other components. Using the following code snippet, we can change the ticket request:

```
public TicketResponse createHdTicket(
        @Context HttpHeaders headers,
        TicketRequest ticketRequest)
        throws ServiceInvocationException{
```

The following adds a new property to the Plain Old Java Object (web model):

```
@Component
  private String emailAddress;
@XmlElement
 public String getEmailAddress() {
        return emailAddress;
    }
public void setEmailAddress(String emailAddress) {
        this.emailAddress = emailAddress;
    }
```

The following code allows us to add logic to the DAO layer to get that property from the database:

```
private String saveToDatabase(TicketRequest ticketRequest){
      //added with existing one
        ticket.setEmailAddress(ticketRequest.getEmailAddress());
}
```

Notice that this ticketing change does not affect any other service. We just need to test this service and deploy it, and we should be good to go. Making this change in a monolithic application would require us to build the complete application and do thorough regression testing, which is time- and resource-consuming. It is a simple example, but it illustrates the difference between making a change in a microservices application and making the same change in a monolithic application.

Now let's go through the same challenges we highlighted with the monolithic application in Chapter 11 to see if microservices really helped solved those challenges:

- **Addressing bugs.** Only the portion of the application that has the bug needs to be fixed. If the bug is in the code of one microservice, then we just need to touch that particular microservice, fix the code, and deploy. Also, since each microservice will be load balanced in a typical deployment, you can deploy the fix serially so as to not impact the application availability. If the bug is in the monolithic code, you still need to follow the normal process, but notice that the microservices remain untouched and no retesting of those components is required; hence, there is a reduced release cycle time.

- **Replacing application components.** Let's assume the same case where we want to use cloud services for ticket management; all we need is a configuration change, as we discussed earlier in the chapter, to point to the cloud service end points. Simple enough!

- **Replacing or adding new technology stack.** If it ever makes sense to develop an existing or new service using a different technology stack, say PHP/NOSQL, the developer has full freedom to do so with minimal dependencies.

- **Scaling selectively.** One of the biggest advantages of microservices is selective scaling. As you noticed in the new architecture diagram, each microservice can be load balanced. If there is more traffic expected on the ticketing layer, you can easily spin up more virtual machines or containers for the ticketing service without touching any other service or monolithic part of the application. This saves time, resources, and expenses on unnecessary scaling of the complete application. We will do this in the next chapter.

- **Handling faults.** An issue or bug in a particular microservice will not impact the whole application if designed properly. The worst-case scenario may be that a particular microservice could be impacted, but the rest of the system will still be functional. Think of an e-commerce site based on a monolithic architecture. Say the product rating part of the application crashes. Depending how the monolithic application is written, this may bring down the whole application even though there were no issues with, say, the cart and checkout part of the application. With microservices, the worst outcome of a product rating microservice crashing would be that users cannot submit ratings. Since shopping cart and checkout services are up, users will still be able to complete the shopping, causing limited impact to business.

Scalability is the biggest challenge. Running a few microservices is fine, but they are meant to comprise large systems, with thousands of microservices and lots of scaling up and down. Let's now go and containerize our microservices in the next chapter so we can scale and manage them more easily.

Chapter 13

Case Study: Containerizing a Helpdesk Application

In Chapter 12, "Case Study: Migration to Microservices," we created three microservices based on our needs and the criteria we learned throughout this book. The next question becomes, how do we scale this model? In the real world, a large-scale application may have hundreds to thousands of microservices. In this chapter, we use our knowledge of Docker containers to deploy and scale the microservices on demand.

The monolithic part of our application will continue to run as is, but we will containerize the microservices part of the application, which includes ticketing, product catalog, and search, and make appropriate changes to the monolithic application.

Containerizing Microservices

In this section, we containerize the product catalog microservice we created in the Chapter 12. Armed with our knowledge so far, containerizing microservices involves the following steps:

1. Make a list of dependencies required for each microservice.

2. Build the binaries, WAR files, and so on, that compose the microservice.

3. Create a Docker image that includes items in the previous two steps.

4. Use the image created in step 3 to launch one or more containers.

Listing Dependencies

Here is the list of software that's required (dependencies) to run the product catalog microservice:

- **Tomcat:** Required to run the application (product catalog) code
- **Java:** A dependency for Tomcat to function properly
- **MySQL connector:** A dependency for Tomcat to connect to MySQL
- **Apache Maven:** To be installed on the system where you are building your microservice (for reference, see https://maven.apache.org/install.html)

Build Binaries and WAR files

Now that we have identified the dependent software required to run the catalog microservice, the next thing we need is the WAR file (binary) itself. Please follow the following instructions to build and produce a WAR file for the catalog microservice. For this task, clone the code from the GitHub repository for our catalog microservice: https://github.com/kocherMSD/Helpdesk_Microservices.git

Since we are building our first microservice, we should take advantage of the latest toolset available. In this case, we use Apache Maven to build the WAR file instead of Apache Ant (as we did for our monolithic application) because Maven is a more advanced build automation tool.. For example, it also downloads the library dependencies required for the project.

The next task is to verify that the Apache POM file is located in the root directory of your cloned code. The POM file consists of the dependencies, such as the Java Runtime version, the Maven central repository information, and a list of required JAR files.

If it is all there, then the next step is to build the WAR file. Run `mvn install` from the command line at the project root directory, or right-click on the POM file in the Eclipse editor and select **mvn install**. A folder named Target should have been created in the root directory, which will have the WAR file.

Creating a Docker Image

Let's look at how to create a Docker image for our product catalog service. The approach to create images for other microservices, such as ticketing, is the same except that you include the appropriate binaries of the chosen microservice and the environment dependencies.

As we learned in previous chapters, the right way to create a Docker image is through a Dockerfile, which includes all the dependencies mentioned previously. Building that Dockerfile will give us the image we need to deploy our service.

Let's start writing the Dockerfile. Please note we'll be building this file in multiple steps so that it is easy to explain the content. Make sure you don't create multiple files if you are executing things in parallel:

```
# Based on Ubuntu 17.04
FROM ubuntu:17.04
# Environment variables to install Tomcat 7; you may change the
# minor version of Tomcat according to your needs. To change the
# major version as well (e.g., to Tomcat 8), you must be sure to
# change the TOMCAT_LOCATION variable as well.

ENV    TOMCAT_VERSION=7.0.81
ENV    TOMCAT_FILENAME=apache-tomcat-$TOMCAT_VERSION.tar.gz
ENV    TOMCAT_DIRECTORY=apache-tomcat-$TOMCAT_VERSION
ENV    TOMCAT_LOCATION=http://www-eu.apache.org/dist/tomcat/ \
tomcat-7/v$TOMCAT_VERSION/bin/$TOMCAT_FILENAME
```

Let's take a closer look at some of the code:

- FROM ubuntu tells what environment the catalog service will run in. In this case, the catalog service will be running under an Ubuntu environment.

- The ENV command defines environment variables that can be used within the Dockerfile.

The next step is to pull and install all the dependencies. Append the following to the existing file:

```
# Fetch Tomcat; install required utilities such as wget & JDK1.8.
# Clean up apt cache, as "apt-get update" is going to bust the
cache
# always.
RUN apt-get update && \
    apt-get install -y wget && \
    apt-get install -y default-jdk && \
    rm -fr /var/lib/apt/lists/* && \
    wget $TOMCAT_LOCATION
```

Here's what we're doing with this code:

- apt-get is the package manager in Ubuntu, which simplifies the lifecycle (install/update/delete) of packages. It is recommended to always do an apt-get update. This command gets the latest list of packages and their versions from the Ubuntu repository.

- The apt-get install command installs the Wget package. Wget is a free utility that's used to download files from the web. We need this utility to download Tomcat from the web.

- The install command installs the Java development kit. This is a dependency for Tomcat.

- When the command apt-get update is run, it downloads the packages from the Ubuntu repository and stores them in the directory named /var/lib/apt/lists. This directory could be large, which can make our Docker image look big too. Since the installation is complete, we can safely remove the contents in this directory, and that's what the rm command does. It's a best practice in writing Dockerfiles.

- wget is the utility we installed earlier in the code, and it downloads Tomcat from the web.

One key thing to note is that all of these commands are run in a single line to reduce the number of layers in the Docker image. RUN is the command that instructs Docker to run any command within the environment (in this case, it's the Ubuntu environment). If we choose CentOS as the environment (e.g., FROM CentOS), then the same command will become RUN yum, because yum is the package manager in CentOS just as apt-get is the package manager in Ubuntu.

Now that we have downloaded Tomcat, let's append the following to the existing file:

```
# Install Tomcat under /opt and rename the directory "tomcat"
RUN tar -xf $TOMCAT_FILENAME -C /opt && \
    mv /opt/$TOMCAT_DIRECTORY /opt/tomcat
```

Here, we are installing Tomcat into our /opt directory and then renaming the directory /opt/tomcat.

Now let's deploy our microservice:

```
# Deploy product catalog service to Tomcat
ADD catalog-svc.war /opt/tomcat/webapps/
```

```
# Expose port to the host system
EXPOSE 8080
```

```
# Run tomcat in the foreground
CMD ["/opt/tomcat/bin/catalina.sh", "run"]
```

Let's look closer at this snippet:

- The ADD command instructs Docker to copy the catalog-svc.war file to the Tomcat webapps directory because we want the catalog service to start as soon as the container is launched.

- Expose is a command that exposes Tomcat's port to the host machine on which the container is running.

- CMD is the default command that gets executed when a container is launched. By starting Tomcat as the default command when a container is launched, we get two things: first, Tomcat is started automatically, and second, the product catalog service is deployed automatically.

Here is the complete file for reference:

```
# Based on Ubuntu 17.04
FROM ubuntu:17.04
# Environment variables to install Tomcat 7; you may change the
# minor version of Tomcat according to your needs. To change the
# major version as well (e.g., to Tomcat 8), you must be sure to
# change the TOMCAT_LOCATION variable as well.

ENV    TOMCAT_VERSION=7.0.81
ENV    TOMCAT_FILENAME=apache-tomcat-$TOMCAT_VERSION.tar.gz
ENV    TOMCAT_DIRECTORY=apache-tomcat-$TOMCAT_VERSION
ENV    TOMCAT_LOCATION=http://www-eu.apache.org/dist/tomcat/ \
tomcat-7/v$TOMCAT_VERSION/bin/$TOMCAT_FILENAME

# Fetch Tomcat; install required utilities such as wget & JDK1.8.
# Clean up apt cache, as "apt-get update" is going to bust the
cache
# always.
RUN apt-get update && \
    apt-get install -y wget && \
    apt-get install -y default-jdk && \
    rm -fr /var/lib/apt/lists/* && \
    wget $TOMCAT_LOCATION

# Install Tomcat under /opt and rename the directory "tomcat"
RUN tar -xf $TOMCAT_FILENAME -C /opt && \
    mv /opt/$TOMCAT_DIRECTORY /opt/tomcat
```

```
# Deploy product catalog service to Tomcat
ADD catalog-svc.war /opt/tomcat/webapps/

# Expose port to the host system
EXPOSE 8080

# Run tomcat in the foreground
CMD ["/opt/tomcat/bin/catalina.sh", "run"]
```

Now let's use this Dockerfile to build a Docker image for the product catalog service.

Building the Docker Image

Using the Dockerfile we just created, enter the following command on the command line:

```
>> docker build -t catalog-svc:1.0 .
```

Let's review what the command does:

- `docker build` is the command used to create a Docker image.
- `-t` is the option to specify a name for the created image (in our case, `catalog-svc:1.0`), which includes `ImageName:<Tag>`.
- The ending `.` tells the Docker `build` command to use the files in the current directory.

To run this command, you need to do the following:

1. Make sure that Docker is installed.

2. Create a directory that has the Dockerfile we created and the WAR file for the catalog service.

3. Run the Docker `build` command from the directory created in step 2.

Now that we have created the Docker image for the product catalog service, we are ready to use this image and spin up the catalog service (inside Docker containers) on the fly. Before we can spin up our catalog service, we need infrastructure where these services can run. We discussed Mesos and Marathon in previous chapters, and we'll be using it to spin up our microservices.

A fast way to get started is to utilize a DC/OS (datacenter operating system), an open source distributed operating system software based on Apache Mesos that provides an easy way to get Mesos, Marathon, and Marathon-lb set up quickly. We'll set up the framework within Amazon Web Services (AWS); the rest of this chapter is based on that. For more information on DC/OS, visit https://dcos.io.

DC/OS Cluster Setup on AWS

To spin up our microservices, we leverage the DC/OS cluster, so let's set it up first. There are a few different ways to set up a DC/OS cluster; the easiest option by far is to spin up a cluster in AWS. (You will need an AWS account to spin up this cluster. For detailed documentation, refer to the following webpage: https://docs.mesosphere.com/1.7/administration/installing/ent/cloud/aws/.)

When accessing the EC2 instances in Amazon, be aware that Amazon enforces best practices such as Secure Shell (SSH) keys instead of using usernames and passwords. It uses public key cryptography to encrypt and decrypt user credentials such as login information.

Let's create a key pair, which we will use during our DC/OS cluster creation:

1. From the AWS console, under Network & Security, click **Key Pairs**. See Figure 13.1.

Figure 13.1 *Representation of AWS console*

2. Provide a name for the key pair to create one.

3. Save the newly created key pair in a secure place. We'll need it during our cluster creation shortly.

Now let's create the DC/OS cluster using the following steps:

1. Launch the DC/OS template at https://dcos.io/docs/1.7/administration/ installing/cloud/aws. Click **Launch the DC/OS template**, which is step 1 under the Install DC/OS section of the page.

2. Choose a cluster type (single or multimaster). For testing purposes, a single master is sufficient. For production systems, multimaster setup is highly preferred to avoid single points of failure.

3. In the next screen, as shown in Figure 13.2, accept the defaults and click **Next**.

4. In the Create Stack page, select **Specify Details** on the left, shown in Figure 13.3. Provide a name for the cluster, and from the dropdown, select the key pair that was created earlier.

5. Next, choose the number of public and private agent nodes, or in this case, leave the default count.

6. Accept defaults in the rest of the screens and finish the stack creation.

   It should take 10 to 15 minutes to create the DC/OS cluster successfully. You may watch the stack creation status at CloudFormation → Stacks, as shown in Figure 13.4:

7. Once the stack creation is complete, go to the Outputs tab and copy/paste the mesos-master URL to your browser. You should see the DC/OS user interface (UI) launched successfully from the system dashboard shown in Figure 13.5:

8. From the cluster UI, go to Universe on the left and search for Marathon. You should see a screen similar to Figure 13.6. Click the **Install** buttons for Marathon and Marathon-lb.

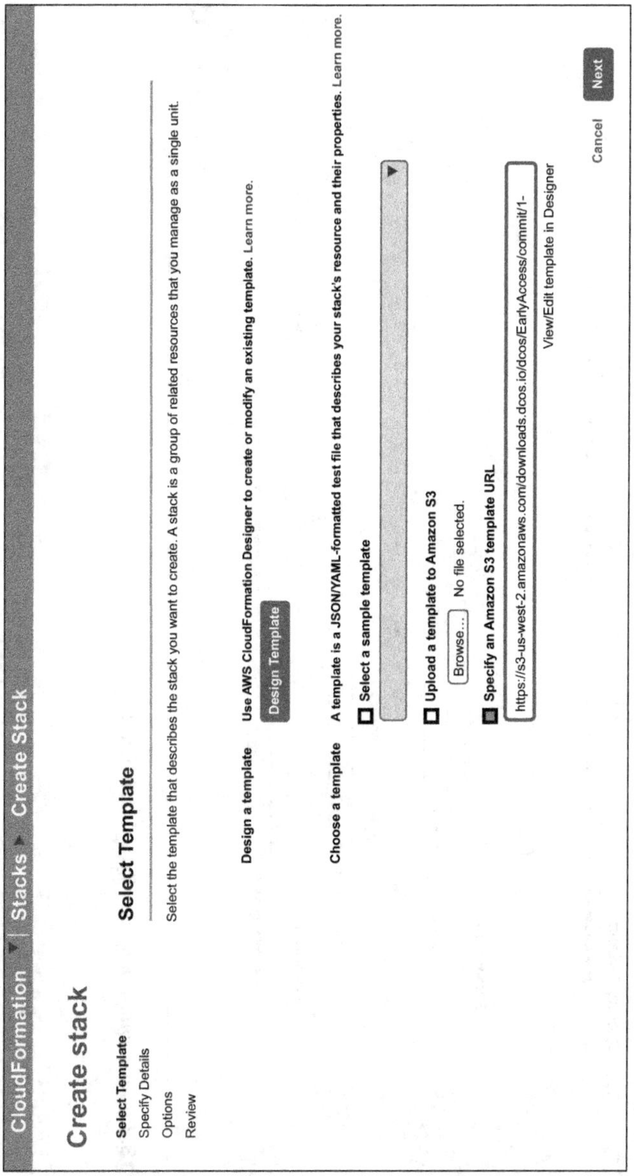

CloudFormation ▸ Stacks ▸ Create Stack

Create stack

Select Template
Specify Details
Options
Review

Select Template

Select the template that describes the stack you want to create. A stack is a group of related resources that you manage as a single unit.

Design a template   Use AWS CloudFormation Designer to create or modify an existing template. Learn more.

[Design Template]

Choose a template   A template is a JSON/YAML-formatted test file that describes your stack's resource and their properties. Learn more.

☐ Select a sample template

[▶]

☐ Upload a template to Amazon S3

[Browse…] No file selected.

☑ Specify an Amazon S3 template URL

[https://s3-us-west-2.amazonaws.com/downloads.dcos.io/dcos/EarlyAccess/commit/1-]

View/Edit template in Designer

Cancel   [Next]

Figure 13.2 *Representation of selecting default template*

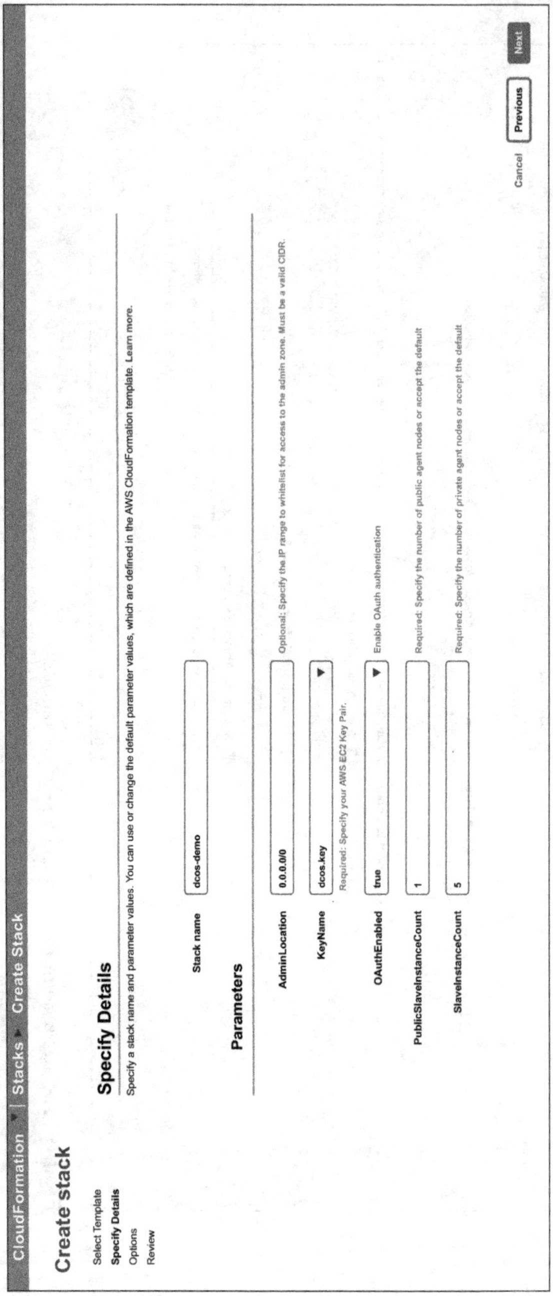

Figure 13.3 *Representation of specifying stack details*

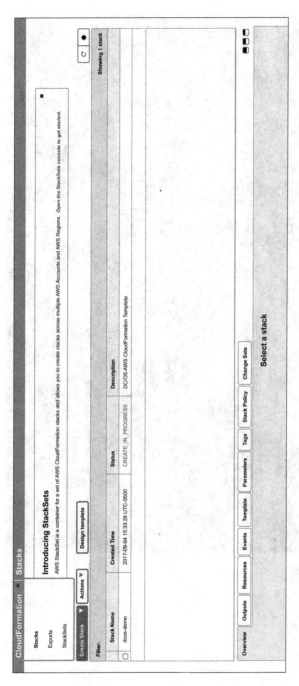

Figure 13.4 *Representation of stack live status*

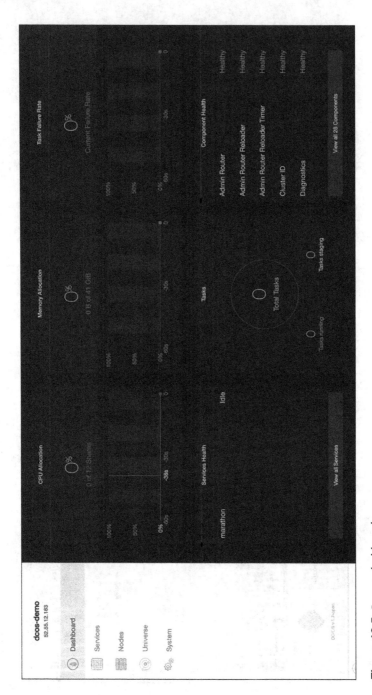

Figure 13.5 *System dashboards*

Figure 13.6 *Installing Marathon and Marathon-lb*

With this, we have successfully installed DC/OS cluster. Let's look at the overall picture of our application using a logical diagram, as shown in Figure 13.7:

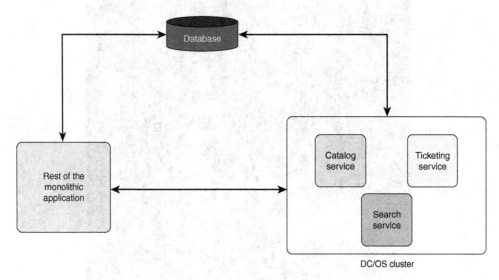

Figure 13.7 *Application logical diagram*

Notice that the services we split and packaged as microservices (catalog, ticketing, search) are the ones that will be deployed and managed within the DC/OS cluster, while the rest of the application will work as is. These microservices will continue to use the same database.

Figure 13.8 shows how our deployment will look logically on the DC/OS cluster.

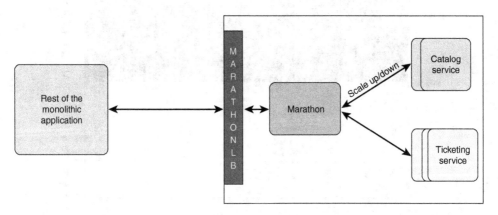

Figure 13.8 *Logical Application view*

Let's review at a high level what we learned in Chapter 9, "Container Orchestration," about Mesos and Marathon, so we can better understand our deployment:

- **Mesos.** This is an open source Apache project that manages resources such as CPU and memory on a cluster of machines. Tasks or services like product catalog and ticketing will be running in the Mesos cluster.

- **Marathon.** This is another open source framework that works closely with Mesos master to schedule tasks in the cluster. In our case, if we have to schedule our catalog service to run inside the Mesos cluster, then we have to go to the Marathon UI, provide the details about the product catalog service (e.g., Docker image for the service, listening port), and click **Submit**.

- **Marathon-lb.** This load balancer is based of the popular load balancer HAProxy, and it works by automatically generating a configuration for HAProxy on the fly. Here is how it works:

  - It communicates to Marathon via APIs to get a list of tasks and services that Marathon scheduled in the Mesos cluster.

  - From Marathon's response, it finds out what services are running in the cluster, where they are running (i.e. which machine in the cluster), which port the service is running on, and so on.

  - It generates an HAProxy configuration, which is simply a request mapping. The configuration has details; for example, "if a request comes to a service endpoint, /abc," then this request may be handled by servers a, b or c, where a, b and c are the machines the service is running to handle the request /abc.

  - External applications will always reach out to Marathon-lb to get the services running in the Mesos cluster.

Now that our cluster is ready, let's deploy our microservices. We deploy the product catalog service here and leave the other two services for you to deploy on your own in a similar fashion.

Deploying the Catalog Microservice

We start by deploying a single instance of the product catalog microservice, and then we scale it up or down according to our needs.

To deploy the service into the cluster, we create a task that has all the details about the service and our needs. This task is then submitted to the cluster through Marathon.

Submitting a Task to Marathon

Let's describe the task for our product catalog service. There are two ways to submit a task to Marathon:

- Using a simple command, you can submit a Docker command directly—for example, `Docker run -P -d nginx`. Simple, small tasks that do not require major configurations can be submitted directly.

- When we want to describe the service with more details, we can use a JSON file. The JSON file is a well-known, standard file format that uses human-readable text to describe data. It uses key-value pairs to describe the data, as we'll see shortly.

We use a JSON file to describe our catalog service in detail and then submit the task through Marathon. Here is our catalog microservice configuration file (JSON):

```
{
 "id": "catalog-external",
 "container": {
  "type": "DOCKER",
  "docker": {
   "image": "kocher/catalog-svc:1.1",
   "network": "BRIDGE",
   "portMappings": [
    { "hostPort": 0, "containerPort": 8080, "servicePort": 10000 }
   ],
   "forcePullImage":false
  }
 },
 "instances": 1,
 "mem": 1024,
 "healthChecks": [{
   "protocol": "HTTP",
   "path": "/",
   "portIndex": 0,
   "timeoutSeconds": 20,
   "gracePeriodSeconds": 10,
   "intervalSeconds": 10,
   "maxConsecutiveFailures": 10
 }],
 "labels":{
     "HAPROXY_GROUP":"external",
"HAPROXY_0_VHOST":"ec2-52-207-255-252.compute-1.amazonaws.com"
 }
}
```

Let's review the submitted task in detail:

- `id` is an identifier for our catalog service. It is used to identify services running in the cluster.
- The `container` section describes the Docker container for the product catalog service. It has the following components:
  - `type` indicates the type of container. It is `DOCKER` by default. Another option is `MESOS`, which, in future Marathon frameworks, may support other container types.
  - `image` indicates which Docker image should be spun up when this task is launched in the cluster.
  - `network` indicates the type of network. We are using `BRIDGE`. There are other types of networks, as we saw in Chapter 8, "Containers Networking."
  - `portMappings`: `hostPort` indicates what port should be exposed within the host on which the container is running. `containerPort`, as the name suggests, is the port exposed within the container. `servicePort` is the port on which this catalog service is accessible via the Marathon-lb load balancer.
  - `forcePullImage`, if set to `TRUE`, forces Marathon to pull the latest image from the Docker registry before it launches the task. The default value is `false`.
- `instances` indicates how many instances of the catalog service must be launched in the cluster.
- `mem` indicates how much memory should be allotted to the catalog service.
- The parameters in the `healthChecks` block section instructs Marathon to perform a health check on the catalog service at the configured intervals.
- The `labels` section has the following labels:
  - `HAPROXY_GROUP`: The `external` label indicates to the Marathon load balancer that this microservice must be accessible to the external world. If it is made internal, then the same microservice will be accessible only from within the DC/OS cluster and not accessible from the outside world.
  - `HAPROXY_0_VHOST` instructs the Marathon load balancer to create a virtual host for the service. Services with this label set will be accessible via the `servicePort` and additionally at ports 80 and 443.

Now let's go to the Marathon UI and submit this JSON file to launch our first microservice in the DC/OS cluster. From the DC/OS UI, go to Services and click the **Marathon** link. Then launch the Marathon UI by clicking **Open Service**, as shown in Figure 13.9:

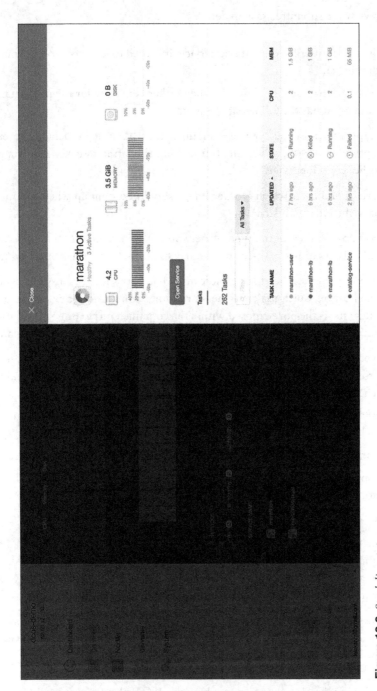

Figure 13.9 *Stack live status*

You should see our running applications, as shown in Figure 13.10. From this screen, launch **Create Application**. Choose **Ports and Service Discovery**, and then click **JSON Mode** to provide our catalog.JSON.

You should see a new Application window similar to Figure 13.11:

Hit **Create Application**, and after a few seconds, you should see that our catalog service is up and running, as shown in Figure 13.12:

Inspecting and Scaling the Service

If you click the catalog-external link from the applications, you will be able to inspect further details about this service. Figure 13.13 shows that one instance of this microservice is healthy. It also provides status, log information, version number, and when it was last updated.

Running a quick `curl` on the instance will return a list of products indicating that the service is up and running normally, as shown in the following:

```
curl http://10.0.0.79:15973/catalog-svc/rest/CatalogService/
getCatalog/pkocher | python -m JSON.tool
```

```
{
  "productFamilyListList": [
    {
      "productFamily": "Phone",
      "productId": "iPhone5",
      "technologySolution": "N"
    },
    {
      "productFamily": "Phone",
      "productId": "iPhone6",
      "technologySolution": "N"
    }
  ],
  "responseErrorCode": null,
  "responseErrorMessage": null,
  "responseStatus": "SUCCESS"
}
```

To scale up this microservice, all we have to do is click **Scale Application** and provide the number of instances. Let's say we want to run two instances of this service. We would click on **Scale Application** and enter **2**. It should scale the application in a matter of seconds, as shown in Figure 13.14. Under the Running Instance column, you should see "2 of 2," indicating that two instances of the catalog service are now deployed in the cluster.

Figure 13.10 *Create application*

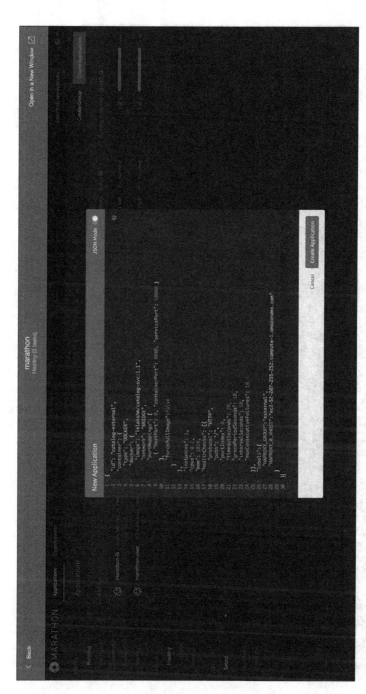

Figure 13.11 *New application*

Figure 13.12 *Running applications*

Figure 13.13 *Catalog external*

Figure 13.14 *Scaling up the microservice*

This is how easy it is to scale up or scale down a microservice within a DC/OS cluster. Now that two instances of our catalog microservice are deployed in the cluster, we will access this service from rest of the application.

Accessing the Service

How do we know where the service is running? If you recall from Chapter 3, "Interprocess Communication," this is one of the most challenging parts in microservices deployment and architecture, as microservices may come up or go down for various reasons, such as node failure or insufficient resources. If a microservice goes down for any reason, then Marathon will detect the failure and will work with the Mesos cluster to spin up another instance. It ensures that the correct number of instances are always running in the cluster.

Marathon-lb, on the other hand, works with Marathon, through Marathon APIs, to discover what services are running in the cluster, on what machines in the cluster the service is running, on what ports, and so on. Once it discovers the services running in the cluster, if `servicePort` is defined, then Marathon-lb exposes that port on itself through which the actual service can be reached.

Given this context, in our case, we have two instances of the catalog service deployed in the cluster, and they have a `servicePort` value 10000, which means the catalog service can be reached at http://<DNS name of the Marathon-lb server>:10000.

To find out the Marathon-lb's host name, you go to the DC/OS cluster running in AWS, select the stack, and choose **Outputs** tab, as shown in Figure 13.15.

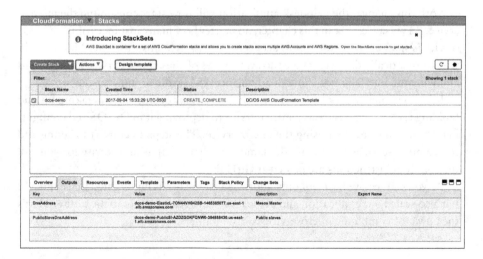

Figure 13.15 *Representation of finding host name*

The host name you see in the second row (PublicSlaveDnsAddress) is the server where Marathon-lb is running. So, to access the catalog service, access this endpoint:

```
curl http:// dcos-demo-PublicSl-1O6EEUP951OVX-628629381.us-
east-1.elb.amazonaws.com:10000/catalog-svc/rest/CatalogService/
getCatalog/<userid>
```

Notice in this URL, port 10000 exposes the catalog service in the DC/OS cluster. No matter how many instances of catalog service are up and running in the cluster, the Marathon load balancer will discover them automatically and expose them via port 10000.

Now that the catalog microservice is up and running in the DC/OS cluster, we have to configure the helpdesk application to start using this microservice. It's a simple configuration change in a property file.

Updating the Monolithic Application

Our helpdesk application maintains a list of URLs for each service in a file called Application.properties. This file is located under /usr/share/tomcat7/lib directory.

You will have to change the property called endPoints.getCatalog with the Marathon-lb URL as follows:

```
endPoints.getCatalog=http://ec2-52-207-255-252.compute-1.
amazonaws.com:10000/catalog-svc/rest/CatalogService/getCatalog
```

With this change, the helpdesk application will now start consuming the microservice. As we saw earlier in this chapter, no matter how many instances of the catalog service is spun up, the endpoint to access the service remains the same. Marathon-lb will automatically discover where those instances of the catalog service are deployed and will automatically route (and load balance) the traffic to those instances.

In this chapter, we looked at the catalog service in detail, from breaking up and building the catalog service as a microservice to deploying it in DC/OS and configuring the monolith to start using the microservice. The steps to convert ticketing and search microservices are exactly the same, and that is left as an exercise for you. All the code and instructions are posted at GitHub.

As you can see, we have not only addressed all the needs highlighted in Chapter 12 but also scaled our application and made it easier to scale further in the future. That's the power of combining microservices and containers.

Conclusion

In the preface, I said that I wrote this with two groups of readers in mind: experienced software and systems engineers looking to roll up their sleeves and get their hands dirty with some real-life examples and a deep-dive case study, and executives and project managers—that is, non-programmers—who want a high-level introduction to the topic. Whichever group you fall into—perhaps you even have a foot in both—I hope you found the pages you read enlightening.

Each subject we covered about microservices and containers—discovery services, API Gateway, Kubernetes, services communication, and more—is worthy of an entire tome on its own. (Indeed, some of those topics already have multiple books devoted to them!) What I wanted to do with this book was provide a higher-level synthesis of those topics, providing you with just enough to make the takeaways you need for your own job or career. Alone, microservices enable the on-demand scaling of various software components. Containers, meanwhile, help with virtualization, keeping everything lightweight along the way. Together, they complement each other beautifully, making one plus one equal three—the ultimate definition of synergy.

What Is DevOps?

In the opening chapters of this book, we examined some of the impacts microservices and containers can have on organizations, but we did not talk much about their potential impact on another hot topic of the moment: DevOps. Today, many software organizations are moving toward the DevOps model, and microservices and containers will be key enablers in this journey.

DevOps is a portmanteau—a hybrid term—that combines two software engineering practices: software *dev*elopment and (IT) *op*erations. The emphasis is on increasing collaboration between these two practices in order to accomplish the following:

- Increase software release velocity.
- Improve the product quality at a faster pace.
- Automate various aspects of these two fields, such as code-building, testing, packaging, releasing, and deploying.

Not surprisingly, the entire tech industry is scrambling to jump on the DevOps bandwagon in order to reap the benefits of all that potential. So, what's the holdup? What challenges are Silicon Valley's best and brightest facing that's preventing them from developing the proverbial golden egg–laying goose? The biggest one is change. Many tools and practices are already in place in these organizations to manage software development, testing, or release, and all these must change. Not only that, organizational change may also impact existing team structures, which in turn can require the recruitment of new skill sets. These challenges should sound similar to those surrounding microservices.

Next, if you look at the goals behind DevOps, you can see microservices can clearly enable this combination of software engineering practices. The complexity of a monolithic architecture is broken down into manageable pieces that provide just one capability each. Those pieces can be divided among multiple teams such that each team can focus on its own piece. The result is shorter development cycles and simpler, quicker deployments, reducing time to market. These advantages, in turn, create the need for operations agility and automation. Microservices need that kind of agile culture to be sustained, and therefore push or enable the DevOps environment.

Given these advantages with DevOps, it might seem as though every developer, architect, or organization would want to transition to a microservices paradigm. Yet as we discussed earlier, it is not for everyone. Microservices are the best fit for complex architectures—that is, software with many functionalities and end users, rapid deployment, and scalability. In the very near future, most companies, including many small and medium-size organizations, will embrace this trend. Why? Five major reasons:

- **An even more complex future of the software industry.** Software-defined networking, software-defined storage, software as a service, the Internet of things, and platforms that handle complex communication between millions of users and devices are some examples that come to mind when you talk about where the software industry is going. There is a plethora of companies, both big and small, getting into these fields, and as they move forward, they will realize the need for a microservices-based architecture coupled with an agile culture.

- **New client types generating new needs.** The most innovative companies are developing solutions that are supported on all kind of new devices and around the globe. Each family of devices has different sets of resources to work with. Memory, processing speed, and storage are limited in some devices and found in abundance in others. When all these devices with different constraints try to access the same software, the software must support their requests by hiding the complexity from the clients. Where is this complexity going to be hidden? In the software itself! Which means the software will become even more complex—hence the need for microservices architecture that can support communication with different clients, as we discussed in earlier chapters.

- **User-driven complexity.** Amazon and Netflix offerings have gotten complex thanks to their innovation in simplifying and enhancing the user experience. They would have probably survived with monolithic paradigms if their numbers of users remained manageable. In fact, they continued on that path in their initial years. As the emerging markets catch up to developed ones and their millions (or billions!) get online, software will continue to grow more complex to address the scalability, performance, and needs of different users. This will cause more and more companies to feel the need for microservices, which can address those issues.

- **Job satisfaction.** Monolithic means one platform worked on by one or more development teams, sometimes divided by work type (e.g., frontend, backend, user experience). One of the issues with this model is that one backend engineering team may be responsible for building all the backend code for required services such as billing, product catalog, shopping cart, and so on (in the example of an e-commerce site). When the code and use cases get complex, the team splits further and divides the work within backend systems (common capabilities and the like). As the complexity increases, they add more people and create new teams and complexity grows to the point that any small feature update requires long cycles and deployment times. Over time, teams become frustrated. Failed builds, rollbacks, and time-consuming debugging can become the norm rather than occasional roadblocks. Miscommunication and lack of collaboration occur, and in particularly fraught situations, can end in finger-pointing, name-calling, and even talent attrition. If implemented well, DevOps and microservices can promote clearer separation of roles and responsibilities, which will enhance collaboration between teams. Collaboration, in turn, drives up productivity, which directly impacts the bottom line. The result? Job satisfaction all the way around.

- **Business benefits.** A smart business will always adapt to new technologies or paradigms if they can improve the bottom line and solve major challenges. Microservices offers one such opportunity to the business to differentiate itself from its competitors.

Time will tell, but given these reasons, the penetration rate of microservices and containers will likely skyrocket over the next few years.

Only the Beginning

Although you have reached the end of this book, my hope is that these words serve as a commencement more than a conclusion. In other words, while you may have "graduated" from the School of Microservices and Docker, I assure you there is still so much more out there to learn. Whether you consider this your main course or merely your appetizer, I hope that I have whet your appetite for more! I encourage you to read more and get involved with various online microservices and containers communities and dive into more case studies yourself. In conclusion, I hope this is both an ending and a beginning for you. Time to get to work!

Appendix A

Helpdesk Application Flow

This appendix provides a functional overview of the helpdesk application. Think of it as the user guide that presents the application capabilities for admin and the customer.

In the real world, most support applications are integrated with order management and customer management systems. As a result, there is a lot of automation in place from the data movement perspective. For example, when a customer is created in a customer management system, the customer information is automatically pushed down to other systems, such as a support application. For our purposes, we are considering the standalone helpdesk application, and we have no integrations with upstream applications, so we will manually create all the required data to explain this application.

There are three main types of users or roles in this application:

- **Administrator.** The so-called superuser, who can create and modify new accounts, users, services, and so on. He or she can see all the data and can access the backend systems such as databases.

- **Customers.** Users who purchased the product or service from the vendor. Customers can create, modify, and check the status of tickets. They have visibility to the tickets that they submit.

- **Support desk engineer.** A user who works on tickets submitted by customers and has visibility to all the tickets.

Administrator Flows

This section lists all the functions available to application administrators to set up and maintain the application.

Login

Every application needs to authenticate so that only legitimate users can use it. The application takes the username and password for authenticating users, as shown in Figure A.1. The username and password should be available in the database. The application is already set up with the username *admin* and password *admin*. You can reset them in the database directly.

Figure A.1 *Application login screen*

On successful authentication, the admin arrives on the landing page; this page will have all the modules on the top menu, as shown in Figure A.2. Let's review each of them.

Figure A.2 *Application capabilities for admin*

Administration and Supported Products

The administrator can add new users (customers and support desk), newly supported products, and sold products within the product catalog for the user, as shown in Figure A.3.

New products are released at regular intervals and old ones taken out of support or service. This is where the admin comes to add new supported products or expire existing products that are going out of support. For example, Figure A.3 shows a list of supported products, where Y is yes (supported) and N is no (not supported).

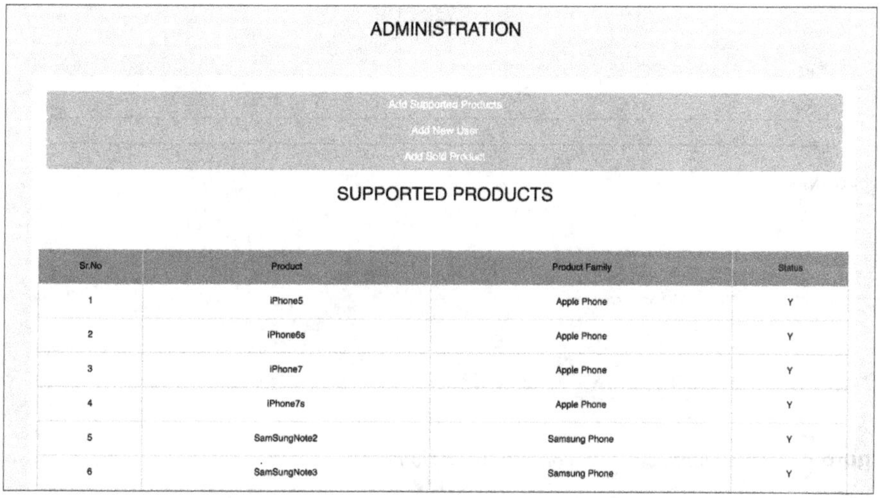

ADMINISTRATION

Add Supported Products
Add New User
Add Sold Product

SUPPORTED PRODUCTS

Sr.No	Product	Product Family	Status
1	iPhone5	Apple Phone	Y
2	iPhone6s	Apple Phone	Y
3	iPhone7	Apple Phone	Y
4	iPhone7s	Apple Phone	Y
5	SamSungNote2	Samsung Phone	Y
6	SamSungNote3	Samsung Phone	Y

Figure A.3 *List of supported products within the Administration control panel*

Add Supported Product

From here, the admin can add new supported products to the catalog, as shown in Figure A.4.

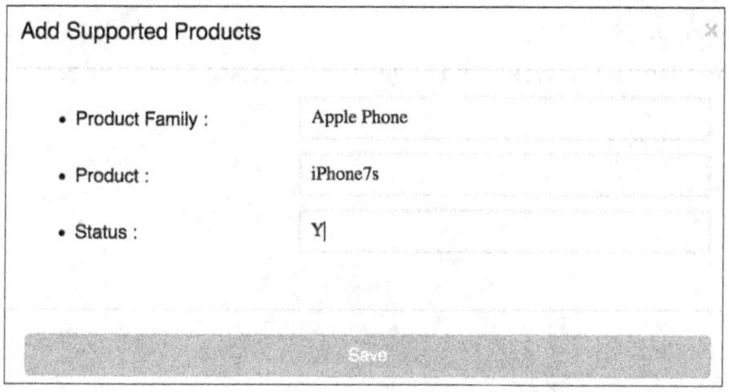

Add Supported Products   ✕

• Product Family :   Apple Phone

• Product :   iPhone7s

• Status :   Y

Save

Figure A.4 *Adding supported products to the catalog*

Add New User

As discussed earlier, usually these kinds of activities will be automated and the data will be entered in the upstream system. For the sake of understanding this application, let's create the data manually. As admin, let's add a new customer user to the helpdesk application, which will enable this particular user to submit tickets. For example, we'll create a customer user named Bob Black with user ID Bblack, as shown in Figure A.5.

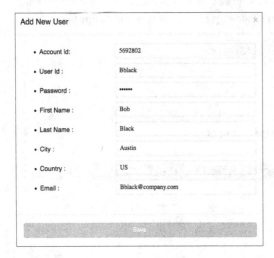

Add New User   ×

  • Account Id: 5692802

  • User Id :   Bblack

  • Password :   ••••••

  • First Name :   Bob

  • Last Name :   Black

  • City :   Austin

  • Country :   US

  • Email :   Bblack@company.com

Save

Figure A.5 *Our sample user's account information*

The user account for Bob has been created, but to enable him to submit a ticket, we need to associate him with the product he purchased. Let's create this entry within Add Sold Product.

Add Sold Product

The admin can manually add the products a customer bought. Let's say he purchased an iPhone 7s, as shown in Figure A.6.

Now that we know about the admin activities, let's get to the customer's role.

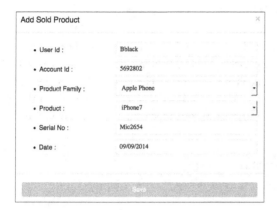

Figure A.6 *Our sample user's iPhone purchase*

Customer Flows

After the customer successfully logs in by using the credentials supplied by the admin, he can see the options on the landing page, as shown in Figure A.7:

Figure A.7 *Application capabilities for customer user*

Let's review these capabilities one at a time.

My Products

This console is called "Product Catalog Service" in our helpdesk application. It is used to view the products available under the account of a logged-in user. It shows the list of supported products he bought. In this example, Bob Black has active support on iPhone 6 and iPhone 7 (the entry we just created in the Administrator section), as shown in Figure A.8.

Sr.No	Product	Product Family	Support Available
1	iPhone6	Apple Phone	Y
2	iPhone7	Apple Phone	Y

Figure A.8 *The My Products console, also known as the product catalog*

Create an Incident

Say this customer wants to create an incident for a mobile device he bought recently: an iPhone 5. Using his identity, the application looks up the products he bought and allows him to create an incident based on his selection. The customer uses the UI screen shown in Figure A.9 to create the ticket. To describe the issue, he fills in the required fields such as title, problem severity, phone model, and issue category; then he submits the incident.

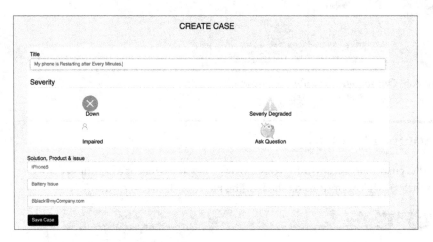

Figure A.9 *Submitting an incident for a product*

View Incident

Through this console, the user can view all historical tickets, as shown in Figure A.10. As the support engineer works on the ticket, the user can view ticket details and updates on the incident by clicking on the ticket number, as shown in Figure A.11.

VIEW ALL TICKETS

Ticket.No	Problem Description	Date
1	Mobile phone is switched of Frequently after 100% charged.	Sun Dec 13 2015
2	Screen resolution dims down after 50% battery is left.	Sun Dec 13 2015
3	Contracts are deleted automaticaly.	Sun Dec 13 2015
4	Call are automatically diverted to voice mails.	Sun Dec 13 2015

Figure A.10 *User's view of his active tickets*

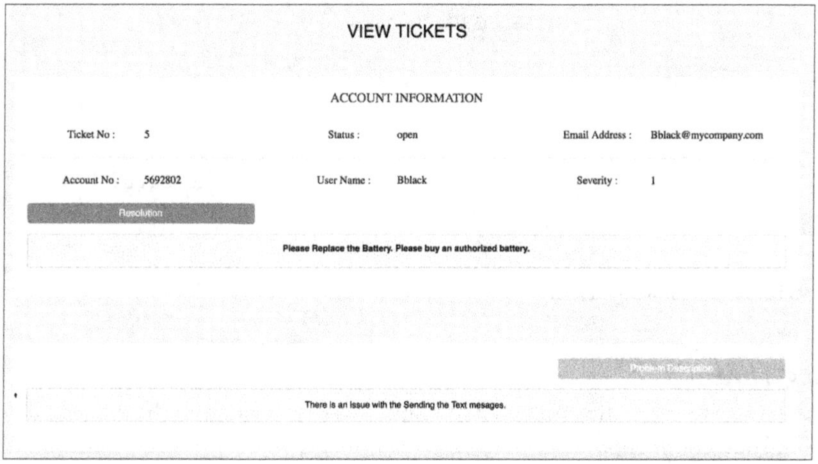

Figure A.11 *Viewing a ticket update*

Message Board

This is very basic message board utility. Users can use message board functionality to get help from the user community. They can post questions and respond to the questions posted on the message board by other users.

The message board console shown in Figure A.12 will display the entire list of messages that are currently open.

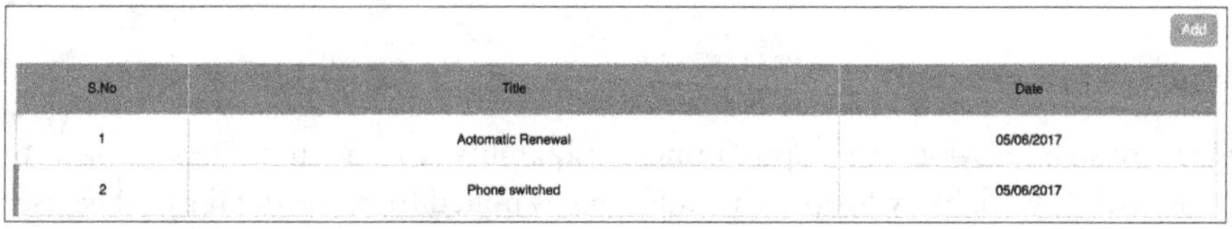

Figure A.12 *Message board*

Let's take a look at what we can do in the message board.

New Message

Clicking on the Add button opens a console to start a new message for discussion, as shown in Figure A.13.

MESSAGE BOARD

Title :-

Case Title

Comments

Enter your Comments here

Comments Date time

Save Message

Figure A.13 *Adding a new message*

Existing Thread

By clicking the Message title, as shown in Figure A.14, you can join the existing discussion and add comments.

Title :- Cell Phone Network

Comment	Date
Cell Phone Network is always weak when ever I am travelling outside.	Mon Oct 09 22:10:52 CDT 2017,Mon Oct 09 22:16:07 CDT 2017
Please save the default settings again.	Mon Oct 09 22:10:52 CDT 2017,Mon Oct 09 22:16:07 CDT 2017

Comments

Enter your Comments here

Comments Date time

Save Message

Figure A.14 *Commenting on existing message*

Make Appointment

This console provides the appointment capability to the users, as shown in Figure A.15. Availability for the date and time is pulled from the database. The user can select time zone, date, and time for the appointment with the support engineer.

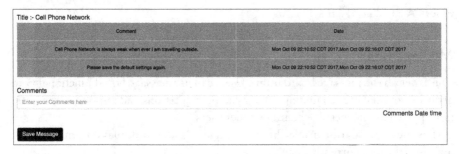

Product :   Black berry Z10

TimeZone :   Eastern Time

Apointment Date: 10/02/2017

Apointment Timeslot :   2:00 PM

Save

Figure A.15 *Scheduling an appointment*

Search

Users can search across the application for issues. The application has three search options, as shown in Figure A.16:

- **Basic Search.** Performs a database scan for the keywords.
- **Wiki Search.** Searches all Wiki data for the keyword.
- **Advance Search.** Uses Solr search, which is a text search and is more accurate than a basic search.

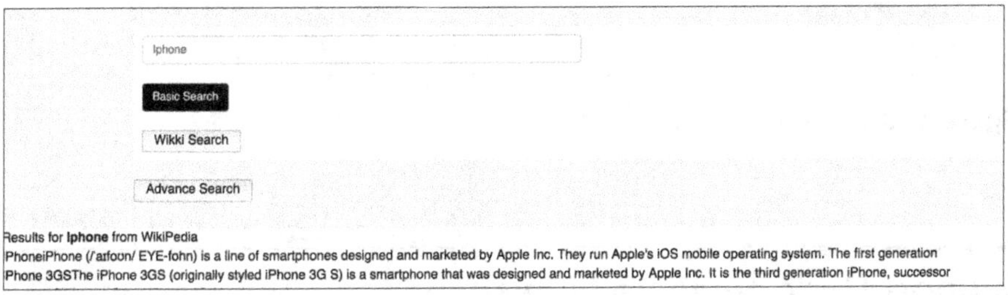

Figure A.16 *Searching the application for issues*

My Profile

These two tabs show the user profile for the logged-in user. The first tab shows the personal information, as shown in Figure A.17; the second shows the account information, as shown in Figure A.18.

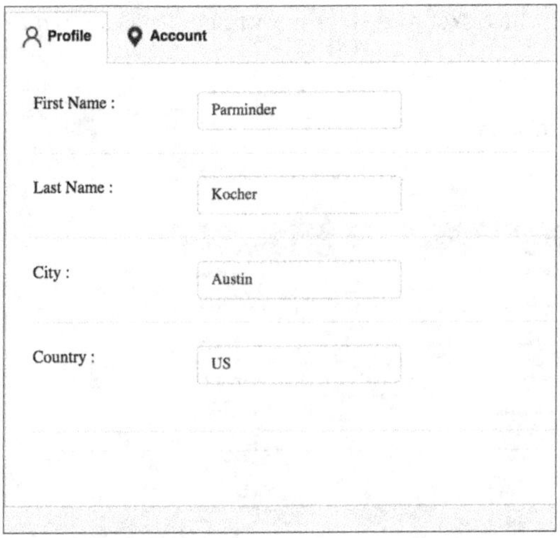

Figure A.17 *User profile*

Figure A.18 *Account information*

Support Desk Engineer Flows

Support desk engineers work on the incoming tickets and help resolve customers' issues. There are two main options: viewing all tickets and viewing and updating a specific ticket.

View All Tickets

In the support desk engineer console, the engineers can see all the tickets, and they can click on the ticket number to open the ticket and start working at it, as shown in Figure A.19.

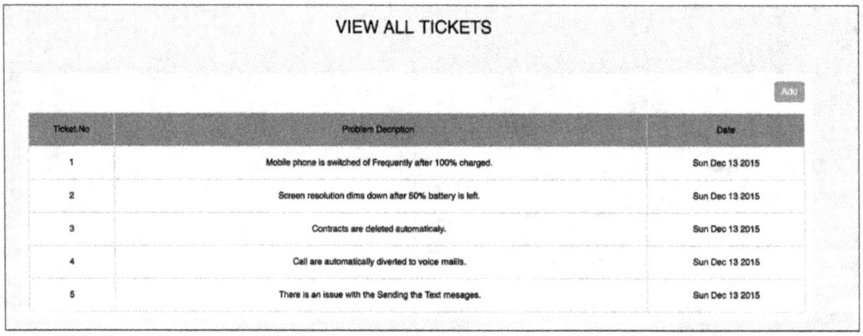

Figure A.19 *Support desk user console*

View Tickets

Clicking on the ticket number in the support console opens the ticket in the update mode. A support desk engineer can add comments, change status, and so on, as shown in Figure A.20.

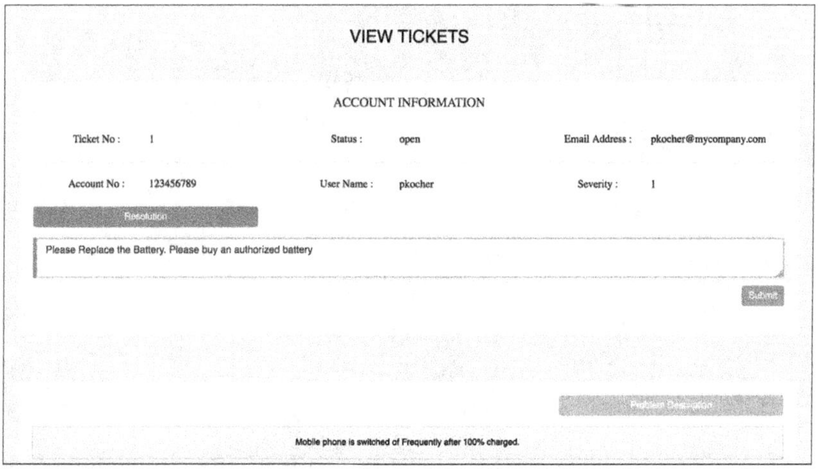

Figure A.20 *Viewing and updating a ticket*

This wraps up our high-level discussion of the functionality of the application. Again, the intent was not to write an industry-grade application but to create an application comprehensive enough for a case study in which you could gain hands-on experience in transitioning a monolithic application to a microservices- and containers-based application.

Appendix B

Installing the Solr Search Engine

This appendix provides step-by-step instructions for installing and configuring Solr to use as our search engine as part of improving the search service part of our case study in Chapter 12, "Case Study: Migration to Microservices." The instructions are applicable to CentOS operating system. If you want to learn more about Solr and explore its capabilities, visit http://lucene.apache.org/solr/resources.html.

Prerequisites

- CentOS Linux box or virtual machine with at least 1 GB of RAM
- python-software-properties package installed
- Latest version of Java installed

Installation Steps

1. Download the Solr tar file from the mirror. You can pull the latest version available, but at time of writing, we worked with version 5.5.

   ```
   wget http://apache.mirror1.spango.com/lucene/solr/5.5.4/
   solr-5.5.4.tgz
   ```

   We'll use the wget utility to download the tar file, as shown in Figure B.1.

```
ANUJSIN-H-T2H9:webapps anujsin$ wget http://apache.mirrorl.spango.com/lucene/solr/5.5.4/solr-5.5.4.tgz
--2017-07-25 22:14:54-- http://apache.mirrorl.spango.com/lucene/solr/5.5.4/solr-5.5.4.tgz
Resolving apache.mirrorl.spango.com... 83.98.147.65
Connecting to apache.mirrorl.spango.com|83.98.147.65|:80... connected.
HTTP request sent, awaiting response... 200 OK
Length: 136766786 (130M) [application/x-gzip]
Saving to: 'solr-5.5.4.tgz'
solr-5.5.4.tgz            100%[====================================>] 130.43M  3.40MB/s    in 28s

2017-07-25 22:15:22 (4.67 MB/s) - 'solr-5.5.4.tgz' saved [136766786/136766786]
```

Figure B.1 *Downloading solr tar file*

2. Unzip the downloaded tar file:

```
tar xzf solr-5.5.4.tgz
```

3. Execute the install script:

```
solr-5.5.4/bin/install_solr_service.sh
```

It may take a minute or so to install. Once it is installed, you can visit http://your_server_ip:8983/solr. The Solr web interface should look like Figure B.2.

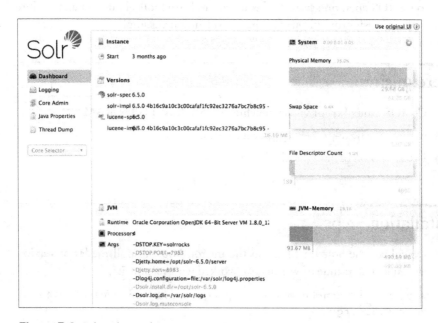

Figure B.2 *Solr web interface*

There will be a separate microservice for the Solr-based search, but we will pull the data from the existing database to be indexed in Solr. There are different utilities available to pull the data from MySQL/PostgreSQL into Solr. (You may also need continuous syncing of the data between the application database and Solr; in this case, you would pull the data only once to keep it simple.) We will use a simple data import handler and import the required table in Solr.

Configuring Solr for Simple Data Import

1. Add the following configuration in solrconfig.xml. This code specifies the path to the data import configuration file. This configuration file is installed as part of Solr. Update the path in this snippet to the location of the file on your machine:

```
<requestHandler name="/dataimport"
class="org.apache.solr.handler.dataimport.
DataImportHandler">
  <lst name="defaults">
    <str name="config">/path/to/my/dbconfigfile.xml</str>
  </lst>
</requestHandler>
```

2. Add the following in the dbconfig file. We are importing the database table to be indexed in Solr. In this snippet, we are specifying the data source along with the data selection query.

```
<dataConfig>
  <dataSource driver="org.hsqldb.jdbcDriver"
          url="jdbc:hsqldb:./example-DIH/hsqldb/ex"
          user="sa" password="secret"/>
<document>

    <entity name="products" query="select * from products "
          deltaQuery="select id from products
          where updated_date >
          '${dataimporter.last_index_time}'">
    />
<document>
<dataConfig>
```

3. Go back to the shell prompt and run following command to import and index the data:

```
bin/solr -e dih
```

Once all the data is indexed in Solr, it is easy to create a RESTful web service that can query the data from Solr and provide fast, accurate, reliable searches. We are ready to go! Now you can create the microservice from the case study described in Chapter 12.

Index

A

account management, helpdesk application
  case study, 175
  addAccount service, 176–177
  deleteAccount service, 178
  getAccount service, 176
  updateAccount service, 177
addAccount service, helpdesk application
  case study, 176–177
addCatalog service, helpdesk application
  case study, 182–183
administration, helpdesk application case
  study, 247, 248–261
Alertmanager and Prometheus, 165–167
Amazon Web Services
  DC/OS cluster setup, 227–235
  service discovery, 138
Apache Mesos + Marathon, container
  orchestration, 129
  agents, 130–131
  frameworks, 131–132
  Mesos master, 130
API (Application Programming Interface)
  gateways
    creating microservices,40
    discovery services and microservice
      communication, 27
  online resources, 149
  REST API, 149
  servers, Kubernetes and container
    orchestration, 124–125
appointments, helpdesk application case
  study, 184–185
  getAvailableDates service, 185–186
  getAvailableTimeSlots service, 185
  saveAppointment service, 186
asynchronous communication,
  microservices, 23–24
authentication, helpdesk application case
  study, 173–174, 248–249
authorization, helpdesk application case
  study, 175
automation, microservices, 38, 39
awslog logging driver, 145

B

backups/recovery, VM, 51
backward compatibility, microservices, 25
binaries, containerizing microservices, 222
bridges
  custom bridge networks, 117–118
  Docker containers, networking, 113–116
  Linux networking, 106
bug fixes, helpdesk application case study,
  200–202, 217–219
building
  binaries, containerizing microservices,
    222
  microservices, 18, 19, 212–213
  WAR files, containerizing microservices,
    222

C

cAdvisor monitoring, 149–150, 155–156
calculator applications, microservices
    versus monolithic applications, 4–5

case studies, helpdesk application, 171, 173
  account management, 175–178
  administration, 247, 248–261
  appointments, 184–186
  architecture of, 172–173
  authentication, 173–174, 248–249
  authorization, 175
  bug fixes, 200–202
  building application, 193–197
  configuring, 198–200
  customers, 247–248
  deploying, 198–200
  Eclipse IDE, 190–193
  flow of, 247–261
  Interceptor, 174
  message board, 186–189
  migrating to microservices, 203–219
  overview of, 171–172
  product catalog, 181–184
  requirements, 200–202
  searches, 189
  support, 251
  ticketing, 178–181
  troubleshooting, 200–202
  user roles, 248–251
changing logging drivers, 146–147
circuit breakers, creating microservices, 40
cluster–wide monitoring
  Heapster, 150–151
  Prometheus, 151–152
    adding targets, 156
    Alertmanager and, 165–167
    cAdvisor and, 155–156
    Grafana user interface and, 157–160
    Node Exporter and, 155–156
    online resources, 167
    running, 152–155
    viewing stats, 160–165
commands (Docker)
  docker attach command, 85–86
  docker commit command, 94–95
  docker cp command, 91–92
  docker create command, 94

docker diff command, 95
docker exec command, 89
docker images command, 76–77
docker inspect command, 87–89
docker logs command, 80–83
docker pause command, 92–93
docker ps command, 79–80, 85
docker pull command, 75–76
docker remove command, 86–87
docker rename command, 90–91
docker restart command, 85
docker rmi command, 77
docker run command, 77–79
docker search command, 73–75
docker stats command, 147–149
communication, microservices, 15
  asynchronous communication, 23–24
  discovery services, 26–27, 28–29
    API gateways, 27
    service registries, 27–28
  maintaining, 25–26
  message buses, 37
  migrating to microservices, 37
  publish/subscribe method, 24
  synchronous communication, 23
  web services
    maintaining, 25–26
    writing, 24–25
compatibility (backward), microservices, 25
complexity of microservices, 11
Compose (Docker), 55, 101–103
configuring
  Eclipse IDE, helpdesk application case
    study, 190–193
  Grafana user interface, 159–160
  helpdesk application case study,
    198–200, 213–217
  microservices, 17, 213–217
containers
  architecture of, 52–53
  defined, 52–53
  Docker containers, 56
    architecture of, 54–57

attaching to running containers, 85–86

bridges, 113–116

cAdvisor monitoring, 149–150

copying files from containers and local machines, 91–92

creating, 94

creating images from container changes, 94–95

custom bridge networks, 117–118

default connection options, 110

deploying, 57–60

efficiency, 57

example of, 57–60

Heapster monitoring, 150–151

host networking option, 111–113

linking, 106–109

listing changed files/directories in, 95

listing running containers, 79–80

logging, 144–147

LXC versus Docker containers, 53–54

metrics collection, 147–149

monitoring, 143–144

monitoring, cAdvisor, 149–150

monitoring, Heapster, 150–151

none (no connection) option, 110–111

orchestration, 123

orchestration, Docker Swarms, 132–136

orchestration, Kubernetes, 123–129

orchestration, Mesos + Marathon, 129–132

overlay network drivers, 119–120

pausing processes in, 92–93

port mapping, 118–119

portability, 54, 56

processes, running, 53

Prometheus monitoring, 151–167

removing, 86–87

renaming, 90–91

REST API, 149

restarting, 85

running commands in, 89

storage, 53

viewing container information, 87–89

viewing log files, 80–83

helpdesk application case study, containerizing microservices, 221–246

LXC, 52–53

Docker containers versus LXC, 53–54

portability, 54

microservices, containerizing, 221

accessing microservices, 245–246

building binaries, 222

building WAR files, 222

creating Docker images, 222–227

DC/OS cluster setup, 227–235

deploying microservices, 235–242

inspecting microservices, 239–245

listing dependencies, 222

scaling microservices, 239–245

submitting tasks to Marathon, 236–242

continuous delivery, microservices, 9

controller manager (replication controller), Kubernetes and container orchestration, 126–127

converting microservices, helpdesk application case study, 206–207

copying files from Docker containers and local machines, 91–92

cost of switching to microservices, 18–22

createMessage service, helpdesk application case study, 188–189

createTicket service, helpdesk application case study, 179

cultural change, switching to microservices, 14–15

custom networks

custom bridge networks, 117–118

overlay network drivers, 119–120

underlay network drivers (Macvlan), 121–122

customers, helpdesk application case study, 247–248

D

daemons/servers, Docker servers/daemons, 54

data migration, microservices migration, 44

data recovery/backups, VM, 51

data segregation, microservices, 10

database-based searches, 211–212

DC/OS (Datacenter Operating Systems), cluster setup, 227–235

decentralization of data, microservices, 10

deleteAccount service, helpdesk application case study, 178

deleteCatalog service, helpdesk application case study, 184

deploying
    Docker containers, 57–60
    helpdesk application case study, 198–200, 213–217
    microservices, 39, 43, 205, 213–217, 235
    VM, 57–58

DevOps, 20–22
    defined, 247–248
    microservices and, 248–250

directories, listing changed files/directories in Docker containers, 95

discovery process, microservices, 15

discovery services, microservice communication, 26–27, 28–29
    API gateways, 27
    service registries, 27–28

Docker
    clients, 54
    containers, 56
        architecture of, 54–57
        attaching to running containers, 85–86
        bridges, 113–116
        cAdvisor monitoring, 149–150
        copying files from containers and local machines, 91–92
        creating, 94

creating images from container changes, 94–95
        custom bridge networks, 117–118
        default connection options, 110
        deploying, 57–60
        efficiency, 57
        example of, 57–60
        Heapster monitoring, 150–151
        host networking option, 111–113
        linking, 106–109
        listing changed files/directories in, 95
        listing running containers, 79–80
        logging, 144–147
        LXC versus Docker containers, 53–54
        metrics collection, 147–149
        monitoring, 143–144
        monitoring, cAdvisor, 149–150
        monitoring, Heapster, 150–151
        none (no connection) option, 110–111
        orchestration, 123
        orchestration, Docker Swarms, 132–136
        orchestration, Kubernetes, 123–129
        orchestration, Mesos + Marathon, 129–132
        overlay network drivers, 119–120
        pausing processes in, 92–93
        port mapping, 118–119
        portability, 54, 56
        processes, running, 53
        Prometheus monitoring, 151–167
        removing, 86–87
        renaming, 90–91
        REST API, 149
        restarting, 85
        running commands in, 89
        storage, 53
        viewing container information, 87–89
        viewing log files, 80–83
    custom networks
        custom bridge networks, 117–118

overlay network drivers, 119–120
underlay network drivers (Macvlan),
      121–122
defined, 49
docker attach command, 85–86
docker commit command, 94–95
Docker Compose, 55, 101–103
docker cp command, 91–92
docker create command, 94
docker diff command, 95
docker exec command, 89
docker images command, 76–77
docker inspect command, 87–89
docker logs command, 80–83
Docker Machines, 55
docker pause command, 92–93
docker ps command, 79–80, 85
docker pull command, 75–76
docker remove command, 86–87
docker rename command, 90–91
docker restart command, 85
docker rmi command, 77
docker run command, 77–79
docker search command, 73–75
docker stats command, 147–149
Docker Swarms, 55, 120–121, 132
      nodes, 132
      services, 133, 135
      Swarm clusters, 133–136
      tasks, 133
Dockerfiles, 55
      commands, 96
      creating, 96–100
      format of, 95
      instructions for, 96
      MySQL Dockerfiles, 96–100
evolution of, 75
images, 54
      creating, 222–227
      reusability, 57
installing

Mac OS X installations, 61–65
Ubuntu Linux installations, 68–72
Windows installations, 66–68
online resources, 60
registries, 55
releases, changes between, 75
servers/daemons, 54
VM advantages, 56–57
docker0. *See* bridges

E

e-commerce systems, microservices versus
      monolithic applications, 6–8
Eclipse IDE
      helpdesk application case study,
            190–193, 213
      microservices, building, 213
efficiency
      Docker containers, 57
      VM, 51, 52
Ethernet devices (virtual), Linux
      networking, 106
examples, Docker containers, 57–60

F

failsafe design
      microservices, implementing, 38
      web services, 25
failure handling, microservices, 17
fault handling, helpdesk application case
      study, 219
fault isolation, microservices, 10
files
      copying from containers and local
            machines, 91–92
      listing changed files/directories in
            Docker containers, 95
flexibility, VM, 51

G

gcplogs logging driver, 145
GELF logging driver, 146
getAccount service, helpdesk application
    case study, 176
getAllMessage service, helpdesk application
    case study, 187–188
getAvailableDates service, helpdesk
    application case study, 185–186
getAvailableTimeSlots service, helpdesk
    application case study, 185
getCatalog service, helpdesk application
    case study, 182
getMessage service, helpdesk application
    case study, 187
Google, Kubernetes and container
    orchestration, 123–124
    kubectl command-line interface, 124
    master node, 124–127
Grafana user interface
    configuring, 159–160
    Prometheus and, 157–160

H

Heapster monitoring, 150–151
helpdesk application case study, 171, 173
    account management, 175
        addAccount service, 176–177
        deleteAccount service, 178
        getAccount service, 176
        updateAccount service, 177
    administration, 247, 248–261
    appointments, 184–185
        getAvailableDates service, 185–186
        getAvailableTimeSlots service, 185
        saveAppointment service, 186
    architecture of, 172–173
    authentication, 173–174, 248–249
    authorization, 175
    bug fixes, 200–202
    building application, 190–197

configuring, 198–200
containerizing microservices, 221
    accessing microservices, 245–246
    building binaries, 222
    building WAR files, 222
    creating Docker images, 222–227
    DC/OS cluster setup, 227–235
    deploying microservices, 235–242
    inspecting microservices, 239–245
    listing dependencies, 222
    scaling microservices, 239–245
    submitting tasks to Marathon,
        236–242
customers, 247–248
deploying, 198–200
flow of, 247–261
Interceptor, 174
message board, 186–187
    createMessage service, 188–189
    getAllMessage service, 187–188
    getMessage service, 187
migrating to microservices, 203
    bug fixes, 217–219
    building microservices, 212–213
    configuring microservices, 213–217
    deploying microservices, 205, 213–217
    fault handling, 219
    helper services, 205
    microservice conversion process,
        206–207
    planning migrations, 203–204
    product catalog, 208–211
    requirements, 217–219
    scalability, 205, 219
    searches, 211–212
    storage alternatives/polyglot
        persistence, 205
    technology alternatives/polyglot
        programming, 205
    ticketing, 211
    troubleshooting, 217–219
overview of, 171–172
product catalog, 181

addCatalog service, 182–183
deleteCatalog service, 184
getCatalog service, 182
updateCatalog service, 183
requirements, 200–202
searches, 189
support, 251
ticketing, 178–179
createTicket service, 179
viewAllTicket service, 180–181
viewTicket service, 180
troubleshooting, 200–202
updating, 246
user roles, 248–251
helper microservices, 5–6
helper services, migrating to microservices, 43, 205
host networking option, Docker containers, 111–113
hybrid approach, microservice creation, 45

I

images
Docker images, 54
creating, 222–227
reusability, 57
MySQL images
reating from container changes, 94–95
listing available images, 76–77
removing from local machines, 77
running, 77–79
searching for, 73–75
implementing microservices, 38
environment security/automation, 38
failsafe design, 38
independency, 38
reusability, 38–39
source control, 38
tagging, 39
installing
Docker

Mac OS X installations, 61–65
Ubuntu Linux installations, 68–72
Windows installations, 66–68
Solr search engine, 247–266
Interceptor, helpdesk application case study, 174
Internet resources
API, 149
Docker, 60
Kubernetes, 129
Prometheus, 167
interprocess communication. *See* communication, microservices
iptables, 106

J

Journald logging driver, 145
json-file logging driver, 145, 146

K

Kubernetes, container orchestration, 123–124
kubectl command-line interface, 124
kubelet, 127
Kubernetes Services, 128
master node, 124
API servers, 124–125
replication controller (controller manager), 126–127
scheduler, 125–126
online resources, 129
pods, 127–129
worker nodes, 127

L

latency, microservices, 11
learning curve, switching to microservices, 15–17
life span of software in monolithic applications, 18

linking, Docker containers, 106–109

Linux

  bridges, 106

  Docker installations, 68–72

  iptables, 106

  namespaces, 105–106

  networking, 105

    bridges, 106

    iptables, 106

    namespaces, 105–106

    virtual Ethernet devices, 106

  virtual Ethernet devices, 106

listing

  available MySQL images, 76–77

  changed files/directories in Docker
    containers, 95

  dependencies, containerizing
    microservices, 222

  running Docker containers, 79–80

log files, viewing Docker containers, 80–83

logging

  awslog logging driver, 145

  changing drivers, 146–147

  Docker containers, 144–147

  gcplogs logging driver, 145

  GELF logging driver, 146

  Journald logging driver, 145

  json-file logging driver, 145, 146

  Splunk logging driver, 145

  Syslog logging driver, 145

LXC (Linux containers), 52–53

  Docker containers versus LXC, 53–54

  portability, 54

  processes, running, 53

M

Mac OS X, Docker installations, 61–65

Macvlan (underlay network drivers),
  121–122

maintaining microservices, 18, 19, 25–26

managing

accounts, helpdesk application case
  study, 175–178

Docker containers

  logging, 144–147

  monitoring containers, 143–144

  microservices, 16

Marathon. *See* Mesos + Marathon,
  container orchestration

marketing microservices, 19, 20–22

Mesos + Marathon

  container orchestration, 129

    agents, 130–131

    frameworks, 131–132

    Mesos master, 130

    submitting tasks to Marathon,
      236–242

message board, helpdesk application case
  study, 186–187

  createMessage service, 188–189

  getAllMessage service, 187–188

  getMessage service, 187

message buses, microservice
  communication, 37

metrics collection and containers, 147–149

microservices

  accessing, 245–246

  advantages of, 9–11

  automation, 38, 39

  backward compatibility, 25

  building, 18, 19, 212–213

  communication, 15

    API gateways, 27

    asynchronous communication,
      23–24

    creating microservices, 37

    discovery services, 26–29

    maintaining, 25–26

    message buses, 37

    publish/subscribe method, 24

    service registries, 27–28

    synchronous communication, 23

    web services, 24–25

    writing web services, 25–26

complexity of, 11
configuring, 17, 213–217
containerizing, 221, 222
continuous delivery, 9
creating
    API gateways, 40
    circuit breakers, 40
    communication, 37
    deployment phase, 39
    hybrid approach, 45
    implementation phase, 38–39
    monitoring, 40
    operational support, 40
    organizational readiness, 36
    scalability, 40
    services-based approach, 36–37
    technology selection, 37–38
data segregation, 10
decentralization of data, 10
defined, 3–4
defining for functions, 44
deploying, 39, 43, 205, 213–217, 235
DevOps and, 20–22, 248–250
disadvantages of, 11
discovery process, 15
e-commerce systems, 6–8
failure handling, 17
fault handling, 219
fault isolation, 10
helper microservices, 5–6
implementing, 38
    environment security/automation, 38
    failsafe design, 38
    independency, 38
    reusability, 38–39
    source control, 38
    tagging, 39
inspecting, 239–245
latency, 11
maintaining, 18, 19
managing, 16
marketing, 19, 20–22
migrating to, 40–42

bug fixes, 217–219
building microservices, 212–213
configuring microservices, 213–217
data migration, 44
defining for functions, 44
deploying microservices, 43, 205,
    213–217
fault handling, 219
helpdesk application case study,
    203–219
helper services, 43, 205
independent builds/deployments, 45
microservice conversion process,
    206–207
modification requests, 43
monolithic code, 44
need for migration, 33–35
performance, 42
planning migrations, 203–204
polyglot programming/technology
    alternatives, 205
product catalog, 208–211
rearchitecting services, 44–45
refactoring code, 44
removing old code, 45
requirements, 217–219
scalability, 42, 205, 219
searches, 211–212
storage alternatives/polyglot
    persistence, 43, 205
technology alternatives/polyglot
    programming, 42–43
ticketing, 211
troubleshooting, 217–219
versioning microservices, 44, 45
modularity, 8–9
monitoring, 17, 25–26, 40
monolithic applications versus, 4–5, 6–8,
    9–11
performance, migrating to
    microservices, 42
scalability, 5, 9–10, 16, 19, 20–21, 37, 40,
    42, 239–245

microservices *(continued)*
  security, 16, 37, 37, 38
  service discovery, 139
  standalone microservices, 15
  switching to
    business case for switching, 17–18, 22
    cost of, 18–22
    cultural change, 14–15
    learning curve, 15–17
    monolithic application attributes, 14
    monolithic application fatigues, 14
    operational processes, 15
  testing, 16
  troubleshooting, 11, 217–219
  updating, 5, 18, 20
  upgrading, 16
  version control, 11
  versioning, 44, 45
migrating
  data, microservices migration, 44
    to microservices, 40–42
    bug fixes, 217–219
    building microservices, 212–213
    configuring microservices, 213–217
    data migration, 44
    defining for functions, 44
    deploying microservices, 43, 205,
      213–217
    fault handling, 219
    helpdesk application case study,
      203–204, 205, 206–207, 208–219
    helper services, 43, 205
    independent builds/deployments, 45
    microservice conversion process,
      206–207
    modification requests, 43
    monolithic code, 44
    need for migration, 33–35
    performance, 42
    planning migrations, 203–204
    product catalog, 208–211
    rearchitecting services, 44–45
    refactoring code, 44

removing old code, 45
requirements, 217–219
scalability, 42, 205, 219
searches, 211–212
storage alternatives/polyglot
  persistence, 43
technology alternatives/polyglot
  programming, 42–43
ticketing, 211
versioning microservices, 44, 45
VM, 51
modification requests, migrating to
  microservices, 43
modularity of microservices, 8–9
monitoring
  cAdvisor, 149–150, 155–156
  Docker containers, 143–144
  Heapster, 150–151
  microservices, 17, 25–26, 40
  Prometheus, 151–152
    adding targets, 156
    Alertmanager and, 165–167
    cAdvisor and, 155–156
    Grafana user interface and, 157–160
    Node Exporter and, 155–156
    online resources, 167
    running, 152–155
    viewing stats, 160–165
monolithic applications
  complexity of, 9
  e-commerce systems, 6–8
  fatigues, 14
  helpdesk application case study, 171, 173
    account management, 175–178
    appointments, 184–186
    architecture of, 172–173
    authentication, 173–174
    authorization, 175
    bug fixes, 200–202
    building application, 193–197
    configuring, 198–200
    configuring Eclipse IDE, 190–193
    deploying, 198–200

Interceptor, 174
message board, 186–189
overview of, 171–172
product catalog, 181–184
requirements, 200–202
searches, 189
ticketing, 178–181
troubleshooting, 200–202
microservices, migrating to, 40–42
    data migration, 44
    defining for functions, 44
    deploying microservices, 43
    helper services, 43
    independent builds/deployments, 45
    modification requests, 43
    monolithic code, 44
    need for migration, 33–35
    performance, 42
    rearchitecting services, 44–45
    refactoring code, 44
    removing old code, 45
    scalability, 42
    storage alternatives/polyglot
        persistence, 43
    technology alternatives/polyglot
        programming, 42–43
    versioning microservices, 44, 45
microservices, switching to
    attributes, 14
    business case for switching, 17–18, 22
    cost of, 18–22
    cultural change, 14–15
    fatigues, 14
    learning curve, 15–17
    operational processes, 15
microservices versus, 4–5, 6–8, 9–11
software, life span in monolithic
    applications, 18
monolithic code, microservices
    migration, 44
MySQL
    Dockerfiles, 96–100
    images

creating from container changes,
    94–95
listing available images, 76–77
removing from local machines, 77
running, 77–79
searching for, 73–75

N

namespaces (Linux), 105–106
naming, Docker containers, 90–91
networking (Linux), 105
    bridges, 106
    custom bridge networks, 117–118
    Docker containers
        bridges, 113–116
        default connection options, 110
        linking, 106–109
        none (no connection) option, 110–111
    iptables, 106
    namespaces, 105–106
    overlay network drivers, 119–120
    port mapping, 118–119
    underlay network drivers (Macvlan),
        121–122
    virtual Ethernet devices, 106
Node Exporter and Prometheus, 155–156

O

old code (migrating to microservices),
    removing, 45
online resources
    API, 149
    Docker, 60
    Kubernetes, 129
    Prometheus, 167
operational complexity of microservices, 11
operational processes, switching to
    microservices, 15
OS freedom and VM, 51
overlay network drivers, 119–120

P

pausing processes in Docker containers, 92–93
performance
    microservices, migrating to, 42
    VM, 51, 52
planning microservice migrations, helpdesk application case study, 203–204
pods, Kubernetes and container orchestration, 127–129
polyglot persistence/storage alternatives, migrating to microservices, 43, 205
polyglot programming/technology alternatives, migrating to microservices, 42–43, 205
port mapping, 118–119
portability
    Docker containers, 56
    LXC versus Docker containers, 54
    VM, 51–52
processes (LXC versus Docker containers), running, 53
product catalog, helpdesk application case study, 181
    addCatalog service, 182–183
    deleteCatalog service, 184
    getCatalog service, 182
    migrating to microservices, 208–211
    updateCatalog service, 183
Prometheus monitoring, 151–152
    Alertmanager and, 165–167
    cAdvisor and, 155–156
    Grafana user interface and, 157–160
    Node Exporter and, 155–156
    online resources, 167
    running, 152–155
    stats, viewing, 160–165
    targets, adding, 156
publish/subscribe method, microservice communication, 24

Q–R

recovery/backups, VM, 51
refactoring code, migrating to microservices, 44
registries (Docker), 55
removing
    Docker containers, 86–87
    images from local machines, 77
    old code, migrating to microservices, 45
renaming Docker containers, 90–91
replication controller (controller manager), Kubernetes and container orchestration, 126–127
requirements, helpdesk application case study, 200–202, 217–219
resource utilization, VM, 52
REST API, 149
restarting Docker containers, 85
reusing
    code, migrating to microservices, 44
    Docker images, 57
    microservices, 38–39
running
    commands in Docker containers, 89
    Docker containers
        attaching to running containers, 85–86
        listing running containers, 79–80
    images, 77–79

S

saveAppointment service, helpdesk application case study, 186
scalability
    helpdesk application case study, 219, 239–245
    microservices, 5, 9–10, 16, 19, 20–21, 37, 40, 42, 205, 239–245
scheduler, Kubernetes and container orchestration, 125–126

searches
    database-based searches, 211–212
    docker search command, 73–75
    helpdesk application case study, 189,
        211–212
    MySQL images, 73–75
    Solr search engine, 212, 247–266
security, microservices, 16, 37, 37, 38
segregation of data, microservices, 10
servers
    API servers, Kubernetes and container
        orchestration, 124–125
    Docker servers/daemons, 54
service registries, discovery services and
        microservice communication, 27–28
services
    Docker Swarms, 133, 135
    service discovery, 136–137
        Amazon Web Services, 138
        client-side discovery, 137–138
        microservices, 139
        server-side discovery, 138–139
        service registry, 139–141
sharing VM, 51
shopping carts (e-commerce systems),
        microservices versus monolithic
        applications, 7–8
SOA-based monolithic applications
    e-commerce systems, 6–8
    fatigues, 14
    microservices, switching to
        attributes, 14
        business case for switching, 17–18, 22
        cost of, 18–22
        cultural change, 14–15
        fatigues, 14
        learning curve, 15–17
        operational processes, 15
    microservices versus, 4–5, 6–8, 9–11
    software, life span in monolithic
        applications, 18
software
    dependencies (containerizing
        microservices), listing, 222

    life span in monolithic applications, 18
Solr search engine, 212, 247–266
Splunk logging driver, 145
standalone microservices, 15
storage
    Docker containers, 53
    storage alternatives/polyglot persistence,
        migrating to microservices, 43, 205
subscribe/publish method, microservice
        communication, 24
support, helpdesk application case study,
        251
Swarms (Docker), 55, 120–121, 132
    nodes, 132
    services, 133, 135
    Swarm clusters, 133–136
    tasks, 133
synchronous communication,
        microservices, 23
Syslog logging driver, 145

T

tagging microservices, 39
technology alternatives/polyglot
        programming, migrating to
        microservices, 42–43, 205
testing microservices, 16
ticketing, helpdesk application case study,
        178–179, 211
    createTicket service, 179
    viewAllTicket service, 180–181
    viewTicket service, 180
transitioning to microservices, 40–42
    data migration, 44
    defining for functions, 44
    deploying microservices, 43
    helper services, 43
    independent builds/deployments, 45
    modification requests, 43
    monolithic code, 44
    need for migration, 33–35
    performance, 42

transitioning to microservices *(continued)*
  rearchitecting services, 44–45
  refactoring code, 44
  removing old code, 45
  scalability, 42
  storage alternatives/polyglot
    persistence, 43
  technology alternatives/polyglot
    programming, 42–43
  versioning microservices, 44, 45
troubleshooting
  helpdesk application case study,
    200–202, 217–219
  microservices, 11, 217–219

U

Ubuntu Linux, Docker installations, 68–72
underlay network drivers (Macvlan),
    121–122
updateAccount service, helpdesk
    application case study, 177
updateCatalog service, helpdesk application
    case study, 183
updating
  helpdesk application case study, 246
  microservices, 5, 18, 20
upgrading microservices, 16
usage examples, Docker containers, 57–60
user roles, helpdesk application case study,
    248–251

V

version control, microservices, 11
versioning microservices, 44, 45
viewAllTicket service, helpdesk application
    case study, 180–181

viewing Docker containers
  container information, 87–89
  log files, 80–83
viewTicket service, helpdesk application
    case study, 180
virtual Ethernet devices, Linux
    networking, 106
VM (Virtual Machines)
  advantages of, 50–51
  backups/recovery, 51
  defined, 50
  deploying, 57–58
  disadvantages of, 49–52
  Docker, VM advantages, 56–57
  efficiency, 51, 52
  flexibility, 51
  migrating, 51
  OS freedom, 51
  performance, 51, 52
  portability, 51–52
  resource utilization, 52
  sharing, 51

W–X–Y–Z

WAR files, building, containerizing
    microservices, 222
web resources
  API, 149
  Docker, 60
  Kubernetes, 129
  Prometheus, 167
web services
  failsafe design, 25
  maintaining, 25–26
  writing, 24–25
Windows, Docker installations, 66–68
WordPress sites, Docker containers
    deployment example, 57–60

Credits

Register Your Product at informit.com/register

Access additional benefits and **save 35%** on your next purchase

- Automatically receive a coupon for 35% off your next purchase, valid for 30 days. Look for your code in your InformIT cart or the Manage Codes section of your account page.

- Download available product updates.

- Access bonus material if available.*

- Check the box to hear from us and receive exclusive offers on new editions and related products.

Registration benefits vary by product. Benefits will be listed on your account page under Registered Products.

InformIT.com—The Trusted Technology Learning Source

InformIT is the online home of information technology brands at Pearson, the world's foremost education company. At InformIT.com, you can:
- Shop our books, eBooks, software, and video training
- Take advantage of our special offers and promotions (informit.com/promotions)
- Sign up for special offers and content newsletter (informit.com/newsletters)
- Access thousands of free chapters and video lessons

Connect with InformIT—Visit informit.com/community

the trusted technology learning source

Addison-Wesley • Adobe Press • Cisco Press • Microsoft Press • Pearson IT Certification • Prentice Hall • Que • Sams • Peachpit Press

 Pearson